Jane Austen:
A Reassessment

JANE AUSTEN:
A REASSESSMENT

by
P. J. M. Scott

VISION
and
BARNES & NOBLE

Vision Press Limited
11–14 Stanhope Mews West
London SW7 5RD

and

Barnes & Noble Books
81 Adams Drive
Totowa, NJ 07512

ISBN (UK) 0 85478 494 2
ISBN (US) 0 389 20282 7

3/19/97

© 1982 by P. J. M. Scott
First published in the U.S.A. 1982

Printed and bound in Great Britain by
Unwin Brothers Ltd.,
Old Woking, Surrey.
Phototypeset by Galleon Photosetting,
Ipswich, Suffolk.
MCMLXXXII

Contents

Note on Abbreviated References

In all that follows, reference to Austen's writings is to the editions of them by R. W. Chapman. Since their first appearance in 1923, his texts of and annotative matter for the novels have been slightly modified not only by his own but in more recent years by another hand also (Miss Mary Lascelles) and those of the *Minor Works* (1954) by B. C. Southam, so I mention here the dates of the issues I have used for this study:

Sense and Sensibility (SS)	— 1978
Pride and Prejudice (PP)	— 1976
Mansfield Park (MP)	— 1978
Emma (E)	— 1978
Northanger Abbey (NA) and *Persuasion* (P)	— 1975
Minor Works	— 1975

Shorthand attribution is also made in a standard manner as denoted parenthetically above, and MW = Minor Works.

I give only the page references for this 'The Oxford Illustrated' account of the canon. For the benefit of readers not using the same series, the chapter numbers preceding such references— though in the interest of relative clarity these are expressed in Roman numerals—are those of most modern editions, where the original divisions of the novels into volumes are ignored.

Reference to Austen's letters is by page to the one-tome recension of his 1932 collection which Dr. Chapman published in 1952 (1959 corrected reprinting); and likewise, lest a par-

7

ticular entry should be sought instead in the 1955 selection ('The World's Classics' issue, Oxford), following his excellent initiative in this manner I supply the numbers of the epistles in question, which are the same in that abridgement and in the complete edition.

Grateful acknowledgement is made by the publishers and author to Professor Marvin Mudrick for permission to quote from his *Jane Austen: Irony as Defense and Discovery* (Princeton, 1952) in the following pages.

1

The Question of a Divided Intention (I): ' "Lady Susan" ', *'Sanditon'*, *Northanger Abbey*

This study has two objects: to present a reading of Austen's work which is different from those hitherto expounded—sometimes drastically different, and to consider what may be meant by such terms as 'author' or 'authorial intention' in respect of imaginative fictions.

The problem of a divided intention comes to the fore promptly and with relative straightforwardness in the cases of the tales named at this chapter's heading. The fair copy manuscript which J. E. Austen-Leigh entitled ' "Lady Susan" ' and which, whether it dates from 1793–94 or 1805,[1] is reasonably to be termed an early work, has a formidable finish in both senses of the word. For ' "Lady Susan" ' ends with palpable abruptness. Yet it would never occur to any reader for whom its provenance and history were all unknown, to deem it some feeble sketch or half-hearted apprentice-effort. It is a powerful novella, equally amusing and of even tone, which has no mark of the 'juvenile' about it, whether in the sense of its vision of life or the technique expressing that vision being immature. It exhibits no patchiness as of a voice which has not yet found its full throat of utterance:

9

quite the reverse. The narrative is first to last quicksilver-adept.

A long short-story, it consists in a judicious selection of letters adumbrating one episode out of a life evidently packed with improper adventures on the part of the lively villainess Lady Susan Vernon. She is a widow who has betrayed her ingenuous husband during his lifetime and, with scant regret for his death, now continues a career of flirtation and other intrigue as well upon her innocent daughter's account, the harassed Frederica, as on her own. At the intermittence of her newest escapade indulged while staying with a family by the name of Manwaring (Mrs. Manwaring's jealousy has been raised to distraction by the conduct of Lady Susan and her host together), the impenitent heroine is obliged to foist herself upon her late husband's brother-in-law and sister Mr. and Mrs. Vernon at their home of Churchill. There she encounters the lady's brother Reginald De Courcy whom, though he arrives in that household replete with her ill-fame and inspired to treat her with a just condescension of contempt, she soon subdues into believing all her explanations of past conduct and into falling in love with her.

In letters to her mother Mrs. Vernon deplores

> the very rapid increase of Lady Susan's influence. They are now on terms of the most particular friendship, frequently engaged in long conversations together, & she has contrived by the most artful coquetry to subdue his Judgement to her own purposes. (Letter 11; MW, p. 259)

But 'those bewitching powers which can do so much—engaging at the same time & in the same house the affections of two Men who were neither of them at liberty to bestow them—& all this, without the charm of Youth' (Letter 4, p. 248) themselves are presently vexed by the news that her only child ('who was born to be the torment of my life' [Letter 2, p. 245]) has run away from the London school where Lady Susan installed her. She deposited her there in the first place with the hope that her confinement and unhappiness in an environment ill-suited to the girl's temperament would mellow the prospect of an arranged marriage, having determined that Frederica will accept the proposals of the almost imbecile Sir James Martin, whose wealth and pliancy are all a flirtatious mother-in-law could desire. She has a comrade after her own

10

heart in the capital, and the missive she addresses to this sister in feeling affords us a glimpse of her glittering multi-faceted personality.

LETTER 16
Lady Susan to Mrs Johnson

Churchill.

Never my dearest Alicia, was I so provoked in my life as by a Letter this morning from Miss Summers. That horrid girl of mine has been trying to run away.—I had not a notion of her being such a little Devil before; she seemed to have all the Vernon Milkiness; but on receiving the letter in which I declared my intentions about Sir James, she actually attempted to elope; at least, I cannot otherwise account for her doing it. She meant I suppose to go to the Clarkes in Staffordshire, for she has no other acquaintance. But she *shall* be punished, she *shall* have him. I have sent Charles to Town to make matters up if he can, for I do not by any means want her here. If Miss Summers will not keep her, you must find me out another school, unless we can get her married immediately. Miss S. writes word that she could not get the young Lady to assign any cause for her extraordinary conduct, which confirms me in my own private explanation of it.

Frederica is too shy I think, & too much in awe of me, to tell tales; but if the mildness of her Uncle *should* get anything from her, I am not afraid. I trust I shall be able to make my story as good as her's. If I am vain of anything, it is of my eloquence. Consideration & Esteem as surely follow command of Language, as Admiration waits on Beauty. And here I have opportunity enough for the exercise of my Talent, as the cheif of my time is spent in Conversation. Reginald is never easy unless we are by ourselves, & when the weather is tolerable, we pace the shrubbery for hours together. I like him on the whole very well, he is clever & has a good deal to say, but he is sometimes impertinent & troublesome. There is a sort of ridiculous delicacy about him which requires the fullest explanation of whatever he may have heard to my disadvantage, & is never satisfied till he thinks he has ascertained the beginning & end of everything.

This is *one* sort of Love—but I confess it does not particularly recommend itself to me. I infinitely prefer the tender & liberal spirit of Manwaring, which impressed with the deepest conviction of my merit, is satisfied that whatever I do must be right;

11

& look with a degree of contempt on the inquisitive & doubting Fancies of that Heart which seems always debating on the reasonableness of it's Emotions. Manwaring is indeed beyond compare superior to Reginald—superior in everything but the power of being with me. Poor fellow! he is quite distracted by Jealousy, which I am not sorry for, as I know no better support of Love. He has been teizing me to allow of his coming into this country, & lodging somewhere near me *incog.*—but I forbid anything of the kind. Those women are inexcusable who forget what is due to themselves & the opinion of the World.

S. VERNON.

This is self-definition by a character as in Restoration Comedy of the very best.

Miss Summers does not agree to take Frederica back, and Lady Susan has to put up with her daughter's sojourning for the while under the same roof as herself and 'actually falling in love with Reginald De Courcy'. Sir James Martin visits unexpectedly. Frederica appeals to Reginald to take her part against the proposed match between her and this 'Rattle' of a baronet—which matrimony the rest of the family at Churchill also view with alarm. It provokes an angry conference between De Courcy and our intrepid Jezebel upon which—to the delight of Mrs. Vernon's family—he resolves to sever the acquaintance by returning to his parents' home immediately. But another conversation with Lady Susan quickly sets this determination on its head. A reconciliation is effected—Lady Susan chooses not to relinquish her conquest albeit at the cost of sending Sir James packing (for the meanwhile), her daughter's hand in marriage (apparently) withheld.

The Vernon family prepares for the worst—the union of their brother and Lady Susan, and Mrs. Johnson herself urges her friend to 'come to Town . . . without loss of time . . . [and] get yourself well established by marrying M^r De Courcy. . . .' Lady Susan nevertheless hopes to secure both Reginald and his father's fortune, and counsels delay of this swain. He rushes to the city to see her and there meets Mrs. Manwaring, Mr. Johnson's ward, who produces irresistible proofs of his intended's depravity. The schemer has to console herself with telling her friend that 'Manwaring is more devoted to me than ever; & were he at liberty, I doubt if I could resist even

Matrimony offered by *him*' (Letter 39, p. 308). A little later in fact—with Frederica 'fixed in the family of her Uncle & Aunt, till such time as Reginald De Courcy could be talked, flattered & finessed into an affection for her'—she opts for marriage with the giddy, fatuous Sir James Martin herself.

And so the story concludes. But matters are wound up by a not lengthy direct authorial narrative with a declaration the beginning of which has helped the whole *nouvelle*'s considerable critical depreciation:

> This Correspondence, by a meeting between some of the Parties & a separation between the others, could not, to the great detriment of the Post office Revenue, be continued longer. Very little assistance to the State could be derived from the Epistolary Intercourse of Mrs Vernon & her neice, for the former soon perceived by the stile of Frederica's Letters, that they were written under her Mother's inspection. . . . (p. 311)

Inevitably the charge not just of a local lapse into perfunctoriness but a more generally unserious intention on Austen's part has been raised. Introducing a recent paperback issue of *Lady Susan, The Watsons* and *Sanditon* its editor comments that

> *Lady Susan* is the earliest and possibly the least satisfactory of the three. . . . The letter form of novel had been popular in the eighteenth century, and was very much a living convention when she tried to use it, but it did not really suit her talents. . . . [The first sentence of the passage quoted immediately above] indicates her sense of unreality in keeping the game up. . . .[2]

Miss Drabble is not alone in these opinions, for this *conte*, far from being recognized as the major thing it is amongst work on its scale, endures the ultimate relegation in esteem, neglect. It gets very fleeting mentions, whether laudatory (e.g. R. W. Chapman[3]) or otherwise (Mary Lascelles[4]) in the 'standard' books on this author, and in most monographs or collections of articles hardly features at all.

Actually it is hard to refine very much upon Marvin Mudrick's assessment in respect of its major theme. As in his other stimulating analyses of this author's fiction, Mudrick is again here guilty of a certain partisanship:

> It is clear that Lady Susan triumphs over Mrs Vernon whenever she wishes to, over Reginald, over everyone else. For Lady

13

Susan is the legitimate beneficiary of the society which moral, sentimental Mrs Vernon indignantly and desperately defends, but which makes no provision for moral or emotional values, for any values at all except those attaching to birth, money, and show—the society which gives Lady Susan her reason, her constant encouragement for being what she is and succeeding as she does.[5]

Is it really very unfair to suspect this critic of regularly liking the *bad* simply, if only they are vital enough? But we get straight at the essence of the work's import when he goes on:

The virtuoso's delight with which Lady Susan achieves and recollects her victories is insufficient, after all, to sustain her. The victories are, in fact, hollow, as victories must be over a world so hollow. . . . She is the only person with passion and will in a milieu of circumscribed and will-less formality; and, alone in such a milieu, the passionate and wilful person must wither, or dissipate his power in cold unfruitful strategies. . . . Energy, in her immobile bounded conventional world, turns upon and devours itself. The world defeats Lady Susan, not because it recognizes her vices, but because her virtues have no room in it.[6]

Energy is exactly what it is all about, and the most impressive thing in the tale is Austen's ability to convey the insipidity of the characters opposing her heroine without making them lay-figures, crude cardboard cut-outs whom the reader's sense of fair play is ultimately impelled to reject as de-natured. Brief as the work is, the punch it packs comes from our not feeling (*pace* Miss Drabble) that Lady Susan has the narrative of events too much on her own terms.

The real criticism which one can make of *Lady Susan* is that it does not give enough weight to the other side of the question. Lady Susan does too much of the talking, and runs away with the novel. In *Mansfield Park* and *Emma*, the two sides are so perfectly balanced that one remark from either faction can shake one's faith: Frank Churchill is at times so amusing, the Bates at times so appalling, Fanny at times so dull, Henry and Mary Crawford at times so delightful, that one's mind is kept in a perpetual unrest, a perpetual reassessment of the central issues. But in *Lady Susan*, the opposition is dull. Frederica, the besieged daughter, is allowed to write only one letter of her own: she spends the rest of the time weeping or playing the pianoforte. Reginald de Courcy is gullible, the deceived wife, Mrs Manwaring, is thin and ugly, the sister-in-law, Mrs Vernon, is motivated against Lady Susan by obvious sexual jealousy. There is no acceptable positive world to set up against Lady Susan's corrupt one. . . . [7]

This seems to me an injustice; if 'The choice, a not particularly attractive one, is between an eighteenth-century London where wives deceive their husbands . . . and a dull country house',[8] that is because reality was a matter of such unattractive alternatives for most women in certain classes of society at that date. We do indeed have only one letter from Frederica but of the forty-one comprising almost all the story, a full score, some of them very lengthy, come from 'the opposition'—Mrs. Vernon and her mother Lady De Courcy, Reginald De Courcy and his father. The awful historical fact rushes out upon us from these pages once again; what on earth was the lively female intelligence, if passably educated and at leisure, then allowed to do with her time in this world? She could enter no profession, nor any trade without heavily losing caste (i.e. her friends' and relatives' countenance also). She was expected to be decorative, unopinionated, and committed to a routine of the most suffocating inanition. The first major feature of remark that one must bring away from reading through Austen's letters is the almost complete triviality of her daily round—the dissatisfying emptiness of it. E. M. Forster, in spite of R. W. Chapman's hurt protests against his harshness, can be said to have hit upon this feature with his most exasperated comment, despite its factual inaccuracy:

> In the earlier letters Lydia Bennet is all pervading; balls, officers, giggling, dresses, officers, balls, fill sheet after sheet until every one except Kitty grows weary.[9]

—an exasperation which is perhaps itself reflected off something rather desperate—at times—in the letters themselves. We know that Jane Austen accommodated herself to her situation and the fact that in her missives 'She has not enough subject-matter on which to exercise her powers.'[10] There was a strong element in her which approved her existence's lack (on the whole) of stirring domestic topics and its general quietude,

15

void of an external career in which to exercise her talents. She lived her life as much by choice as otherwise and very positively (one way in which she made it tolerable of course was by almost continuously writing imaginative prose from first to last).[11] I believe D. W. Harding has best reached the kernel of the matter with this commentary upon her nephew's Memoir of her:

> He also offers an idealized view of her life within her family and immediate circle of friends. When he wrote the *Memoir* he was 71 and under strong persuasion from other members of the family towards reticence and discretion. He followed the family practice of completely ignoring the existence of her defective or handicapped brother [George] and he played down her love affairs. Her sister Cassandra had done much to the same end by her ruthless destructions and excisions amongst the letters. But the chief responsibility for this polite conspiracy to idealize her situation must rest with Jane Austen herself; Cassandra's censorship was in the spirit of her sister's own tact and gratitude as a poor relation and adored spinster aunt and the patient daughter of a mother who was constantly unwell (and lived to be 88). No one who reads the *Memoir* can doubt that she followed this programme naturally and well and that it reflected part of her personality. It is equally evident that the novels would not have been what they are unless she had at the same time been a very different person.[12]

Her attitude was inevitably complex and ' "Lady Susan" ' dramatizes more exclusively than any other of her fictions this predicament of the disablingly thin outlets for female energy (at a median social level) in the life of her time.

Now we accept it as a convention of this novella that its reference is deliberately restricted. Only those items of correspondence are 'reproduced' out of the characters' lives which reflect the latest series of Lady Susan's escapades, and to some such extent one can allow that her victims are trapped by the author's chosen framework or leading-strings. Yet for two reasons our impression is the stronger that her dreaded minx of a guest is the first thing of real moment to happen to Catherine Vernon in an age. First, Austen is very fair to that lady—and to the other *dramatis personae*. Second, it is their *codes* which damn them.

There is no case for being sure that Mrs. Vernon is sexually jealous of her visitor. Her complaints do not reflect that kind of illicit animus, but only what of its nature does well deserve censure. All along the hostess of Churchill comes across as intelligent and committed to her duties. No mere mean spiteful worldling (quite the contrary—like her father-in-law her objections to the probable match between Lady Susan and Reginald are based only upon the former's character and have nothing to do with her comparative indigence) she is a woman rationally unhappy at the absolute exploitation of her husband, her brother, his family and her niece. Yet even as late as Letter 20 when she recounts the tale Lady Susan has spun her about the intended match between Frederica and Sir James Martin, she is ready to waver doubtfully and be uncertain still as to her sister-in-law's sincerity: 'What can one say of such a Woman, my dear Mother?—such earnestness, such solemnity of expression! & yet I cannot help suspecting the truth of everything she said' (p. 278). In fact Austen shows herself to have chosen just the right form for her story by the way she enlists its intrinsic subjectivism. The epistolary mode tends of itself to offer us images of life through glimpses discrete, fresh and first-hand from characters whose vision is inevitably partial and perceptibly unauthoritative. The second best subtlety of the tale is that in reading it we take quite some time to get our bearings as to the various participants' moral value; the very best is that this too is not overdone. We are not left blundering about in an unknowable world (in which case why, to begin with, waste people's eyesight on the business?); but we do undergo the salutary shock of adjusting and re-adjusting our sense of the drama's various agents as we progress through their accounts of each other.

Frederica for instance is written off in the early pages; by her mother, who calls her 'the greatest simpleton on Earth' (Letter 2, p. 245); by Mrs. Vernon, supposing 'a girl of sixteen who has received so wretched an education would not be a very desirable companion here' (Letter 3, p. 247); and by Reginald De Courcy who has heard that 'she has not even Manners to recommend her, & according to Mr Smith's account, is equally dull and proud' (Letter 4, p. 248). But when she comes to Churchill in person her aunt-by-marriage quickly develops a

17

very different impression:

> Lady Susan is surely too severe, because Frederica does not
> seem to have the sort of temper to make severity necessary. She
> looks perfectly timid, dejected & penitent. . . . Her Mother has
> insinuated that her temper is untractable, but I never saw a
> face less indicative of any evil disposition than her's; & from
> what I now see of the behaviour of each to the other . . . I am
> led to beleive as heretofore that the former has no real Love for
> her daughter & has never done her justice, or treated her
> affectionately. (Letter 17, p. 270)

The Churchill family is charmed by 'her artless affection'
(p. 272) which they hope will gradually engage Reginald's and
she becomes the object of their solicitude and protection as
simply a very sweet girl whose character, despite its cruel
upbringing, is all the more remarkably unspoiled—and we
would leave our kaleidoscopes fixed at that view but for the
fact that the hard evidence is open in some degree to different
interpretations.

True it evidently is, the poor lass deploys her acres of
solitude upon the quiet wholesome pastime of reading and she
certainly seems to the Vernons mild, good-natured and un-
affected. But we may note that in the contest between her
untutored arts and her mother's expertise in social manipula-
tion, *she is the winner* and with no small instinct of address.

Her applying to De Courcy for his intervention against the
suit of Sir James Martin *is* 'no better than equivocation' given
that she has been 'forbidden ever speaking to [her] Uncle or
Aunt on the subject' (Letter 21, p. 279) and we might remark
that the hardihood—or toughness—she shows in approaching
anybody at all for such help does not entirely match the
impression the rest of her letter gives—is designed to give?—
of being a cowering resourceless bread-and-butter miss. 'I am
aware how dreadfully angry it will make Mama, but I must
run the risk.' It may also not have passed unnoticed by us that
for all her ignorance of the world and its ways, she well knows
whom to solicit in her cause: 'No human Being but *you* could
have any chance of prevailing with her.' Her opportunities of
observing what is really going on at Churchill—and of estimating very exactly Reginald's personality and her mother's

motives, equally of romance and fortune, for not being willing to alienate De Courcy even at the cost of the designed union for her daughter—have hardly been wasted.

Equally it can be maintained, against such cynical aspersions, that the girl *is* all-artless and good, but goaded to desperate insights and measures by her horror of enforced wedlock to a half-idiot baronet. A worm will turn, very properly, and *aux grands maux les grands remèdes*. Perhaps both these appraisals are not incompatible; maybe the innocent can possess an element of slyness which will be driven to use when they are sufficiently oppressed, the artful supposably may choose to deploy their disingenuousness only to humble and worthy ends. It does not seem likely Frederica will in future lead the kind of life her mother has elected.

The fact is, we never are able to intuit this young lady's character as a moral entity. Unlike all the 'hard evidence' in her mother's case, the means of doing so definitively are withheld from us—are arguably not available yet in her career to any of her acquaintance. Time, actions alone will show where her loyalties abide; but we are not to know what they will be since this is not Frederica's story. In similar fashion Lady Susan may well be on the mark when she writes to her friend Mrs. Johnson:

> She is exactly the companion for Mrs. Vernon, who dearly loves to be first, & to have all the sense & all the wit of the Conversation to herself; Frederica will never eclipse her. (Letter 19, p. 274)

Mrs. Vernon *may* be patronizing, Frederica may be administering to her aunt's conceit. It is entirely possible they each indulge such aptitudes without being aware of it. We find ourselves not competent decidedly to determine the matter and are thus thrown back upon the complexity of human nature—are reinvested with a new active sense of this, so that these personages affect us as different indeed from the two-dimensional types or sketches one might expect in relatively so brief a treatment of their doings as the novella compacts. (We shall find a similar difficulty upon our hands if we attempt to resolve whether Reginald De Courcy is a gullible ass or a rather impressive and likeable young man.)

Yet the tale does not lapse into hapless subjectivism. The

proofs are many and absolute that Lady Susan for her part has opted to be an unscrupulous adventuress; and the reason why such a choice and the brilliant perversity of her achieved identity exhilarate us, is because these things oppose a way of life which is torpid. Letter 24 from Mrs. Vernon to her mother Lady De Courcy is over two thousand words long; and yet she has no item of news or reflection on any topic other than the doings of her delinquent guest. That throughout the story all the correspondence of 'the opposition' is similarly obsessed we come to feel not simply as a function of the narrative mode Austen has imposed upon her characters, but also as—damningly—a concomitant of their culture's emptiness. Catherine Vernon is utterly boring, like all that part of her social sphere which is respectable. For hers is not a world of initiatives. The same codes which prevent her from driving this unwanted succubus from her house (she might otherwise have had spirit enough to do it) paralyse every kind of spontaneous endeavour and self-expression in her ambit, except the under-hand. If her husband Mr. Vernon 'lived only to do whatever he was desired' (Conclusion, p. 311) his pliancy is practically a mere extension of the whole ethos of his class, in its aspect of waiting upon others' initiatives, not originating developments of one's own. Mrs. Vernon attends upon events at her rogue sister-in-law's hands because she has been bred to a series of forms and taboos which are so many shackles and manacles of the free spirit and which leave the individual with one choice; to become almost completely resourceless as a human being or outright to rebel.

Lady Susan, as we see, takes the second course and her performances (as in Letter 16) satisfy so greatly because there, albeit in perverted form, liveliness, a much ampler range of energy than polite society will allow to a woman of her station, is being called up and opposed against the deadly inertia. Yet such truancies are self-defeating, '[Her] victories are, in fact, hollow, as victories must be over a world so hollow'; since all baseness, all privation of good means self-thwarting. The practice of cheating, lying, exploitation, whether in one's attitudes to other people's property, one's child or towards suitors, denies real human mutuality at its very source and turns the larger human currents of feeling and purpose into very shallow rills.

That same sprightly intellect which prides itself on seeing through all other folks' pretensions contracts, as this narrative closes, another loveless marriage and with a semi-imbecile. This mother is estranged from her daughter and shunned by her relatives. Intrigue has inevitably long since become Lady Susan's *raison d'être*, and we are sure that were her every present desire to be crowned in having the opportunity to be wedded to the attractive Manwaring and his fortune, she would soon tire of this bond and flirt with the idea of others.

I cannot forbear to laugh out loud, however, and it is a laughter of delight, at her parting shots themselves; *viz.* her wish for Mrs. Manwaring's death and her quite unabashed suggestion to her colleague Mrs. Johnson that she might help bring it about:

> This Event, if his wife live with you, it may be in your power to hasten. The violence of her feelings, which must wear her out, may be easily kept in irritation. I rely on your friendship for this. (Letter 39, p. 308)

Her solemn perverse posture of injured virtue maintained to the end—'I have given up too much—have been too easily worked on; but Frederica shall now find the difference' (ibid.); or the notion in such a circle as she forms, whenever possible, with her London cronies, of what constitute pleasing salutations and kind regards—[speaking of Mrs. Johnson's husband] 'May the next Gouty Attack be more favourable' (ibid.); such outrageous utterances gratify by their irreverence towards the inert goodness and stolid pointless rectitude in the social scene with which they are at odds; pointless because it is a scene without livingness. Yet their whole relation to that environment is parasitic, as is their speaker's, and the exquisite aptness for me of this tale's dénouement *is* its very 'lameness'. Some games have been lost by Lady Susan, some have been won; she is in trim, as we take our last look at her, for another circuit of adventures. But her predicament is precisely that she is locked into her society and that there can be no satisfactory outlet for her energies as long as she possesses them; i.e. while she lives. Complete scandal, banishment and ostracism (which she is therefore careful to avoid) would only mean an intensification of their imprisoned condition; and there is no happy means—i.e.

21

licit and creative—of their deployment. In any case the world about her being thus, her real vitality has long since been radically corrupted to mischievous uses, which no doubt she now would not exchange if she could. All that abides is the treadmill, equally of her existence as of Mrs. Vernon's and the rest, its continuity and monotony, diversified to Lady Susan's sense only by the variety of her stratagems and the ingenuities of her treachery. The tragedy—of this individual and of her society alike—is that this cannot be the kind of story which *has* a resolution. The clarifications implied whether in a happy wedding or a wretched funeral marking a period or a development in certain human affairs are not available here. Nothing has changed at the end of this particular series of plots and contrivances, nothing can, with regard to the fundamental vacuity of such existences; not until the heroine's class and its *mores* themselves are radically altered.

In that sense it is pertinent for the author to have offered us with these pages one of those concatenations of artifice, and its outcome, which is the nearest approach to a completed action Lady Susan's career could show, but no less appropriate so to abrupt her sequence as she does—and as, indeed, with an air of sudden impatience or fatigue—at the earliest opportunity. For the endlessly active essential sterility of Lady Susan's lot and contribution in life must eventually become wearisome—to an intelligent onlooker, to any sentient being; *that is the point of the tale*.

Now admittedly Austen did not, as far as we know, seek the work's publication (though she was proud of it enough not to destroy but to make a careful fair copy of it). Also she did not even give it a title—' "Lady Susan" ' is the heading bestowed by her nephew in his *Memoir* of her life (1871 edition). Our problem with the *nouvelle* therefore is one of as it were extrinsic authorial intention. We should know for sure her attitude towards it only if she had left orders for its destruction (Virgil's decision about the *Aeneid*, one may recall) or if we could verify that she had hoped for its printing one day.

The matter is complicated. Interviewed in the act of composition at the time, she might indeed have confessed 'Oh yes, I am winding up this letter-series in the hurry of satiety. I *have* "lost patience with the device".[13] I *am* "tidying up"[14] the business as rapidly as may be. I am bored now with my story.' But that would only throw us back upon the question, whether such *ennui*, or 'her sense of unreality in keeping the game up'[15] has no valid creative function for the text in itself. (These caveats proffered by modern critics may well be officiously otiose in any case.) My own view is that ' "Lady Susan" ' is a fully accomplished and important piece of fiction and I do feel, given the all-round aptness of its ending, we should conclude at the very least that the author was writing here better than she knew.

To other studies of '*Sanditon*'[16] my account has only a little to add. As is well known, this last work was begun by Austen on 17 January 1817 and abandoned on 18 March, the month when her niece Caroline first realized just how stricken was the health of its author.[17] Since full publication in 1925 it has received much critical notice and from eminent hands. The most interesting reading of it I have yet met with is Mr. B. C. Southam's '*Sanditon*: the Seventh Novel', a paper delivered to the Jane Austen Bicentennial Conference at the University of Alberta. Admitting 'there is a limit to what can be said about a fragment only eleven and a half chapters long, a manuscript whose status is anyway questionable',[18] this works from the premise that 'the text is reasonably close to the form in which it would one day have been sent to the printer.'[19] Southam ranges over each of the social topics and satires that the fragment ventilates: Improvement (in the Repton, Rumford and analogous senses); the commercial development of new seaside resorts—'an elegant but depressing symbol of the new cash nexus . . . Unlike the humble fishing villages they replaced, the resorts had no dependance [*sic*] on the life of the land or the sea';[20] on the Parker sisters' style of Charity ('the rise of philanthropy, of organized charity, was another attribute of Regency enlightment'[21]); on the rage for motion and busy-ness in the post-(Napoleonic) War era indulged by a landed gentry idle and bored; and so forth. This commentator sees Austen's attitude towards some of these changes as quizzical, critically attentive, but open-minded; so that we can find recreation in such a scene as that where Charlotte Heywood looks out over

the now considerably altered coastal township, its 'miscel-
laneous foreground of unfinished Buildings, waving Linen, &
tops of Houses, to the Sea, dancing & sparkling in Sunshine &
Freshness' (ending of Chapter IV; MW, p. 384).

Elsewhere the drafted portion has been censured as 'remi-
niscent from first to last':

> Clearly, so far as character-drawing is concerned, Jane Austen is
> here completely in the grip of her previous novels. She writes out
> of what she has written, and anyone who has himself tried to
> write when feeling out of sorts will realize her state. The pen
> always finds life difficult to record; left to itself, it records the
> pen.[22]

This criticism I cannot endorse and Southam makes an
impressive case for believing it derived from a radical misreading. In *'Sanditon'* he sees Jane Austen's entry into the
lately revived mode of the discussion-novel, as exhibited in
Peacock's brilliant but novelistically limited *Headlong Hall* and
in the not brilliant but thematically somewhat kindred *The
Magic of Wealth* of Thomas Skinner Surr (both published
1815).

It is a plausible argument; it would account for the fact of so
little dramatic development in this earlier part of the tale—'its
twelve chapters give us no certain clue to the way in which it
was going to develop' as Miss Lascelles has remarked[23]—
which yet consorts with its real vitality, a livingness which I
don't find in the linguistically lame and structurally inert *'The
Watsons'*.[24] It would explain the so large and detailed range of
social and literary reference deployed. One after another
different types, representatives both of contemporary preoccupations and perennial fixations are exposed—not only for
their faults but also in some cases their virtues—by being
brought together to one artificial meeting-ground and made to
speak or act out with a heightened clarity their ruling ideas (it
is unfair to call either Peacock's method or that of Jane Austen
here mere 'caricature').

One thing seems supremely likely. The opening sequence
probably contains in germ-form the essential pattern of the
tale and its major nexus of interests, at least as they would
have been embodied in this first draft had *it* been completed.

For it is strange but true, how invariably the first lines of novels of impressive quality do feature in embryonic or miniaturized version their creative idea-emotion and narrative trajectory. Is not *Emma* about an indulged woman's self-will? *Persuasion* centres upon people's concern for social status and security and the various notions of identity—real and vain— which inhere in differing lives. This 'law'—unless it exists only as a figment of highly generalizing imagination—seems to hold good with all, even the longer, more compendious fictional accounts of our human sphere.

If we look at the first paragraph of *War and Peace* (I have italicized those words which in the original text are in French, not Russian):

> '*Eh bien, mon prince, so Genoa and Lucca are now no more than private estates of the Bonaparte family*. No, I warn you—if you are not telling me that this means war, if you again allow yourself to condone all the infamies and atrocities perpetrated by that Antichrist (upon my word I believe he is Antichrist), I don't know you in future. You will no longer be a friend of mine, or my "faithful slave", as you call yourself! But how do you do, how do you do? *I see I'm scaring you*. Sit down and talk to me.'
>
> [It was on a July evening in 1805 and the speaker was the well-known Anna Pavlovna Scherer, maid of honour and confidante of the Empress Maria Fiodorovna. With these words she greeted the influential statesman Prince Vasili, who was the first to arrive at her *soirée*.][25]

Does not this touch upon the major themes of the long volumes ahead?—Napoleon's career and the recurrence of warfare which will be joined on that account; the uncertain cultural identity and basis of the Russian aristocracy, as expressed in this speaker's typically using the Gallic tongue in converse with her equals, not that of her native land, the very country where she talks and has her being; the different kinds of friendship that there are, superficial and deep; historical change (the once great and powerful Genoa now just a private fief of an upstart conquering clique); and—with the reference to Antichrist—Tolstoy's abiding absorption in the question of religious faith, in Christian revelation and eschatology. Is Anna Scherer right? Will the French dictator become The Antichrist in very deed and by so doing retrospectively vindicate the New Testament as true? Is it all, is such belief, the giddy exaggeration of unsteady feminine minds, an Old Wives' Tale? Or is there a real sense in which both positions are correct?—Napoleon *is* Antichrist (that monster exists in every generation and every life), albeit that we don't have historical 'signs and wonders' (in spite of the comet at the end of Book Two) to confirm the Gospels' narratives and affirmations.

Pari passu considering its opening paragraph we see in microform the interests and procedure of *In Search of Lost Time*[26].—The question of consciousness and self-definition. The way in which each of us is not one unitary identity through his lifetime but many (the desires of yesterday we do not have today and the obsessions of a decade ago now strike us as dull and void). Our idealization of external objects—and of abstract ideas (will not 'what his reading-matter spoke of' reappear as the Church of St. Hilaire at Combray with Mme. de Guermantes kneeling there; as Vinteuil's septet with its transfiguring 'little phrase'; as the self-idealization in the role of august Plantagenet prince, the very embodiment of all that is illustrious from France's monarchical past in the snobberies of M. de Charlus?). The heightening of a particular scene or act by its past associations (dipping the madeleine into his tea, the woods seen from his railway carriage *en route* to Balbec, stumbling in the courtyard of the Prince de Guermantes); and ultimately the 'metempsychosis' which the whole novel is to accomplish. As the child 'Marcel' his character here dreams, so Proust the author will indeed become what his work speaks of; his soul's transmigration upon his death, will be into the pages of his book.

We may even note the employment of his mother-tongue's most ambivalent tense (is it working here in a 'past continuous' or a 'past historic' mode?) as indicative of how habitually his world will be one where individual occurrences illustrate—will be shown as illustrating—general laws. 'Le sujet du livre se détach*ait* de moi'; 'j'entend*ais* le sifflement des trains.' The doubt whether such things happened every night during all that lengthy period of his existence when 'je me suis couché de bonne heure', whether these events were occasional, were rare or were even unique, is allowed to vibrate at leisure. The narrator is already depicting his childhood consciousness as answering to general rules.

26

And already around all this, creating it, weaving it and through it is the unwearied song of his prose, hypertactic and long-breathed (more sonorously euphonious of course in the original French than any translation will satisfactorily suggest), which like Homer's poetry portrays the terms of our life in this world as hellish really but yet of its own beauty steps no inconsiderable way toward redeeming the experience. So much is all logically palpable, since this very beauty must be a correlate of something which is also there in human existence, as well as indignity, incoherence and defeat.

The opening of *'Sanditon'* may be considered as typifying Austen's daylight, normative and largely, though by no means exclusively, a-lyrical style.

> A Gentleman & Lady travelling from Tunbridge towards that part of the Sussex Coast which lies between Hastings and E. Bourne, being induced by Business to quit the high road, & attempt a very rough Lane, were overturned in toiling up its' long ascent half rock, half sand.—The accident happened just beyond the only Gentleman's House near the Lane—a House, which their Driver on being first required to take that direction, had conceived to be necessarily their object, & had with most unwilling Looks been constrained to pass by—. He had grumbled & shaken his shoulders so much indeed, and pitied & cut his Horses so sharply, that he might have been open to the suspicion of overturning them on purpose (especially as the Carriage was not his Masters own) if the road had not indisputably become considerably worse than before, as soon as the premises of the said House were left behind—expressing with a most intelligent portentous countenance that beyond it no wheels but cart wheels could safely proceed. The severity of the fall was broken by their slow pace & the narrowness of the Lane, & the Gentleman having scrambled out & helped out his companion, they niether of them at first felt more than shaken & bruised. But the Gentleman had in the course of the extrication sprained his foot—& soon becoming sensible of it, was obliged in a few moments to cut short, both his remonstrance to the Driver & his congratulations to his wife & himself—& sit down on the bank, unable to stand. (MW, pp. 363–64)

No ambiguous tenses in this author's narratives; for here we are in a world which is presented as available to analysis. Fanny Price and Emma Woodhouse, for example, do indeed pass through some pretty complex states of feeling; but these can be 'parsed' as it were, ratiocination on our part may disentangle and measure every thread in the complicated knot of their sensations and attitudes at such times. Likewise Austen does not record her characters' night-thoughts, they do not have dreams, and (except in *Northanger Abbey* where the whole business of the occulted is spoofed) none of her episodes take place after the extinction of the day's activity. Emma does not come downstairs uncertainly awake at 'half past two o'clock in the morning' like Abbey Flintwinch in *Little Dorrit* (Book I, Ch. IV), to find herself participating in a hallucinated reality, a preternatural heightening of the everyday world which is also an image of her own mind realized as it were externally (which she might do in Dostoyevsky as well). One of Austen's major gifts to prose fiction is to bring into it the virtues and commitments of Augustan poetry. The subliminal, subconscious and mysterious is not shut out as non-existent in our human dimension, but it is relegated to a fugitive role in this artist's pictures of life. Order is created by being imposed. Just as her characters' normal idiom is a prose of high collectedness—Sir Thomas Bertram speaks an English which even in reading we enjoy the artificial properties of; its decorum, antithetical balance, complete articulateness in short—so the conventions of her work insist that we see the world as a place where behaviour and feeling can be rationalized; that the openness of experience to full articulation, makes it manageable. This is the strength of Dryden which T. S. Eliot was referring to when he said 'Dryden's words . . . are precise, they state immensely'.[27]

That Jane Austen was aware of other aspects or possibilities of consciousness we can see in such hilarious outbursts as the following, in a letter of 3 July 1813. Writing to her brother Frank about the woman she has heard a former suitor of her own is now ultimately to marry,

> I would wish Miss Lewis to be of a silent turn and rather ignorant, but naturally intelligent and wishing to learn;—fond of cold veal pies, green tea in the afternoon, and a green window blind at night. (*Letters*, No. 81, p. 317)

The comic richness of that and exuberant vitality, the secure

energic sanity expressing itself in (what offers itself superficially as) erratic and cheerfully a-rational utterance (pure
Dickens for that matter) would repay a long page of appreciation—in between one's gusts of laughter—of what its finely
harmonized complication of tones is achieving.

But this sort of thing she suppresses on the whole in her
fiction. There her concern is with society and human moti-
vation as something which it is the duty, and within the
competence, of men to know and know thoroughly. (If it be
objected that this constitutes a limitation—in outlook, in
art—the answer is very ready; what other mode of responsible
living can be proposed?) Such a posture is clearly enough
intimated by the very syntactical signs themselves, as one may
say, of this exordium for her last work.

Tony Tanner has well remarked:

> Not, indeed, that Jane Austen refers specifically to social
> change. . . . But she does seem to catch some crucial alteration
> of psyche in people which, in little, reflects a radical shift in
> national behaviour. . . . Unlike most of her other novels (which
> usually start with some statement about the social position of a
> person or family) this fragment opens with a dramatic incident.
> A couple in a carriage travelling too fast along a rough road on
> 'Business' are 'overturned'. The commercial spirit is abroad
> and in its haste it has crashed![28]

This surely is one of the scene's 'typal' significances and so far
as that goes substantiates Mr. Southam's reading. Indeed, the
latter may well be justified in pointing to the similarity, a
deliberate reflection on Austen's part, of the preliminaries of
Peacock's lately issued *exposé*:

> [*Headlong Hall*] opens with four 'illuminati' on board a coach
> beginning a lively discussion on 'improvements'. . . . The fourth
> of the illuminati, the Rev. Dr Gaster, has only time to clear his
> throat and begin to complain at [their] 'very sceptical' and
> 'atheistical conversation' when the coachman announces break-
> fast, and in his eagerness to get out, Dr Gaster twists his ankle.
> The coachman has an intrusive presence in this first chapter; and
> it looks very much as if Jane Austen is reminding us of *Headlong
> Hall* at the beginning of *Sanditon*, where in the opening sentences
> there is an otherwise puzzling focus upon the coachman, and
> then the injury to Mr. Parker's ankle. These resemblances could

well be Jane Austen's declaration that she was beginning her own style of discussion novel. . . .[29]

If the echo be unconscious, this supports his case no less. But another equally important feature here and in what we have of *'Sanditon'* as a whole, is the difficulty of getting scenes and personages into focus. In hope of a relief for his sprain Mr. Parker points, for instance, to

> the neat-looking end of a Cottage, which was seen romantically situated among wood on a high Eminence at some little Distance—'Does not *that* promise to be the very place [where the surgeon will reside whom he and his wife have anyway come in search of]?' (I, 364)

Yet a couple of pages later we are assured on the reliable authority of the solid Mr. Heywood, his opposite in type,

> But as to that Cottage, I can assure you Sir that it is in fact— (inspite of its spruce air at this distance—) as indifferent a double Tenement as any in the Parish, and that my Shepherd lives at one end, & three old women at the other. (Ibid., 366)

Charlotte Heywood the heroine who visits Sanditon, comes disposed to view Lady Denham, that district's 'great lady', as a tyrannous dragon ruling her dependant niece-by-marriage Clara Brereton with a high hand. In fact this preconception at first seems not to meet the case.

> She c^d see nothing worse in Lady Denham, than the sort of old fashioned formality of always calling her *Miss Clara*—nor anything objectionable in the degree of observance & attention which Clara paid.—On the one side it seemed protecting kindness, on the other grateful and affectionate respect. (VI, 392).

A little further on, however, a conversation between them persuades us that Lady Denham fulfils the initial idea Charlotte brought to the place of the 'stock' appropriate character for her role of wealthy dowager.

> She is thoroughly mean. . . . I can see no Good in her.—Poor Miss Brereton!—And she makes every body mean about her.— This poor Sir Edward & his Sister,—how far Nature meant them to be respectable I cannot tell,—but they are *obliged* to be Mean in their Servility to her.—And I am Mean too, in giving her my

attention, with the appearance of co-inciding with her.—Thus it
is, when Rich People are Sordid. (VII, 402)

Yet, later again, Lady Denham's identity as avaricious takes a
knock for us, when we are shown into her home (at the very
end of the fragment): 'The House was large & handsome; two
Servants appeared, to admit them, & every thing had a
suitable air of Property & Order' (XII, 427). It may well be,
as Austen goes on to suggest, that it is her egotism which 'had
great enjoyment in the order and the Importance of her style
of living.' But maintaining a 'liberal Establishment', for whatever reason, is not easily reconcilable with the notion of Lady
Denham's ruling passion being miserliness, as was Charlotte's
just impression in Chapter 7.

In like manner Clara Brereton's is not a portrait which
gains a settled focus, albeit that when we put down what has
been achieved of this last novel we have advanced by some
23,000 words into it. (An equivalent progress through *Mansfield
Park* takes us up to the horse-riding episode in Chapter 7, when
Fanny is looking down on Dr. Grant's meadow and watching
the distant Miss Crawford exercising with Edmund Bertram's
'poor mare'. Do we not by then have established, i.e. not
contradictory, ideas of the characters of Sir Thomas and Lady
Bertram and their children; of Mrs. Norris; even of the
Crawfords—as personalities intrinsically dappled, brighter
and darker than the rest?) Clara, having been eulogized by the
sanguine Mr. Parker in Chapter 3, seems indeed to justify all his
praise on her first appearance later.

> Elegantly tall, regularly handsome, with great delicacy of com-
> plexion & soft Blue eyes, a sweetly modest & yet naturally
> graceful Address. . . . She seemed placed with [Lady Denham]
> on purpose to be ill-used. Such Poverty and Dependance joined
> to such Beauty & Merit, seemed to leave no choice in the
> business. (VI, 391)

By the way she (apparently) depresses the faluting attentions
of Sir Edward Denham she distinguishes herself from his
sister, whose haughtiness in the Parker home and cringing
servility to Lady Denham the next morning, as that magnate
and her three young relatives sit on a bench with her in the
Terrace, 'was very striking—and very amusing—or very

melancholy, just as Satire or Morality might prevail' (VII, 396).

Miss Denham's character may indeed be 'pretty well decided', by this, with Charlotte. But the next glimpse we get of Clara Brereton leaves *her* essential attitude obscured to us. Charlotte Heywood of a misty morning catches sight of her having a *rendezvous* with the same impoverished blade of a fatuous baronet who, the author has already informed us, entertains the scheme of carrying her off (and so fulfilling his ideal imagination of being another Lovelace as in *Clarissa*). Either Miss Clara therefore is playing a double game of her own, since we have also been securely told that she 'saw through him, & had not the least intention of being seduced' (VIII, 405) or we can throw up our hands on the supposition that this was indeed very much a first draft and that Austen herself was still fluidly experimenting at this stage with a situation and set of characters whose parts she had not yet determined.

Yet that theory is difficult to reconcile with the calibre of the prose by which this later episode, for example, in which Clara features, is embodied. Writing of how in this author's development 'The settings of the novels begin increasingly to participate in the action, to symbolise and comment upon it', Yasmine Gooneratne has aptly noted that the *mise-en-scène* of this 'stolen Interview'

> has been visualised in great detail, as we can recognise from the care with which, even in this preliminary outline of a novel, the description has been set out and its peculiarities 'stipulated' for. Despite the 'Beauty & Respectability' of the scene, it has been chosen by supposed lovers for a secret meeting; although sympathetic, Charlotte cannot wholly approve. Her *moralising reflection* makes clear that she imagines the relationship existing between Miss Brereton and Sir Edward Denham to be a mixture of intimate freedom and furtive guilt—an impression created in her mind by the two principal features of the hiding-place they have chosen—the open field and the fence protected and reinforced by thorn trees, whose cover has proved inadequate. Charlotte instinctively feels that the landscape before her reveals the motives and feelings of the two people who have chosen to meet each other there—*but the description tells us something of Charlotte, too.*[30]

(It is only Charlotte Heywood's assumption that Sir Edward and Clara *are* 'secret Lovers', we must remember.)

Alongside the novel's satires on hypochondria and other ruling ideas, this dramatization of phenomena which do not yield a secure interpretation also prevails, as a leading interest, through these eleven-and-a-half chapters. It is even comically constituted in the two natures, uncompromisably conflicting, which reports from different sources have accorded to the one Mrs. Griffiths about whose affairs Diana Parker has busied herself (with such 'Unaccountable Officiousness!—Activity run mad!') previous to coming to Sanditon herself.

> It would not do.—Not all that the whole Parker race could say among themselves, c^d produce a happier catastrophée than that the Family from Surry & the Family from Camberwell were one & the same.—The rich Westindians, & the young Ladies Seminary had all entered Sanditon in those two Hack chaises. The Mrs G. who in her friend Mrs Darling's hands, had wavered as to coming & been unequal to the Journey, was the very same Mrs G. whose plans were at the same period (under another representation) perfectly decided, & who was without fears or difficulties. (Beginning of Ch. XI, 420)

And we can catch this issue on the wing in the proemial passage quoted before (the very opening of the book). Just as the Parkers have there come upon a village called 'Willingden' but it is not the Willingden they have been looking for, so Austen's disclaimers only make us entertain the doubt whether or not their coachman *is* 'open to the suspicion of overturning them on purpose'. We cannot know, we probably should not have known had the tale been completed. But that is already of a piece with our being launched into a picture of the world where many motives are hard to penetrate, however much attention (and intelligent attention) be brought to bear on them.

This does not disable Austen's opportunities of humour. We have her own characteristic slyness at work again in the quiet bland collocations, so close in their observingness—'He had . . . pitied & cut his Horses so sharply . . .' or 'the Gentleman . . . was obliged . . . to cut short . . . his congratulations to his wife & himself', just as we have comedy in much that follows. Not all the characters have the ambiguity I am speaking of, by no means; but it is difficult to envisage how the large element of complex ambivalent portraiture frequent in this text would have 'squared' with a fiction of the kind B. C. Southam anticipates (though his case is a strong one too): a discussion-novel with plenty of fixed types in it representing not only perennial 'humours' but particular preoccupations of the epoch, in association (inflammatory no doubt) at this seaside resort.

What remains certain and worthy of emphasis is something Mr. Southam has said elsewhere:

> . . . it is worth remembering that as far as Jane Austen was concerned, *Persuasion* was not her last word. Virginia Woolf's speculation about the novels unwritten may also be a fanciful distraction. But it is salutary fantasy if it reminds us that Jane Austen hurried on to *Sanditon*, that her creative energies were set on the future. To celebrate *Persuasion* as a swan-song, a final statement, is unhistorical and untrue to the sequence of events as we know it.[31]

So much *'Sanditon'* certainly of itself asseverates. What else we may want to know of Austen's intentions here—whether these *were* fundamentally divided, whether her thematic interests (if, as elicited above, I *have* adumbrated them aright) would have proved uncombinable—given this work's incompleteness, must hang like most other notions about it, in a perpetual abeyance.

> *Pandarus:* But there was such laughing, Queen Hecuba laugh'd that her eyes ran o'er.
> *Cressida:* With millstones.
> > Shakespeare: *Troylus and Cressida*, II, i.

It is quite easy to make out an image of Austen's work as a repository of dark insights and bitter feelings lapped under the clever handling of a comic surface. And quite false. The most central feature of her art is its sane balance. Charity, the right kinds of acceptance, her pages distil in practically as fine a measure as she prayed for (in paragraph 2 of the third of the Prayers she composed: MW 456). With her we have a keenly critical intelligence which is also more than just critical—

censorious and frustrated. So let me here be anecdotal for the sake of a later thematic point.

F. R. Leavis has done the state more than 'some service', and I am certainly one of many very grateful for much in his writings, but a limitation was well characterized when one day at Cambridge I was fulminating to E. M. Forster about Leavis's (it seemed to me) very inadequate essay on his novels in *The Common Pursuit*. Said Forster twinkling, at the end of my breathless torrent, solely—'Leavis is always so *angry*, isn't he?'

The wholeness I want to talk about does disappear from *Emma*, it lapses and fails us there, but in her most important works—*Sense and Sensibility, Pride and Prejudice, Mansfield Park* and *Persuasion*—it inhabits *par excellence* and is the quality most worth reading this author for. Few artists have so looked at reality, at life as it actually is and people as they are, undistorted, unromanticized, few have had her degree of moral realism or turn a light so searching into the human heart. Not only are its dark places exposed, and thoroughly; we are also able to go on living with that organism shown in its interest and resourcefulness as well. Misanthropy, optimism, pessimism—these are terms no more worth invoking in connection with Austen than 'sentimentality'; such tendencies are for lesser thinkers.

Alone with E. M. Forster among the English novelists, she achieves something remarkable and precious; 'an easy commerce' of commentary and presentation. Her characters are substantiated, her situations evolve, her actions are realized and the various scenes of her works are there, living, self-existent (as it were) before us, nowise wounded but remarkably harmonized with her interference as a commentator. Mrs. Norris in *Mansfield Park* is not at all diminished or encroached upon by all that the narrator in that book has to say at her expense. Rather, *she* exists—as who should say, independently—*and* the author's comic/critical insights, in one translucent ray of full human attentiveness.

This is so difficult of achievement and it implies on the part of the fictionist such a suppression, in fact, of mere babbling self, that Forster's value as one of the great novelists is quite securely guaranteed, I think, in spite of the fact that yes, his pages are sometimes marred by whimsy and yes, he is fairly feeble on sex, politics and religion (three pretty large matters, agreed) *as topics*.

The narrators' intrusions in the works of George Eliot and Fielding, Thackeray and Zola, by comparison, are relatively heavy-handed and troublesome; and for that matter who among the important novelists dares be half so moralizing, let alone brings it off, as do Austen and Forster continuously? (A clue exists equally in the fact that Forster listened to people with an unusual complete attention, as his biographer has remarked,[32] in his conversation generally. Even though I knew him *aet. suae* 89–91, he spoke in real life exactly as his novels read—with the same pith and exactness of insight, economically expressed in the same quiet conversational manner.)

What both these authors have most in common is a peculiarly close observation of motive—motive as we offer it to public view, what we acknowledge to ourselves and the real impulses lying underneath. Austen will regularly pack the intimation of two or all three of these aspects of incentive into one description or phrase the relative brevity of which answers to the attempted sleight, morally speaking, which it treats of. The consequence for the reader is something like a stylistic depth-charge; to put the process in slow motion, one reads on with a sense of something having been not quite right in the previous sentence, some intimation at war with its superficial meaning, one goes back and rethinks the *mores* or ethos in question—which in turn is a paradigm of what the novel as a whole is inviting us to do.

> The charming Augusta Hawkins, in addition to all the usual advantages of perfect beauty and merit. . . . (E, XXII, 181)

> Emma did not repent her condescension in going to the Coles. The visit afforded her many pleasant recollections the next day; and all that she might be supposed to have lost on the side of dignified seclusion, must be amply repaid in the splendour of popularity. She must have delighted the Coles—worthy people, who deserved to be made happy!—And left a name behind her that would not soon die away. (XXIX, 231)

The arch slyness of such a method of disclosure is tonic. We are actually gratified, I think, to see that our common human nature is able to match in subtlety and rigour of honesty the ingenuities of its own deceitfulness. Thence derives the *comic* 'charge' of such writing. Austen by her very method brings into comprehensive focus the two sides of our nature and is exhilarating in enlisting the resources of one to expose those of the other. Cf. from *Where Angels Fear To Tread* (Ch. 6)— 'Harriet, though she did not care for music, knew how to listen to it.'

Yet such wholeness of outlook may not have come to her adult career so easily as we might suppose from the brilliant wit of the *juvenilia*. That much is hinted, it seems to me, by the performance which is *Northanger Abbey*. All in all it is not a very interesting book. Those critics who speak up for it would have us find there a coherent and illuminating treatment of such themes as the nature of fiction itself, the art of the novel, and innocence abroad among the manipulations and greeds of society. Katrin Ristkok Burlin for example speaks of ' "The pen of the contriver": the four fictions of *Northanger Abbey*'[33] as

> (1) the absurd extravagance of sentimental Gothic fictions; (2) the satiric, educative fictions of Henry Tilney; (3) the manipulative, egotistical fictions of the Thorpes; and (4) the satiric and realistic fiction of *Northanger Abbey* itself.

But this will not justify the novel as something of weight. Catherine Morland is simply not intelligent enough a heroine for the adventures she has to gain a general significance. Don Quixote's reading in the medieval romances of chivalry balloon him off into a series of extravagant behaviour—and significantly—because in Everyman there is a fantasist-aspirant longing for a life of derring-do and illustrious simple action upon the open road glamorously rewarded. The tales larger than life which he has studied are but the trigger to a deep human desire's unlatching which would be there whether or not authors fed it with literary fictions.

> When the knight of La Mancha gravely recounts to his companion the adventures by which he is to signalize himself in such a manner that he shall be summoned to the support of empires, solicited to accept the heiress of the crown which he has preserved, have honours and riches to scatter about him, and an island to bestow on his worthy squire, very few readers, amidst

37

their mirth or pity, can deny that they have admitted visions of the same kind; though they have not, perhaps, expected events equally strange, or by means equally inadequate. When we pity him we reflect on our own disappointments; and when we laugh, our hearts inform us that he is not more ridiculous than ourselves, except that he tells what we have only thought.[34]

Nothing of comparable value is in question in Catherine Morland's case. She is not a young woman in need of a heroic plane of action, of enlarged self-expression, finding this in the Radcliffean tale of terror and sentiment and then appropriating its referents too literally to her own outer sphere. Miss Morland plainly does not have the problem of feeling her diurnal round banal and unfulfilling. She has periods of boredom in Bath, granted, but mostly her hands are full—with the variety and interest of new scenes, 'coming out' therein, falling in love for the first time in the real world, coming to terms with the real world's behaviour (not all of it accountable). Her absorption in *The Mysteries of Udolpho* is most largely, on her part, attention simply to another new pleasure hitherto untried, and the way she seeks parallels between events in her world and those of the Gothic stories derives from her being so very innocent a country girl whose ability to compare different *kinds* of experience is so far insufficiently developed.

Her attitude to written fiction is like that of audiences in remote rural districts of the globe seeing a play enacted for the first time—say, *Othello*—and who, half way through, can bear it no longer, either shrieking at the hero advice about not being gulled or falling upon the hapless man playing Iago to tear him limb from limb. It is *il*literacy in short. Catherine Morland gets pleasure from her reading—the pleasures proper to Gothic fiction of delectable *frissons*, interesting antiquities etc.—so she looks for literally matching pleasures from reality. And just as until we learn to read, the hieroglyphs on white paper presented to our eyes are so many meaningless squiggles, then afterwards one bunch of squiggles (a word) detaches itself to our gaze from another, we having gained the skill meanwhile of interpreting them, so Catherine has to learn that literary fictions, especially in certain kinds, do reflect the actual world outside them but not as in a mirror or on the basis of a one-for-one correspondence.

General Tilney *is* a Montoni[35] in the sense of a domestic tyrant, even though he is not—and would be very unlikely to be—a wife-murderer. Society—as represented in the Thorpe siblings, for instance—*can* be treacherous, even if not peopled by 'such noblemen and baronets as delight in forcing young ladies away to some remote farm-house' (NA, II, 18). Duennas, confidants and chaperones *can* be incompetent to the point of being harmful, as Mrs. Allen is with her inanition of mind (she is like Lady Bertram of *Mansfield Park*) but it is unlikely they will actually be in cahoots with villains to have their charges abducted.

Yet all this is pretty simple stuff. It is sad if you and I, hearing Spanish spoken, cannot understand it; but it is not very significant; and that is the order of incapacity in question with *Northanger Abbey*. Austen is not evolving a profound, or even fairly interesting, fable on the theme of the gap between the worlds of art and the life outside them, e.g. the real dangers inherent in too much reliance on the imaginative faculty (? *The Tempest*), the megalomaniac tendency latent in artistry (Thomas Mann's *Dr. Faustus*), art as constituting consciousness in its most valuable aspects (Proust) or any other theme of remotely equivalent import. The distinction here is mainly between expertise and its absence in a skill the possession or lack of which does not connote *moral* capability. And the ease and speed with which the heroine moves from one of these positions to the other is of a piece with the relative triviality of her book's central issue.

Its story is not very complicated. Catherine Morland, the daughter of a sizeable clergy family which is neither wealthy nor poor, is invited to go to Bath with Mr. and Mrs. Allen, friendly neighbours in their Wiltshire village of Fullerton. During the course of her sojourn in the city of fashion and cures Catherine, absolutely an *ingénue*, meets with the Thorpe family, whose Isabella and her brother John befriend and deceive both her and her brother James Morland. Isabella professing artlessness in everything and devotion to the young man, becomes engaged to James but her ardour quickly cools when his marriage settlement does not match her expectations. (The Thorpe siblings have misconstrued the Morlands' financial resources.) Catherine also encounters Henry Tilney, a young clergyman, in the Lower Rooms, who is witty and unconventional in his address and she begins to fall in love with him. Invited to abridge her stay in Bath by only a fortnight and spend a lengthy period in the home of his father and sister, Northanger Abbey in Gloucestershire, she delightedly accepts and on the way Henry teases her hopes of finding the Abbey something out of the repertoire of the Gothic novels then fashionable, into the reading of which Isabella Thorpe has guided her. In spite of such monitory chafing, Catherine does indeed absurdly deduce that her host, the tall, very attentive and dominating General Tilney, whose presence itself represses the spirits and cheer of his children, is of a piece with the miscreants in the Radcliffean school of fiction; that his wife is either murdered or languishing 'shut up for causes unknown, and receiving from the pitiless hands of her husband a nightly supply of coarse food' (NA, XXIII, 188); and in attempting to gain access to that secluded portion of the building where she deems the hapless woman's apartments to be, both her person and her fantasy are stumbled upon by Henry Tilney:

> Dear Miss Morland, consider the dreadful nature of the suspicions you have entertained. What have you been judging from? Remember the country and the age in which we live. Remember that we are English, that we are Christians. Consult your own understanding, your own sense of the probable, your own observation of what is passing around you—Does our education prepare us for such atrocities? Do our laws connive at them? Could they be perpetrated without being known, in a country like this, where social and literary intercourse is on such a footing; where every man is surrounded by a neighbourhood of voluntary spies, and where roads and newspapers lay every thing open? Dearest Miss Morland, what ideas have you been admitting? (XXIV, 197–98)

'With tears of shame' the reign of delusion is over; but Catherine's worries are not. The General proceeds positively to encourage matrimony between his fair young guest and her friendly admoniser, only suddenly to abrupt Catherine's stay at Northanger with rudest lack of ceremony and have her bundled home, travelling alone, on the morrow of his return from a visit he has made to London.

It transpires in fact that he had been misinformed by John Thorpe at the theatre in Bath of the extent of Miss Morland's fortune. He thought her a fine catch of an heiress for his son, and being a proud mean mercenary spirit, only on that account invited her to visit. In the capital he has met Thorpe again who, now disappointed of his own hopes in the matter, has depreciated the Morlands' title to wealth almost with as much exaggeration as before he had inflated it.

In the event Henry is outraged at his father's behaviour when he learns of it upon returning there after a weekend in his own parish of Woodston. Such brutality only speeds his proposal of marriage to Catherine which he comes directly to Fullerton to make. Faced with his son's defiance and an advantageous wedding to a Viscount on the part of his daughter Eleanor, the General gives his consent after all, and Henry and Catherine are married 'within a twelvemonth from the first day of their meeting' (XXXI, 252).

Essentially it is all fairly pointless, since, as well as treating the theme of fiction *versus* life at a level too rudimentary to matter, the author is not raising other insights of significance out of her material. It has the same principal weakness as *The Tenant of Wildfell Hall*—and, for that matter, of most 'pulp' fiction in any age—it is a story and little else; and probably answers to Forster's thought about the creative impulse in respect of one of his own tales:

> The Rock was the title of this ill-fated effort. It was a complete flop. Not an editor would look at it. My inspiration had been genuine but worthless, like so much inspiration. . . .[36]

We are not made to feel new ideas about 'parental tyranny' or 'filial disobedience', nor very upset (as we are in Fielding) by the presentation of innocence adrift in a world of rapacious deceit and exploitation. It is all too bland and mild for that— superficially. Yet underneath the gentle satire upon various types of pretension—especially literary and sentimental—by which the first and larger part of the novel is distinguished, there sounds a submerged work and theme, of which the author was probably at best half-conscious, and which sinks away as Catherine travels to Northanger. *This* (other) book is redolent of a suppressed disenchantment with everything, is

41

impatient as with a final impatience of the treachery and vacuity of social life. The Henry Tilney of the first five-eighths of *Northanger Abbey* is the hero of an Austenian *Nausée* and this Henry has very little common ground for mutual contentedness with Catherine Morland.

At first sight the author's irony seems to have a limited scope—to be genial banter at the expense of such things as, in the opening chapters, the sentimental and 'romantic' fictive writing of her earlier day, in the 1790s:

> No one who had ever seen Catherine Morland in her infancy, would have supposed her born to be a heroine. . . . Her father was a clergyman, without being neglected, or poor. . . . he had never been handsome . . . and he was not in the least addicted to locking up his daughters. . . . [Catherine] was fond of all boys' plays, and greatly preferred cricket not merely to dolls, but to the more heroic enjoyments of infancy, nursing a dormouse, feeding a canary-bird, or watering a rose-bush, etc. (I, 13)

But the chafing goes on—and on. It animadverts one specious aspect of contemporary existence after another, whether fictional or real, with a sense of the *déjà vu*. From irony at the cost of the age's stock features for a heroine in a novel, and the implausible (and dubious) human characteristics of which these at once reflected and elevated the admiration, we go on to the fatuities of the actual Bath social circus.

> After chatting some time on such matters as naturally arose from the objects around them, he suddenly addressed her with—'I have hitherto been very remiss, madam, in the proper attentions of a partner here; I have not yet asked you how long you have been in Bath; whether you were ever here before; whether you have been at the Upper Rooms, the theatre, and the concert; and how you like the place altogether. I have been very negligent— but are you now at leisure to satisfy me in these particulars? If you are I will begin directly.'
> 'You need not give yourself that trouble, sir.'
> 'No trouble I assure you, madam.' Then forming his features into a set smile, and affectedly softening his voice, he added, with a simpering air, 'Have you been long in Bath, madam?' (III, 25–6)

This would be agreeable simply but that everything *en passant* has the taint of the wearily expectable or the already more than sufficiently known. People and events are seen to perform only as types:

> Sally, or rather Sarah, (for what young lady of common gentility will reach the age of sixteen without altering her name as far as she can?). . . . (II, 19)

> Mrs Allen was one of that numerous class of females, whose society can raise no other emotion than surprise at there being any men in the world who could like them well enough to marry them. . . . (Ibid., 20)

The instances are too many to quote, and may make us recall that little moment in *The Tempest* which expresses its duality of vision:

> *Miranda:*   O brave new world,
>   That has such people in't!
> *Prospero:*   'Tis new to thee. (Act V)

For this whole first half of the book especially has a very peculiar *timbre* from simultaneously presenting the world through the eyes of a young inexperienced and fascinated girl, to whom its social stage and general possibilities alike are new and exciting, and yet insinuating a really radical fatigue almost at the very processes of life:

> Monday, Tuesday, Wednesday, Thursday, Friday and Saturday have now passed in review before the reader; the events of each day, its hopes and fears, mortifications and pleasures have been separately stated, and the pangs of Sunday only now remain to be described, and close the week. (XIII, 97)

On its own this would of course be a simple good-humoured tilt at Fanny Burney's type of stolidity of minuteness in marking fictional time, but in its context of everything seen as *vieux jeux*, it carries a hint of world-weariness itself.

I am not thinking that Austen certainly knew what she was about in writing like this. That a great author as often as not produces something other or deeper than he or she probably consciously intended is one of the themes of this monograph. But such is the effect of the prolonged irony upon all the commonplaces of life and art with which *Northanger Abbey* is

43

imbued, particularly up to Catherine Morland's journey into Gloucestershire, that in the sum total of its achievement it effectually breathes nothing so much as 'the insufficiency of human enjoyments'.

Practically everything ministers to this imaginative impression. On one level the exaggerations of John Thorpe and his sister are those of a lout and a cheat respectively. Austen signalizes with the case of Isabella her view that large professions of sentiment most frequently are uttered by the selfish and calculating. But in this other dimension of the novel which is the cumulative impact of its various impatience, the Thorpes' extravagance of address, exorbitancy of speech-figures, their general histrionics strike one not only as a function of their accomplishment in lies and self-deception—this indeed—but also of a suppressed hysteria inescapable for anybody with a lively personality which has been trapped in the scenes of an unsatisfactory world for a longer period than Catherine Morland has yet experienced.

The discussion of the usage of 'nice' between the heroine and Henry and Eleanor Tilney (Chapter 14) will be seen firstly as a balanced weighing of issues, humorous and good-tempered on the part of author and characters alike:

'But now really, [says Catherine] do you not think Udolpho the nicest book in the world?'

'The nicest;—by which I suppose you mean the neatest. That must depend upon the binding.'

'Henry,' said Miss Tilney, 'you are very impertinent. Miss Morland, he is treating you exactly as he does his sister. He is for ever finding fault with me, for some incorrectness of language, and now he is taking the same liberty with you. The word "nicest", as you used it, did not suit him; and you had better change it as soon as you can, or we shall be overpowered with Johnson and Blair all the rest of the way.'

'I am sure,' cried Catherine, 'I did not mean to say any thing wrong; but it *is* a nice book, and why should not I call it so?'

'Very true,' said Henry, 'and this is a very nice day, and we are taking a very nice walk, and you are two very nice young ladies. Oh! it is a very nice word indeed!—it does for everything.' (pp. 107–8)

Primarily the book's rational attack upon contemporary

faluting, its 'general mess of imprecision of feeling, undisciplined squads of emotion', is here being extended, via Henry Tilney's pertinent protest; and not without acknowledgement on Austen's part also that spoken intercourse is a business dependent on an attitude not too punctilious, that real conversation can exist only on the basis of mutual linguistic charity. Yet there is an undertone of larger exasperation: 'and this is a very nice day, and we are taking a very nice walk, and you are two very nice young ladies.'

In the discussion of the picturesque almost immediately following, the novelist takes a broader stance than that either of Catherine's ignorance or Henry Tilney's knowledge. The inadequacy of certain features of Gilpin-style thought about and terms for Nature is neatly focused:

> The little which she could understand however appeared to contradict the very few notions she had entertained on the matter before. It seemed as if a good view were no longer to be taken from the top of an high hill, and that a clear blue sky was no longer a proof of a fine day. (XIV, 110)

but we are also made to feel the advantages of that kind of approach to landscape with its equipment of artistic terms and insights:

> and a lecture on the picturesque immediately followed, in which his instructions were so clear that she soon began to see beauty in every thing admired by him . . . He talked of foregrounds, distances, and second distances—side-screens and perspectives—lights and shades. . . . (Ibid., 111)

Criticism of criticism, of the wrong kind of discriminative *sensoria*, is on offer too—

> her attention was so earnest, that he became perfectly satisfied of her having a great deal of natural taste. . . . and Catherine was so hopeful a scholar, that when they had gained the top of Beechen Cliff, she voluntarily rejected the whole city of Bath, as unworthy to make part of a landscape. (Ibid.)

One can see if one will the main 'thrust' of this scene as a kindly mockery of Henry Tilney's youthfulness which shows itself, in his assurance and security of affable condescension to a pupil not so very many years his junior, for not much less un-selfcritical than Catherine's wild misconceptions at North-anger later. It is all very genial and delicately done; a subtle play of reactions is elicited from us by the author's skill. Nevertheless this is a famous view which the trio have walked to, a noble scene for its own sake, and given that it is mediated to us—*its* lights, shadows, perspectives—only by such means as these, the whole episode catches up organic and mineral Nature, man's external environment itself, into the book's general process of presenting all phenomena as known and already articulated and exhausted in their ability to speak freshly to a human spirit. For we are offered Henry Tilney's version of what the landscape artists' views are or would be of Beechen Cliff, not some first-hand sensation of that precipice. And the fact that a generic feature of Austen's creative personality is that

> the material solidity and circumstantiality of this world is some-thing that she had relatively little interest in rendering; there is in her novels almost none of the minute description of externals—people and their dress, houses and furniture and landscapes—that is such an important element in creating the fictional worlds of Dickens and George Eliot and Hardy[37]

will not, as an observation, true as it is, mitigate the actual effect of *this* piece of abstractness, this instance of detachment from the particular and *sui generis* for a reader of *Northanger Abbey*.

Other instances proliferate which in different ways, from different angles as it were, collectively build and fortify the through-running undertone of *accidie*: for example, the next phase of talk in the scene already canvassed. The explanation of Henry Tilney's extraordinary statement, 'Government . . . neither desires nor dares to interfere in such matters. There must be murder; and government cares not how much' (XIV, 112), is dislocated, delayed just sufficiently to make this of itself very cynical utterance reverberate with a life of its own that the elucidation on the page following never quite cancels. (And see also B. C. Southam's pertinent essay ' "Regulated Hatred Revisited" ' which treats of the uglinesses which historically speaking, for a contemporary reader must have lain under Tilney's only half-pleasant jesting in this scene on the subject of a London riot.)

It is not so much that Austen has an animus against particular human identities or failings, against the Government or the mob, against the *ton* or the sillier novelists of her day, or certain types of pretension and vanity. It is rather as if individual vents are being found to relieve a deeper exasperation, a sense of spiritual death in the face of all existence.

This must not be overstated. Let me repeat that the element I am speaking of has a sort of submerged career through the larger portion of the book and finally, as the story gains momentum, it sinks more or less out of range. But with it the novelist's interest in her tale also seems to disappear. The truly radical perfunctoriness with which the later stages of the plot are dispatched has not the intrinsic artistic function of the comparable phase in *Mansfield Park*. There (Chapters 47 and 48) the speeded wind-up of events is purposive, has a proper role with respect to that novel's central themes. In *Northanger Abbey* the scantings of the dénouement are almost an authorial recognition that her work has lapsed into merely an individual love story voided of any general significance—just as Henry Tilney has dwindled into being correct and dull. Even so late as towards the very end of the book, Austen has to explain how he could be attracted to Catherine Morland:

> She was assured of his affection; and that heart in return was solicited, which, perhaps, they pretty equally knew was already entirely his own; for, though Henry was now sincerely attached to her, though he felt and delighted in all the excellencies of her character and truly loved her society, I must confess that his affection originated in nothing better than gratitude, or, in other words, that a persuasion of her partiality for him had been the only cause of giving her a serious thought. (XXX, 243)

This is really an attempt to persuade us that the Henry Tilney we have previously known *could* have given her a serious thought, that he *is* attracted to her; and though doubtless such a motive of amorous regard is not 'new in common life' (ibid.) it does not carry conviction in this case.

Indeed the novelist gets so bored with her story that she actually admits the *ennui* of its working-out:

47

I leave it to my readers' [*sic*][39] sagacity to determine how much of all this it was possible for Henry to communicate at this time to Catherine, how much of it he could have learnt from his father, in what points his own conjectures might assist him, and what portion must yet remain to be told in a letter from James. I have united for their ease what they must divide for mine. (Ibid., 247)

She develops almost a wild abandon of 'the rules of composition', as if acknowledging in a paroxysm of self-discredit her present achievement's weightlessness:

[Elinor Tilney's] husband was really deserving of her; independent of his peerage, his wealth, and his attachment, being to a precision the most charming young man in the world. Any further definition of his merits must be unnecessary; the most charming young man in the world is instantly before the imagination of us all. Concerning the one in question therefore I have only to add—(aware that the rules of composition forbid the introduction of a character not connected with my fable)—that this was the very gentleman whose negligent servant left behind him that collection of washing-bills, resulting from a long visit at Northanger, by which my heroine was involved in one of her most alarming adventures. (XXXI, 251)

That Jane Austen could emerge from the sense of *tedium vitae* meant a series of major gains for the rest of us, and indicates something too about the partiality and less than final or authoritative nature of that experience, *that* valley of the shadow. But she had walked there and, however intermittently, *Northanger Abbey* lets us know it. Interestingly it is something else she has in common with her best disciple (one thinks of Mrs. Moore in the Marabar Cave), and I am minded of another Forsterian insight about the destructive vision which, with the bright and creative, this later novelist sees near the heart of our dispensation:

. . . the music started with a goblin walking quietly over the universe, from end to end. Others followed him. They were not aggressive creatures; it was that that made them so terrible to Helen. They merely observed in passing that there was no such thing as splendour or heroism in the world. After the interlude of elephants dancing, they returned and made the observation for the second time. Helen could not contradict them, for, once at all events, she had felt the same, and had seen the reliable walls of youth collapse. Panic and emptiness! Panic and emptiness! The goblins were right. . . .

Beethoven chose to make all right in the end. He built the ramparts up. He blew with his mouth for the second time, and again the goblins were scattered. He brought back the gusts of splendour, the heroism, the youth, the magnificence of life and death, and, amid vast roarings of a superhuman joy, he led his Fifth Symphony to its conclusion. But the goblins were there. They could return. He had said so bravely, and that is why one can trust Beethoven when he says other things.[40]

NOTES

1. The briefest exposition of this crux is to be found in B. C. Southam's headnote to the Oxford Illustrated text (as cited in my *Note on Abbreviated References* above): 'R. W. Chapman judged that the work was composed and transcribed about 1805. But the 1871 *Memoir* [by Austen's nephew J. E. Austen-Leigh] refers to a family tradition that it was "an early production" (p. 52); and according to the *Life* [*and Letters* by R. A. Austen-Leigh and William Austen-Leigh, 1913; these were the said nephew's sons] it was written about the same time as "Elinor and Marianne" (the first version of *Sense and Sensibility*), that is about 1795. My study of the juvenilia and the associated manuscripts leads me to judge that "Lady Susan" was probably written about 1793–94 (see [B. C. Southam: *Jane Austen's*] *Literary Manuscripts* [London, 1964] Ch. 3).' (MW, p. 243)
2. Penguin text, ed. Margaret Drabble (Harmondsworth, 1974) pp. 9–10.
3. R. W. Chapman, *Jane Austen—Facts and Problems* (Oxford, 1948), p. 52: '*Lady Susan* may have had a literary origin. The story is in a manner which the author did not repeat, but which she here handles very unlike a novice. It is as brilliant as its central figure. Its manner is no doubt superior to its matter. The tale is not, as a tale, too convincing, and the characters are not very well individualized. But the hard polish of the style creates a vivid illusion.'
4. Mary Lascelles, *Jane Austen and Her Art* (Oxford, 1939), p. 13, footnote— 'For all its sharp wit, I do not think it very different, in ability or temper, from the corrected version of [Austen's own juvenilium] *The Three Sisters*.'

My not adverting to Q. D. Leavis's acclaiming reference in her 'Critical Theory of Jane Austen's Writings' (*Scrutiny* X: 1941–42; XII: 1944) is intentional. The self-contradictoriness which features elsewhere in these papers—'*Lady Susan* was a remarkable feat, there is no sense of strain apparent in it anywhere . . .' (Part II, Section ii, p. 285); '. . . as unsympathetic as *Lady Susan* . . . *Lady Susan*, a slight but accomplished piece of writing . . .' (Part I, p. 65)—is anyway engulfed in the general theory which strikes me as too fanciful and uncertain for debate. The novella is in Mrs. Leavis's account subsumed, cannibalized, into her treatment of *Mansfield Park*. 'But', as she herself says, 'the very great difference that we find between [what she considers] an earlier draft of a story, and its final form, such as between *The Watsons* and *Emma*, between *Lady Susan* and *Mansfield Park* (so elaborate a change that I cannot after all even summarize it here), and no doubt between *First Impressions* and *Pride and Prejudice*, among others, is a proof of the deliberate change of intention which must have impelled the novelist to a radical overhauling of her materials and to evolve in consequence a new technique for reassembling them on each occasion' (Part I, pp. 81–2). Even if we allow, for instance, that in some sense *Emma* did have its creative germ in *The Watsons* (and I do not see why we should), such a manner of evaluating these works, where the 'changes' have been so many and radical, surely goes far to denature each of the texts in their turn.

5. Marvin Mudrick, *Jane Austen: Irony as Defense and Discovery* (Princeton, 1952), pp. 136–37.
6. Ibid., p. 138.
7. Drabble (ed.), *Lady Susan etc.*, pp. 14–15.
8. Ibid., p. 15.
9. E. M. Forster, *Abinger Harvest* (London, [pocket edition] 1945), p. 155.
10. Ibid., p. 156.
11. She seems to have been writing such things as the preserved items of her *juvenilia* c. 1787 (aet. 12!)–1793. If ' "Lady Susan" ' does date c. 1793–94 in composition (see Note 1 to this Chapter, above) then there is but a brief 'gap' in her creative activity before

> First Impressions [was] begun in Oct 1796. Finished in Augt 1797.
> . . . Sense and Sensibility begun Nov. 1797. [Cassandra Austen's note of the date of composition of her sister's novels, (reproduced between pp. 242–43 of MW); and even this gap may be accounted for by what she says in continuation—] I am sure that something of the same story & character had been written earlier & called Elinor & Marianne. . . .

'North-hanger Abbey was written about the years '98 & 99 [she concludes]', so that takes us up to the end of the old century. We do not know, presumably we never shall, how much fictive writing (including re-writing) Jane Austen did in the years following her removal, upon her father's retirement, from Steventon to Bath (1801–9). 'The Watsons' was composed then, we are given good authority to believe (see MW, p. 314). Its author herself assures us *Northanger Abbey* 'was finished in the year 1803, and intended for immediate publication' (NA, p. 12). In April 1811 she is correcting the proofs of *Sense and Sensibility* (see Letter 70). And from well before that date (we must assume), certainly thereafter for the remainder of her life, she was at work upon imaginative prose more or less continuously.
12. D. W. Harding (ed.), *Jane Austen: 'Persuasion'; with 'A Memoir of Jane Austen' by J. E. Austen-Leigh* (Harmondsworth: Penguin, 1965), pp. 267–

68. This is the edition of the Memoir to which I make reference throughout the present study.
13. *JA and her Art*, p. 14.
14. Ibid., p. 206.
15. Drabble (ed.), *Lady Susan etc.*, p. 9.
16. This title was also conferred by her family, there is no authorial imprimatur for it (see MW, p. 363).
17. *Memoir*, p. 384.
18. In Juliet McMaster (ed.), *Jane Austen's Achievement* (London, 1976), p. 1.
19. Ibid.
20. Ibid., p. 19.
21. Ibid., p. 20.
22. *Abinger Harvest*, pp. 149–50.
23. *JA and her Art*, p. 39.
24. *'The Watsons'* to my sense is principally undistinguished by being too much in a style of semi-synoptic reportage. It does indeed, at certain points, convey the terrible frustrations of the cramped social life, the existence which has strongly delimited options amidst malefic companions; see for example the last section, with the visit of the Robert Watsons and Margaret (his sister and Emma the heroine's) from their more prosperous home at Croydon. That these personages, like Emma's other injurious sibling Penelope, are arguably more crudely cruel than the villains or inadequates of the finished novels may suggest that in the process of working on her stories Austen learned to assimilate to herself and sympathize with their mischievous characters. Even Mrs. Norris is very much seen in the round and treated with a scrupulous justice. More generally, the relatively unfocused quality of 'The Watsons', the way its author goes from one episode to another, evidently with some scheme of her own in hand but in its execution too much telling her tale uneconomically, her picture a rather randomly juxtaposed mosaic of events; this can spur the critic to conclusions about the methods of Austen's art. If we take this surviving fragment as a representative early draft, we may suppose she developed her novels like a spider, creating the human depth of each by an enormous process of rough first outlines, accretions, excisions and revisions. Her statement to her nephew and biographer would harmonize with this assumption: 'What should I do with your strong, manly, vigorous sketches, full of variety and glow? How could I possibly join them on to the little bit (two inches wide) of ivory on which I work with so fine a brush, as produces little effect after much labour?' (*Memoir*, p. 380). The whole question is very interesting but essentially unanswerable.
25. *War and Peace*, translated by Rosemary Edmonds ([rev. ed.] Harmondsworth: Penguin, 1978), p. 3.
26. Here it is (translation by the present author): Longtemps, je me suis couché de bonne heure. Parfois, à peine ma bougie éteinte, mes yeux se fermaient si vite que je n'avais pas le temps de me dire: «Je m'endors.» Et, une demi-heure après, la pensée qu'il était temps de chercher le sommeil m'éveillait; je voulais poser le volume que je croyais avoir dans les mains

et souffler ma lumière; je n'avais pas cessé en dormant de faire des réflexions sur ce que je venais de lire, mais ces réflexions avaient pris un tour un peu particulier; il me semblait que j'étais moi-même ce dont parlait l'ouvrage: une église, un quatuor, la rivalité de Francois Ier et de Charles-Quint. Cette croyance survivait pendant quelques secondes à mon réveil; elle ne choquait pas ma raison, mais pesait comme des écailles sur mes yeux et les empêchait de se rendre compte que le bougeoir n'était plus allumé. Puis elle commençait à me devenir inintelligible, comme après la métempsycose les pensées d'une existence antérieure; le sujet du livre se détachait de moi, j'étais libre de m'y appliquer ou non; aussitôt je recouvrais la vue et j'étais bien étonné de trouver autour de moi une obscurité, douce et reposante pour mes yeux, mais peut-être plus encore pour mon esprit, à qui elle apparaissait comme une chose sans cause, incompréhensible, comme une chose vraiment obscure. Je me demandais quelle heure il pouvait être; j'entendais le sifflement des trains qui, plus ou moins éloigné, comme le chant d'un oiseau dans une forêt, relevant les distances, me décrivait l'étendue de la campagne déserte où le voyageur se hâte vers la station prochaine; et le petit chemin qu'il suit va être gravé dans son souvenir par l'excitation qu'il doit à des lieux nouveaux, à des actes inaccoutumés, à la causerie récente et aux adieux sous la lampe étrangère qui le suivent encore dans le silence de la nuit, à la douceur prochaine du retour.

(For a long time I went to bed early. Sometimes, with my candle only just put out, my eyes would close so quickly that I hadn't time to tell myself: 'I am going to sleep.' And, half an hour later, the thought that it was time to court unconsciousness would wake me; I wanted to lay down the volume which I believed to have in my hands and blow out my light; asleep I hadn't stopped reflecting upon what I had just read, but these reflections had taken a slightly peculiar turn; it seemed to me I was myself what the work spoke of: a church, a quartet, the rivalry between Francis I and Charles V. This belief would survive for several seconds on my awaking; it did not shock my reason, but weighed like scales upon my eyes and prevented them from taking account of the fact that the candlestick was no longer illuminated. Then it began to seem unintelligible to me, like the thoughts, after metempsychosis, of a previous existence; the book's subject would detach itself from me, I was free to identify with it or not; at the same time I would regain my sight and was truly surprised to find a darkness around me, sweet and restful to my eyes, but perhaps still more so for my spirit, to which it seemed a causeless thing, incomprehensible, as something verily obscure. I would ask myself what time it could be; I heard the whistling of trains which, now nearer and now farther off, like the song of a bird in a forest, deepening the distances, would show me in perspective the empty countryside where the traveller hurries to the next station; and the little path he takes is going to be etched in his memory by the stimulus it owes to new places, to unusual deeds, to the conversation just past and the farewells under the strange lamp which still follow him into the night's silence; to the next sweetness, that of his return.)

52

27. T. S. Eliot, *Selected Essays* (London, 1934), p. 315.
28. 'Jane Austen and "The quiet thing"—a study of "Mansfield Park"' in *Critical Essays on Jane Austen*, ed. B. C. Southam (London, 1968), p. 159.
29. *JA's Achievement*, pp. 17–18.
30. Yasmine Gooneratne, *Jane Austen* (Cambridge, 1970), pp. 45 and 46.
31. In the Introduction to his (ed.) *'Northanger Abbey' and 'Persuasion'—A Selection of Critical Essays* (in the Macmillan 'Casebook' series: London, 1976), pp. 31–2. I refer whenever possible to this volume (as 'NA Casebook') and (under the short title 'Collection of Essays') to the equally handy and worthy *Jane Austen—A Collection of Critical Essays* (in the Prentice-Hall 'Twentieth Century Views' series), ed. I. Watt (New Jersey, 1963), which also collates at low price and in easily accessible format some of the most significant critical comment published on Austen, in little space.
32. P. N. Furbank, *E. M. Forster: A Life*, Volume Two (London, 1978), pp. 293–94.
33. Her essay in John Halperin (ed.), *Jane Austen—Bicentenary Essays* (Cambridge, 1975); my quotation is from p. 90 of this book.
34. Samuel Johnson, *The Rambler*, no. 2.
35. The sinister villain of *The Mysteries of Udolpho*.
36. E. M. Forster, *Collected Short Stories* (London, 1947), p. vi.
37. Norman Page, *The Language of Jane Austen* (Oxford, 1972), pp. 56–7.
38. *NA Casebook*, pp. 122–27.
39. Probably the Penguin editor is right—*reader's* should be *readers'*, with respect to the sentence which follows, 'I have united for their ease what they must divide for mine.' As Mrs. Ehrenpreis remarks, 'Compare on [her] page 246 [250 of Chapman], "my readers, who will see in the tell-tale compression of the pages before them".' (p. 26 of her *Northanger Abbey* [Harmondsworth, 1972].) Yet this 'reader's' of the original 1818 text and Chapman's almost has the air of an authorial slip, at least as credibly as one by a printer; which in its tiny way would further substantiate my argument. See also, with regard to Chapman's letting it stand, note 1 to my Chapter 5 below.
40. *Howards End*, Ch. 5.

2

The Question of a Divided Intention (II): *Pride and Prejudice* and *Emma*

<blockquote>
'I suppose
There's no balance without the possibility
Of overbalancing.'
Count Peter Zichy in Christopher Fry's
The Dark is Light Enough, Act Two
</blockquote>

Pride and Prejudice and *Emma* are the two other novels in this canon which are felt to lie in the domain of genial comedy—by which blandness is not suggested. Like *Northanger Abbey*, 'light, and bright, and sparkling'[1] indeed, they have plenty of acerbic social criticism. But their temper is as of Thalia's ringleted locks shaken in pealing mirth, they are like remembered sunshine in most readers' recollection; and certainly *Pride and Prejudice* has the gaiety, the tonic influence of Comedy itself newly refined for the generations of men. In mercurial restraint, austerely charming, its vitalities of intellect and feeling are wonderfully harmonious.

This would be the more remarkable save for Austen's faithful moral realism, given that, like the story of *Jane Eyre*, its essential plot is an almost shamelessly juvenile phantasy. It is surely *the* adolescent girl's daydream. Her family life at home is felt to be dissatisfying (in more extreme versions, like that of Charlotte

Brontë, she is cruelly oppressed); her role in the society it admits her to is frustrating; and she has conversely the desire to achieve distinction, comfort and her womanhood's fulfilment by meeting and gaining the affections of a man who is handsome but aloof, rich but mysterious, a being (with a heart of gold in fact) whom the rest of his society holds in slightly frightened awe. (There is thus a courtship opened to her more piquant and illustrious than one leading at length to engagement with a simple straightforward sunny soul—like Jane Bennet's Mr. Bingham.) The banality of this daydream is to be observed from such details as that the hero in it is usually figured as dark (the colour of mystery) and always as tall (= dominant, not easily tamed); while in real life one knows of ladies wedded with no trivial happiness to gentlemen short and dumpy and fair-haired.

There are three reasons why *Pride and Prejudice* does not strike us as merest female castle-building in the air. First, Austen plays artful variations upon the immemorial Cinderella-story clichés which underlie her scheme. Second, this archetypal fable has of itself a real potency, it celebrates one of what Thomas Hood finely called 'the great human currents'.[2] Third, there is a lot more to the work than 'just' the ideal romance of feminine wish-fulfilment which is its structure.

Elizabeth Bennet is not the youngest of three but the second of five daughters. Her older sister is less intelligent than she; the younger siblings, in different ways, much sillier. She is not otherwise persecuted by them, though the disadvantages of being associated with her family's temperaments do in fact prove considerable. The role of domestic tyrant is fulfilled in her case, not by a step-parent actively malign but in a mother who is 'a woman of mean understanding, little information and uncertain temper. When she was discontented she fancied herself nervous. The business of her life was to get her daughters married; its solace was visiting and news' (I, 5). Her father is guilty of some of the traditional neglectfulness which disgraces the paternal figure in the fable's prototypes, but this is in subdued riposte to the mistake of having taken such a personality as Mrs. Bennet's to wife in the first place. He cultivates irony and detachment as a palliative for the really acute wound of his union and he is, as a moral agent, though much to blame in his daughters' upbringing, no entirely useless or destructive resource. He gives Lizzie all the comfort of opposing with her any idea of her marrying Mr. Collins—against the bleatings of his wife on this score—and is properly insistent that this favourite child should seriously know her own heart and enter the married state rationally, when she announces her willingness to accede to Darcy's proposals near the end (Chapter 59).

The public dance in the old folktale had the same function as it has in Austen's novels; an event both permitting a relatively intimate encounter between the hero and heroine, yet withholding equality as to their social positions *vis-à-vis* one another. Elizabeth's meeting with Darcy at the Meryton ball (Chapter 3) reverses the process of Cinderella's début. Far from spending the evening waltzing with the unknown beauty of the scene, and so preferentially as to raise the talk of the assembly, *this* Prince Charming cannot be prevailed on to dance with his future wife and only gradually and at first against his will finds her attractions irresistible. The story develops not with her closest relatives opposing a match between them or attempting to prefer her sisters in his favour, but with them constituting the difficulty of being the off-putting alliance they are and the lovers-to-be divided by misapprehensions of each other's innermost attitudes. When Darcy proposes to Elizabeth for the first time his remarks, far from being the considerate address of courteous sensibility, bristle with an ill-digested pride which in his acquaintance with this Miss Bennet he has to unlearn; while she on her side gradually discovers the sensitive, kindly and affectionate heart within his cold reserve and supercilious hauteur through observing his behaviour towards his sister and her own. Not only as Lydia Bennet's rescuer but as a man who sloughs his snobbery and shows himself genuinely feeling and considerate, he gains her respect and devotion.

And so forth; Austen inverts, rings changes upon and generally subtilizes the basic features of her poor-girl-meets-and-captivates-rich-boy story in a manner wittily amusing. The Alternative Suitor of the piece, for instance, with whom the heroine is threatened, is not simply a lesser choice in the manner of a clotpoll (like Tony Lumpkin in *She Stoops to Conquer*, for example, or John Thorpe in *Northanger Abbey*)—nor a sly villain (Blifil in *Tom Jones*, Mr. Eliot in *Persuasion*)—nor a worthy but limited being (Paris in *Romeo and Juliet*, Colonel Brandon in *Sense and Sensibility*). He is one of the richest comic creations in our literature.

Most novelists reluctantly agree to modify life and tone it down so as to make it credible in fiction. (Dickens is a glorious exception here.) Jane Austen had this scruple as much as any. Sending comments on Anna Austen's novel-in-progress which her niece had solicited, we find her in August 1814 making the usual acknowledgement that life *is* stranger than fiction and that most story-tellers, if they tell it 'like it is', will run a great risk of not being believed:

> I have scratched out Sir Tho: from walking with the other Men to the Stables &c the very day after his breaking his arm—for though I find your Papa *did* walk out immediately after *his* arm was set, I think it can be so little usual as to *appear* unnatural in a book—& it does not seem to be material that Sir Tho: should go with them. (*Letters*, No. 98, p. 394)

Yet with the portrait of Elizabeth Bennet's clerical cousin, our author casts such restraint to the winds and, which is more, carries conviction. Mr. Collins is egregious and credible. (As to a real-life original in this case, it has been suggested much of his character is a satirical portrait of Sir Samuel Egerton Brydges.[3])

> 'I have more than once observed to Lady Catherine, that her charming daughter seemed born to be a duchess, and that the most elevated rank, instead of giving her consequence, would be adorned by her.—These are the kind of little things which please her ladyship, and it is a sort of attention which I conceive myself peculiarly bound to pay.'
>
> 'You judge very properly,' said Mr. Bennet, 'and it is happy for you that you possess the talent of flattering with delicacy. May I ask whether these pleasing attentions proceed from the impulse of the moment, or are the result of previous study?'
>
> 'They arise chiefly from what is passing at the time, and though I sometimes amuse myself with suggesting and arranging such little elegant compliments as may be adapted to ordinary occasions, I always wish to give them as unstudied an air as possible.' (XIV, 67–8)

Such a colloquy exhibits in little the great distinction of this novel; that it affords as one unitary experience the dark side of social living and a compensating buoyancy which can be derived athwart its current. As we are here invited to derive laughter from watching this clergyman's 'mixture of servility and self-importance' in full cry, so generally *Pride and Prejudice* festivates the possessing a fine sense of humour, the cultivation of a subtle eye to the absurd and mirth-provoking in mortal postures. Whether in the form of characters drawn or commentary thereon, this novelist makes available a mode of genuine exhilaration, a real and substantial re-charging for our depleted energies of perception. It is not that the author's wit offers spurious mitigation of the truly dire future Charlotte Lucas has stepped into when she becomes William Collins's wife. Indeed Austen keeps that quietly in focus in the episode where Elizabeth stays at Hunsford rectory. But with the portrait of Elizabeth her creator suggests the possibility of inhabiting a narrow sphere, of reacting to its frustrations and coping with its oppressions, in the manner of her own narrative's attention to human behaviour. Impenitently independent of spirit, Elizabeth Bennet is bloodied at times but unbowed, owing to the kinds of observation she elects and the uses to which she puts them.

Now any theory of comedy is as suspect, it seems to me, as any psychological or sociological reading of behaviour—the theoretician inevitably brings from his analysis the deductions with which his mind's bent and interests are in accord. Sigmund Freud, for instance, summed up his account of the psychogenesis of the joke thus:

> For the euphoria which we endeavour to reach by these means is nothing other than the mood of a period of life in which we were accustomed to deal with our psychical work in general with a small expenditure of energy—the mood of our childhood, when we were ignorant of the comic, when we were incapable of jokes and when we had no need of humour to make us feel happy in our life.[4]

Given the great predilection for jokes, quizzing riddles, mockery and the rest which characterizes the 4-, 5- and 6-year-olds I have known, this conclusion carries little conviction into my own breast, but there it is. The human mind is like Nature.

The questions you ask about it determine the answers you will get, since both have an endless amount of evidence in stock.

Yet I do think the comic in *Pride and Prejudice*, at least, chimes with some notion of the spirit asserting itself as free. Austen does not illustrate the most public forms of tyranny, the political, those of the state. She is an analyst of the human heart as such and the constraints which operate at a personal level in the societies we make up, whether they be free or bond. Like all her heroines, Elizabeth Bennet's predicament is that of staying intellectually, emotionally, morally alive—which also includes managing to keep sufficiently happy, of course— in a space very much restricted by the misbehaviour of some of her associates and the inadequacy of others; and she does it largely by having the same kind of personality as her book's narrator. As Marvin Mudrick has remarked,

> In *Pride and Prejudice*, for the first time, Jane Austen allows her heroine to share her own characteristic response to the world. Elizabeth Bennet tells Darcy: '. . . Follies and nonsense, whims and inconsistencies do divert me, I own, and I laugh at them whenever I can . . .' (p. 57). The response is not only characteristic of Elizabeth and her author, but consciously and articulately aimed at by both of them.[5]

With good reason. It is their lifeline. They oppose to the very real pressures of their world integrity and a wholesome kind of ironic wakefulness. Elizabeth rightly refuses Mr. Collins's offer of marriage, she rightly refuses Darcy's to begin with and these are serious steps. Mr. Bennet has correctly remarked to his wife and daughters—with the sort of perverse cheer which actually aggravates for us, as often as it redeems, his (in several aspects) ugly failings—how, when he dies, 'my cousin . . . may turn you all out of this house as soon as he pleases' (XIII, 61). But even so she survives and succeeds, equally in 'finding some mode of existence for her critical attitudes'[6] and in deriving interest and stimulus thereby from persons and situations otherwise merely inane and cramping.

Early and late the narrator's wit and Elizabeth's are in happy counterpoint and sympathy. Austen offers us a multitude of her 'depth-charges':

> Sir William Lucas had been formerly in trade in Meryton, where he had made a tolerable fortune and risen to the honour

of knighthood by an address to the King, during his mayoralty. The distinction had perhaps been felt too strongly. (V, 18)

> Miss Bingley's congratulations to her brother, on his approaching marriage, were all that was affectionate and insincere.
> (LX, 383)

and throughout affords humorous perceptions of character in a fashion excellently distinguished by Professor George Whalley:

> We cannot doubt that much of what imparts electrical vitality to Jane Austen's style was her delight in effortless vituosity, in catching by an impossible fraction of a hair's-breadth the savour of a nuance of implication.[7]

An example which answers to that fine emphasis is surely the ending of Chapter 16, when the Bennet girls are driving back with Mr. Collins from their aunt Mrs. Philip's supper party:

> ... but there was not time for [Elizabeth] even to mention [Wickham's] name as they went, for neither Lydia nor Mr. Collins were once silent. Lydia talked incessantly of lottery tickets, of the fish she had lost and the fish she had won, and Mr. Collins, in describing the civility of Mr. and Mrs. Philips, protesting that he did not in the least regard his losses at whist, enumerating all the dishes at supper, and repeatedly fearing that he crouded his cousins, had more to say than he could well manage before the carriage stopped at Longbourn House.
> (XVI, 84)

Elizabeth is principally associated with this quality of outlook by being the consciousness through which most of the action and commentary passes, but her independent existence as a character 'out there' before us, and her lively depth of humorous perception is assured by her own speeches and 'indirect reported' thoughts:

> 'Your examination of Mr. Darcy is over, I presume,' said Miss Bingley;—'and pray what is the result?'
> 'I am perfectly convinced by it that Mr. Darcy has no defect. He owns it himself without disguise.' (XI, 57)

> Elizabeth longed to observe that Mr. Bingley had been a most delightful friend; so easily guided that his worth was invaluable; but she checked herself. She remembered that he [Darcy] had

yet to learn to be laught at, and it was rather too early to begin.
(LVIII, 371)

This is the novel in which Austen celebrates wholeheartedly
the possession of her own intelligence, the resource for coping
with life, especially other people, which such a faculty confers;
and its functions are appropriately bifurcated, being allotted
to her heroine's and the narrator's parts both.

Elizabeth eventually escapes the too limited sphere of her
home into an ideal marriage; and this is in the spirit of the
book. Since the purpose of *Pride and Prejudice* is to jubilate the
means by which awake and upright consciousnesses may find
'salutary refuge from all these vulgarities and pains'[8] imposed
by frustrating social life, it is apt enough that this resource,
also very real, should be focused. From time immemorial 'the
marriage of true minds' has been a sanctum of revivifying
intellectual and emotional resource for two people whose other
fulfilments in the world are less than sufficient. The question
here is not, as who should say—What would Eliza Bennet do
if the possibility of wedlock between her and Darcy lapsed;
what sort of a future would she have to look forward to, how
would she cope if it seemed empty of a satisfactory companion
(and establishment)? Nor does this novel address itself to the
issue, what she would have been like had the constraints in her
upbringing been more restrictive of the very development of
self in her case. (From the evidence quietly afforded us we may
often acknowledge that Mrs. Bennet has in fact half a point—
though by the wrong end—and this is not least so when she
cries to her daughter, 'Lizzy . . . remember where you are, and
do not run on in the wild manner you are suffered to do at
home' [IX, 42]. Fanny Price in *Mansfield Park* crucially has
lacked certain of Elizabeth's advantages here.)

No, *Pride and Prejudice* does not deal in a history of perpetual
privation; we must turn to *Sense and Sensibility* if we want that
bleakness 'straight'. But the general rapacity and cruelty of
the social world it does vividly establish, and the frustration it
would mean to Elizabeth *not* to find a good marriage. The
closeness, whether for comfort or oppression, of her human
ambience is the more enforced indeed by the novel's being so
constructed as to suggest a timeless changeless world. As Tony

Tanner has remarked in his edition,

> It is perhaps worth commenting on just how little requires, or would profit from, annotation in this book. References to topical events, or other writers, are almost totally suppressed, in spite of the fact that this was the age of Napoleon and the heyday of Romanticism.

Also, let us parenthesize, the Industrial Revolution had got well into its stride by now—yet this does not really feature in English fiction, though its radical alteration of the nature of life on earth was perceived by every participant and onlooker early, for yet another quarter-century. Tanner continues,

> This perhaps contributes to the element of timelessness in the novel, even though it unmistakably reflects a certain society at a certain historical moment. Chapman showed that, going from dates in the book, it is possible to demonstrate 'Miss Austen's punctilious observance of the calendars of 1811 and 1812', though he wisely added that 'We are still free . . . to suppose, if we choose, that she at all times conceived the events as belonging to the closing decade of the eighteenth century.' Military camps, and a 'peace' are mentioned, but so vaguely as almost to de-historicize them. Just as Jane Austen specifically excludes from this novel the possibility of purely descriptive writing ('It is not the object of this work to give a description of Derbyshire . . .'), so she is careful to keep out the clamour of large public events by allowing no references to them to distract attention from the quieter drama being enacted by Elizabeth and Darcy.[9]

In this *exemplum* legitimately the emphasis falls upon those human qualities which the author herself possessed in their fullness—at least as embodied in the narrator of her novels; for neither the voice of the book nor its heroine are 'pictures of perfection', or their offered presentments a counsel of the same. The human centrality which is Jane Austen's witty conscience, humorous perception, her comic instinct and morally responsible irony is here the asset we are to make our own.

Emma offers us the other side of the coin, exactly part of the novelist's nature which is not an asset and which ought to have come in for a lot more decisive depreciation than it has earned hitherto. Full as it is of a technical accomplishment most novelists could never match, a score of wonderful things glistening out at us from every chapter, regularly very funny and with a mirth that is healthily to be enjoyed, it is essentially a nasty book, and in evident demonstrable ways; though this only becomes determinate to the view, admittedly, over the course of its concluding phase.

Much of the work, certainly its opening, appears on a first reading to engage with Austen's regular preoccupations in a most promising fashion. Always she dramatizes the 'ordeal of consciousness' incident to a sensitive personality begirt by a society less than exhilarating—which is as much as to say, the only kind of encompassment most of us ever know. But in the other novels that individual is represented as relatively weak and powerless; economically, in status or prestige. Here she reverses the terms of the equation most interestingly:

> Emma Woodhouse, handsome, clever, and rich, with a comfortable home and happy disposition, seemed to unite some of the best blessings of existence; and had lived nearly twenty-one years in the world with very little to distress or vex her.

is how the novel begins. We are shown a young lady who is practically the absolute monarch of her condition. Much too wealthy ever to fear encountering Miss Bates's difficulties and contrivances, for the most part she is unhampered by restraints at home. As the story opens, the governess Miss Taylor, now Mrs. Weston, has left Emma's Hartfield to set up in an establishment of her own. Emma's elder sister Isabella is also married and departed. (Thus the heroine can enjoy some of the pleasures of motherhood on her nephews' and nieces' visits without the commitments and fatigues.) Hartfield is the second house of importance in this Surrey neighbourhood. The local township of Highbury which it adjoins can offer Mr. Knightley, Emma's brother-in-law and the proprietor of Donwell Abbey, the big landowner thereabout, only a shade more of respect than to the Woodhouse establishment; so that effectually in this district Emma is Queen; for her father, a valetudinarian old woman, imposes upon her few significant curbs and all the other local inhabitants have a lower social station.

The book begins fairly proposing to consider the issue— What would it mean to *be the ruler* of one's own immediate world, to have all those impediments set aside which are at the behest of fortune simply? And at first Austen does seem to be tracing with a full fine fidelity the contours of the fact that, even so circumstanced, there would still be the self to come to terms with, one has to become inwardly competent also, integrated and disciplined, to 'get the good of' one's happy fate.

Getting the good of it would doubtless mean sharing it, and Emma imagines herself in the role of generous patron when she plucks up from Mrs. Goddard's local school a Harriet Smith, the natural daughter of some unknown parents, and begins match-making for her. In fact Miss Woodhouse is in the grip of delusion. Among her acquaintance only she cares for Harriet's 'soft, blue eyes' (III, 24) or deems her a high-born changeling whose true future will disclose impressive lineage (which it ultimately does not). The matrimonial schemes she contrives for this protégée are really attempts at gaining experience by proxy. Emma is frightened of the wedded state—it would mean restraint in no little measure, for she could not be attracted to a man feeble and pliable like her father. So she puts poor Harriet through the mill; and still more Robert Martin, the local young farmer, modestly circumstanced but very respectable, who alone of the men in this vicinage is interested in Miss Smith and seeks her hand in marriage. Emma gets Harriet to abjure his offer and in its place fabricates the illusion of a courtship from Mr. Elton, the new young vicar of Highbury. This latter is much too worldly so to abase his opportunities of gain, assumes the heiress has been making up to him; suffers, as he inflicts, the humiliating discovery of their mutual mistake one night driving home from a party with her; and to Harriet's wounded feelings Emma soon enough offers the dubious consolation of encouraging her in hopes of another, better catch. Upon the identity of this possible suitor there is between the two young ladies, as between so many people on major issues in this story, a misunderstanding; Emma assumes Harriet's affections have turned towards Frank Churchill, her former Governess's stepson, the heir destined by adoption to a Yorkshire fortune. But Harriet is not thinking of him; and he has a plot of his own, having contracted a secret engagement at Weymouth the previous summer with a Miss Jane Fairfax, the almost portionless but well-bred orphan niece of the good-natured Highbury chatterbox Miss Henrietta Bates, and at present (as has often been the custom) a guest with her aunt. Churchill has been remiss enough in not visiting Highbury through the long years he has left his father Mr. Weston for his adoptive northern household; but now he does come to stay, ostensibly to pay his respects to his new stepmother, in reality principally motivated by the wish to see Jane (who for her part is on her last sojourn at her grandmother Bates's here, before going forth to her mean doom as a governess). Emma's delusions multiply. She and Churchill flirt together, which naturally, unbeknownst, makes heartache for Miss Fairfax, but on his going away for a spell, recalled by his jealous adoptive aunt Mrs. Churchill, Miss Woodhouse finds her heart unengaged. (Frank, as he is ironically named, indulges his teasing spirit in this fashion in order to give his secret better cover, but also for its own sake.) Nevertheless our heroine designs him for Harriet when he returns again, continues to flirt with him also, is rude to Miss Bates; and gets a big shock when she discovers (a) that Harriet's devotion has all along been transferred to Mr. Knightley, not Frank Churchill at all, and (b) that this latter has been leading their whole community by the nose all year. The revelation of his hidden understanding with Miss Bates's niece is made as swiftly as may be, upon the death of Mrs. Churchill and following *contretemps* between the two lovers due to which Jane has attempted to break off their pact. Harriet meanwhile, having made Emma wretched with the supposition that George Knightley may indeed return her protégée's affection, is consoled very swiftly with a renewed offer of marriage from Robert Martin, after a further *éclaircissement* unites the mistress of Hartfield and the master of Donwell Abbey.

It is the most brilliant of all detective stories; Austen's technique of revealing character and relationships, covert inclinations and activities here is at its uttermost. A diligent scanning might reveal several thousand instances in the book as a whole where hints and ligatures of motive are ambiguously glanced at or disclosed in an artful way, the hidden life of the place, its surfaces and depths glinting in the minutiae of its conversation. Here are united this novelist's principle of creating identities by making them talk and also her present theme of egotism and its solipsistic errors.

Yet its brilliant plot, its myriad echoic effects and ingeniously implanted clues entirely satisfy only if you are reading it as a detective story *tout court*. The moral attention of the author 'fluctuates' (to put it kindliest) across the trajectory of her work—indeed in a degree which to my mind makes most of the criticism on this novel shameless issue-dodging. Stein Haugom Olsen's article of recent date, 'Do you like Emma Wood-house?',[10] will stand in this respect for almost all printed appreciation of the book. He purports to take the bull by the horns and face up to the unlikeable aspects of Emma Wood-house squarely. He argues that the novel as a whole is about the assimilation of the younger generation in Highbury society. Emma can either accept her typal role and proper obligation to this society, i.e. marriage to Mr. Knightley and all that that portends, or become a self-frustrated and frustrating organism in the social body. The matter of how much we like her is much less relevant:

> Towards the end of Emma's growing-up period, marked by the termination of Mrs. Weston's pregnancy, the prospect facing Emma as a result of her egocentric behaviour is one of isolation and wretchedness.
>
> 'The child to be born at Randall's must be a tie there even dearer than herself; and Mrs. Weston's heart and time would be occupied by it. They should lose her; and, probably, in great measure, her husband also.—Frank Churchill would return among them no more; and Miss Fairfax, it was reason-able to suppose, would soon cease to belong to Highbury. They would be married, and settled either at or near Enscombe. All that were good would be withdrawn; and if to these losses, the loss of Donwell were to be added, what would remain of cheerful or of rational society within their reach?'
>
> (XLVIII, 422)
>
> As the young generation matures and marries, new nuclei of social intercourse are formed and those who refuse to accept the social code necessary for the survival of social intercourse are in the end excluded from it. However, at this stage of the novel, Emma is ready to act as a social being rather than as an un-attached individual. She has recognized the responsibilities and claims of her position as well as the nature of her predicament and is ready to fill her place in the social order. . . . The question, what sort of character Emma is and how she develops, can only be settled through an argument of the above type.'

66

Nothing of the kind can be settled before we have decided just how much growing-up Emma has really done; and it is here that the novelist is herself most dishonest.

George Knightley's embittered remarks on Frank Churchill as 'the favourite of fortune' (XLIX, 428) could be paraphrased for Emma's case also:—She plays the very deuce early and late with Harriet's possibilities of future happiness and all is absolved. Just as Mrs. Churchill miraculously dies at exactly the right moment, so the upright and manly Robert Martin, having received treatment which would have put fire into the belly of a cringing court sycophant, goes to London, there meets Miss Smith and yet again renews his addresses to this weak-headed girl who was very lucky to be offered marriage by him once—and this just at the time that Emma is otherwise to ruin Harriet's peace of mind all over again by announcing her engagement to the man she has encouraged her dupe to hope for.

And it is not simply a case of one series of injury and insult. Always, in small matters Emma's behaviour is punctilious, in large ugly, because she is a pampered egoist. Mrs. Elton's vulgarity is affronting indeed, but Emma very particularly dislikes Mrs. Elton, as Marvin Mudrick has effectually pointed out,[11] because Mrs. Elton is a caricature of the mistress of Hartfield herself. Emma has all the right-minded feelings about the interference of the vicar's wife in the affairs of Jane Fairfax—positively oppressing that poor spinster with offers of work as a governess in a *parvenu* Somerset circle—because this does not cost her, Emma, anything. But it would cost her something, a little self-gratification, to hold her tongue about Miss Bates's ridiculous way of talking, at the Box Hill picnic party, so restraint is thrown aside and the leading lady of Highbury insults this weak and senior member of its society, to her face and in a heterogeneous gathering. Mr. Knightley protests afterwards to Emma, and she pays a call on Miss Bates the next morning, first thing, by way of a covert but sincerely meant apology; and in that spirit the difficulty is closed between them. Yes, certainly Emma is shocked and hurt by her own behaviour. She is good at being very upset by it, when reason and penitence obtrude. But as in all other cases of her doing and contriving, we are to note that the price she pays for her conduct

67

is small and temporary, when for others it may prove permanent and heavy. How does the call she offers her wounded neighbour the next morning after the ill-managed trip wipe out the following consequences of her self-indulgence?—

> 'It was badly done indeed! [says Mr Knightley.]—You, whom she had known from an infant, whom she had seen grow up from a period when her notice was an honour, to have you now, in thoughtless spirits, and the pride of the moment, laugh at her, humble her—and before her niece, too—and before others, many of whom (certainly *some*,) would be entirely guided by *your* treatment of her . . .' (XLIII, 375)

Does not Miss Bates have to go on living for the rest of her life in Highbury and with this result of Emma's selfishness?—The novel is unfairly silent on such a score.

My complaint against the story's management in its later phases, the desire that Emma should suffer larger and less fleeting penalties for her generally delinquent attitudes is not a crude vindictiveness. For such in sophisticated form is the fictive mode to which Austen has committed herself, elsewhere in this novel as in the rest of her work. Other people in *Emma* pay for their experience, *pay* for being what they are, in a heightened image of the way they pay in ordinary life. Their faults, greeds, blindnesses are felt to be dangerous and threatening, yes; but these are also seen as literally contemptible, concomitants of a limited way of life and cramped kinds of consciousness. For example, Mr. Woodhouse hardly lives anything worth the name of a 'life'. We shall indeed fear as well as laugh at the Eltons, that sort of people in our world are fearful, but the novelist also makes us recognize how narrowed and *silly* a form of existence the Elton-style of one is. Frank Churchill and the heroine are spirits with much in common and it is irresistibly indicated to us that, just as Jane Fairfax's period of betrothal has been fraught, so her marriage will not be serene; even near the very end where, after all the pain he has caused his fiancée, Frank still gladly enjoys making the less savoury aspects of their engagement a matter for teasing:

> Jane was forced to smile completely, for a moment; and the smile partly remained as she turned towards him, and said in a conscious, low, yet steady voice,

'How you can bear such recollections, is astonishing to me!—
They *will* sometimes obtrude—but how you can *court* them!'

He had a great deal to say in return, and very entertainingly;
but Emma's feelings were chiefly with Jane, in the argument;
and on leaving Randall's, and falling naturally into a comparison of the two men, she felt, that pleased as she had been to
see Frank Churchill, and really regarding him as she did with
friendship, she had never been more sensible of Mr. Knightley's
high superiority of character. The happiness of this most happy
day, received its completion, in the animated contemplation of
his worth which this comparison produced. (LIV, 480)

The kind of resolute commitment to moral realism implicit
in this our last view of them is at work through the whole
portrayal of Jane Fairfax's relations with her husband-to-be.

Comparison may be made with the career of the earlier
witty heroine of this author's *oeuvre*. Elizabeth Bennet is also
very highly favoured by fortune. It is estimated that only some
400 individuals would have had Darcy's kind of income in the
England of the turn of the nineteenth century;[12] and perhaps
still fewer of these combined as he does the advantage (to a
middle-class radical Tory like Austen) of being untitled, with
the grace nevertheless of coming from an ancient and respectable family, great landowners from of old. The actual chances
for a young woman of meagre dowry, however pleasing she
might be, to find herself the wife of such a man were probably
as remote then as for any single punter in our time to win a
football pool jackpot. Yet that is not a proper subject for
critical complaint, and for the reasons remarked above. In a
celebrative comedy it is apt that the most valuable character,
with her life ahead of her, should be unusually blessed. All the
Bennet sisters present variant alternatives to the problem of
perception (so does their father): Lydia has no discrimination,
Kitty is too easily led, Mary speaks morality in the void, Jane
is *too* uncensorious; Elizabeth is right to be as critical as she is
of other people—the world shown about her justifies this
reaction—but she has to learn too that character is a thing of
layers and also may develop (as is the case with Darcy). *And
she does learn it.*

The important distinction between Elizabeth Bennet's good
fortune and Emma's is that her magnificent matrimony is the

fitting *terminus ad quem* of the earlier heroine's career, at the conclusion of the 'many blows and banes' she has undergone and in respect of the excellent though not faultless personality she has developed athwart her situation. In Miss Woodhouse's case, 'the perfect marriage' comes as yet another glittering prize in a continuous career of self-absorption, destructive attitudes and acts.

Emma's endeavours in respect of Harriet Smith are self-indulgence. Harriet is the vehicle through which her own timidity and snobbery express themselves. Harriet has to undertake, by transference, Emma's ripostes to the commonplaceness of her local community (hence the spurning of Robert Martin) and the whole business of marriage itself (the loss of domination, love in a physical aspect). That Harriet may get hurt in this process will just have to be her bad luck; each time Emma finds she has made a mess of things, she is very sorry, gets over it, turns the other person's cheek, and begins a new mischievous scheme of legislating (like Mrs. Elton) for lives other than her own. This does not make her unsympathetic or uninteresting as a principal character. On the contrary, the book's appeal begins by being grounded in her human representativeness. Few among us, alas, are wholly free from her faults and it is of great moment to every reader to see these common central traits of our common nature anatomized in her history. Nor is she without excuse. Trying to live life by deputy is a likely enough reaction on the part of our human fearfulness, and Emma's snobbery is equally a matter of asserting her Queenship (the Sovereign Baby refuses to give up ruling, even after leaving the nursery) and a flexure of her not unjustified resentment at the feebleness of her neighbourhood's weak intellectual pulse. Mr. Weston's 'unmanageable good will', at first something which seems genial and pleasant, becomes cumulatively irritating over the story as a whole. The utter triviality of outlook which it reveals eventually makes him simply an irritation. His wife's talk, though san*er*, is by no means exhilarating; and the same can be said for the whole Highbury set. Emma is a much more exciting conversationalist than the rest of them:

If it would be good to her, I am sure it would be evil to himself

70

[Mr Knightley]; a very shameful and degrading connection. How would he bear to have Miss Bates belonging to him?—To have her haunting the Abbey, and thanking him all day long for his great kindness in marrying Jane?—'So very kind and obliging!—But he always had been such a very kind neighbour!' And then fly off, through half a sentence, to her mother's old petticoat. 'Not that it was such a very old petticoat either—for still it would last a great while—and, indeed, she must thankfully say that their petticoats were all very strong.' (XXVI, 225)

This is witty, it is skilful mimicry indeed, as well as only half fair.

We feel for her in her loneliness and boredom—the lack of interesting equals. If she takes out so good a whack of her resentment, as here above, on the one person who makes a big job of being contented in this uninspiriting social echelon— Jane Fairfax's aunt—that is understandable. But understanding does not mean exoneration in Austen—one of the marks of her profundity as a mind everywhere else in her work. *Emma* purports to be a study, like the other novels, of the difficulties and rewards incident to a sensitive spirit coming to terms with life, the life of society. But in fact the matter is fudged. Not only does the heroine achieve wishes beyond her deserts, we are asked to believe that she knows how to enjoy them aright, the first seven-eighths of the book having shown just the reverse. She has abused the privileges of her single life all along, yet now we are to believe in 'the perfect happiness of the union' once she is Mr. Knightley's bride. No authorial irony surrounds this statement, any more than it comes into play in the final sequences of their courtship. The marriage is creditable in so far as we well appreciate that Miss Woodhouse also has qualities to do it credit; but it is not credible, as a match noble, gracious and happy, given the habit of reducing others' identities to extensions of her own—or (like Mrs. Elton) angrily rejecting them—in which Emma's faculties have long since been ingrained. The achievement of that kind of 'durable fire', the notion of nuptials deeply felicitous and symbolically healthy Austen's subtlest art is most speciously enlisted to impose.

It does so in ways I have already glanced at. Inconvenient questions—like the one about the buffet Miss Bates's social position has taken at the Box Hill party—are ignored.

Wondrous convenient 'reversals—like Harriet's renewed proposal from her young farmer—are provided at the level of plot.
Everybody is catered for, every difficulty smoothed over, so that
Emma will not seem guilty of being the really ruinous creature
she is.

Why Austen should have pressed ahead with erecting this
structure for an unreal daydream in which egoism is critically
identified but essentially endorsed—just in the manner that
Emma handles her own self-knowledge—I do not know. I do
not believe in bringing biographical elements into literary
commentary—they have to be essentially impertinent, in both
senses, if the text is really worth thinking about at all—but
there may be a clue in the author's alleged remark, 'I am going
to take a heroine whom no one but myself will much like.'[13]
Maybe it was a bank holiday trip for her very intelligence, a sort
of ethical blow-out. We all betray our best insights from time to
time and perhaps even Jane Austen, born into frailty like the
rest of us, had her lapses of the spirit. What I really must rub my
eyes at is the reputation of this one among her fictions.

Arnold Kettle and Marvin Mudrick are not part of the
conspiracy of approval. Their memorable essays at least go so
far as sharply to recognize that features of the work are unpleasant, though still they writhe upright meanings out of it by
wire-drawn processes. There is a lot more to say about the
novel's virtues and strengths of course—and such praises have
been omitted here because these and its general brilliancy of
address have been sung by everyone everywhere else. Yet if the
essential revolt it inspires in my nerves be still to justify, then
there is a lot more that could be said about that too.

There is, for instance, the failure of the portrait of Jane
Fairfax—rather a gap in Austen's plan. On the one hand
Emma is supposed to convict herself ultimately of having been
unfair to Miss Bates's niece: uncharitable and ungenerous to
her from no better motive than jealousy. And it is true she has
resented all along Jane's self-discipline and accomplishments,
is not particularly fond of the aunt's constant eulogies or the
girl's own beauty, and seizes on Frank Churchill's churlish
'blind'—the idea that Miss Fairfax has retreated to Highbury,
on this latest visit, from a love-entanglement with another
man—as a way of exercising her spleen against a young woman

72

whose possible rivalry as the local cynosure the lady of Hartfield is not ready to enjoy.

So the authorial writ is to run. Yet in fact this scheme breaks down. We do not, we cannot, indict Emma in this case of grievous impetuous misjudgement, for one of her principal complaints against Miss Fairfax—'she did not know how it was, but there was such coldness and reserve—such apparent indifference whether she pleased or not' (XX, 166)—the novel at large justifies. It is no good the narrator insisting this 'was a dislike so little just—every imputed fault was so magnified by fancy' (ibid., 167), for until the scurried tidyings-up of the end Jane Fairfax is only mediated to us in that frigid character. Emma's resentment is valid, not merely on grounds of her own piqued vanity, but because 'coldness and reserve' as characteristics, 'such apparent indifference whether she pleased or not' as Jane Fairfax does display through almost all the tale, *are* mortal affronts, certainly in a society restricted like Highbury's where in the arts of cheering human intercourse most human resources are invested.

With the benefit of hindsight we are supposed to see it is simply or mainly that Jane has dwelt under heavy duress— from the fact of her secret engagement, from Churchill's behaviour and his aunt's caprice, from the ever-approaching misery of the governess-condition—but her each appearance being distinguished by coolness, *and not only to her apparent threat Emma*, her character as a cold fish in our view cannot retrospectively be undone; not even by the appearance of a new Jane Fairfax who looks differently and speaks with a different syntax and is motivated on different principles from of yore, when in the conclusion, with her engagement declared, she talks to Miss Woodhouse on Miss Bates's stairs (LII, 459). That scene, worth marvelling at only as a piece of legerdemain, is another gross instance of the artfulness which conceals artfulness on the novelist's side in this book. The matter cannot so be blurred with one closing episode. Emma's original condemnation, we should recall, dated from and refers to the period of her acquaintance with Jane Fairfax before Frank Churchill was ever known to either of them.

There is the wound of Mr. Knightley's characterization— the one figure of power and possessions who does arouse a 'political' irritation in this student of the Austen novels. If he is so woodenly perfect and supplied with all life's answers why is he silent about the economics of a society where, according to his own recognition, the likes of Miss Bates (let alone the poorer folk of the district) are to slip further and further downhill?

There is the almost incestuous element in the novel's technique, which is wonderful but overblown; the begetting of itself upon itself, so that ultimately it invites some such comment as F. R. Leavis's upon *The Ambassadors*: 'Isn't . . . the energy of the "doing" (and the energy demanded for the reading) disproportionate to the issues—to any issues that are concretely held and presented?"[14] It is, for instance, clever, amusing, satisfying, that in one particular chapter (21) Mr. Woodhouse is twittering on about the necessity for the Bateses'—or anybody's—health not to eat roasted the pork Emma has in fact sent them, and certainly not the loin to be so cooked, when Miss Bates walks in and later in the scene, all disconnectedly and after a maelstrom of her thanks and chat—which is still more full of unconscious point and import for the attentive reader—indicates that that is just what she and her mother are going to do: 'My dear sir, if there is one thing my mother loves better than another, it is pork—a roast loin of pork—' (p. 175). We enjoy our own archness eyeletting these details together, doubtless in a fashion correspondent to that of the author in writing the scene. But as a characterizing gesture, as yet another scintilla proleptic of the book's larger movement as a whole—here the idea that Mr. Woodhouse proposes but the people around him dispose—it does not tie in. At the end still one more *deus ex machina*—the unprecedented visitation of pilferers to the neighbourhood's poultry-yards (Chapter 55)—has to be wheeled on to gain his consent to his daughter's marriage. And this example is only one of an innumerable multitude of such phenomena in the text, to each of which an ideal reader would be awake. Repeat such acts of attention on his part a thousand-fold, the holding of them all up in the air, like a juggler's trick, from first to last, so that a multitude of early evidences modify a multitude of late, and, given that the text as a whole is destined to slide into a simple women's magazine love-story, so far as its credibility and significance are concerned, is it all worth that kind and degree of mental effort?

Emma is indeed a failure, but of a special kind. Arguably Austen well knew what naughty deed she was about in penning it.

> . . . I will do myself the justice to declare that, whatever may be my wishes for its success, I am very strongly haunted with the idea that to those readers who have preferred 'Pride and Prejudice' it will appear inferior in wit, and to those who have preferred 'Mansfield Park' very inferior in good sense.[15]

My whole objection to the book is not that it suffers from inadvertence or oversight on the author's part; rather, that with a breath-taking technical achievement, it is deliberately and (speaking again for my own nerves) unenjoyably perverse. Yet in the same paper in which one critic speaks of Elinor Dashwood's secretive silence and its consequences as 'one of the most complete messes in fiction',[16] *Emma* is (inevitably) praised to the skies; not but what his masterly elucidation of the complex play of tones in the extended passage where this heroine, newly delivered from her delusion about Mr. Elton's feelings for Harriet, sits and broods over her error, I can only applaud;

> . . . the registration of Emma's mind in action . . . as she deals with the incontrovertible facts of the case, has an intensity, a complexity, a vocal power that makes it the comic equivalent, in both method and value, of Macbeth's 'If it were done when 'tis done.'[17]

Bating his point about the scene's absolute value and yet sifting the said chapter (16) how we may, it simply is not possible to conceive any fictionist in prose more subtly tracing the velleities, impetuses, side-winds, now wayward now resolute intermixture of these impulses, in a mind at debate with itself. The constantly changing kaleidoscope of Miss Woodhouse's reactions, to her situation and her own character, are created with an authenticity which other novelists possibly may equal but it is unimaginable any talent should every surpass, whether realizing this or whatever other kind of psychological moment. And it is equally a measure of novelistic control that the inward dialogue so presented affects us as comic and serious, delinquent and sympathetic, by turns and all together.

The issue raised by that episode of (as it were) soliloquy is the question of Emma's honesty with herself, but to a central crux herein Professor Garis does not address himself, though that crux is well expressed in Marvin Mudrick's chapter on the novel:

> It is a very circumscribed honesty, it operates characteristically in the trough of failure and disaster, before the next rise of confidence and self-delusion; and it is another inextricable strand in the complex ironic web. Emma can recognize how badly her matchmaking schemes have turned out and resolve never to attempt them again—*but without recognizing why she attempts them at all* and keeps coming back to them.[18] (Emphasis added)

The fact is that, at any level sufficiently deep to be worth talking about, this heroine is allowed by her author *not* to recognize 'why she attempts' her various interferences 'and keeps coming back to them'; and, equally unnaturally within the pattern of Austen's style of fiction, she is not forced to encounter a proportionate defeating result of such escapes from self-knowledge. The conclusion of Mudrick's study is itself specious:

> The irony of *Emma* is multiple; and its ultimate aspect is that there is no happy ending, easy equilibrium, if we care to project confirmed exploiters like Emma and Churchill into the future of their marriages.[19]

That is true of Frank Churchill, because in his case the author has held to the guiding light throughout of her other fictive endeavours—moral realism—and she certainly does imply the volatile, by no means sufficiently reassuring and kindly marriage Jane Fairfax has to look forward to, in the latter phases of this story. But the notion of Emma's ironic presentation itself suggesting a complex future in her case cannot be so extrapolated.

For one thing it is more her book than Frank Churchill's; his is definitely a subplot; and her appearances before the reader end with wedding-bells in the traditional manner of the most relaxed and approving kind of comedy. There is not even with the last sentence, as in *The Bostonians*, a minatory note struck by the novelist. Here, rather, the story-teller's full privilege is enlisted to authorize the most contented afterlife for Miss Woodhouse:

> ... the wishes, the hopes, the confidence, the predictions of the small band of true friends who witnessed the ceremony, were fully answered in the perfect happiness of the union. (LV, 484)

Not that this needs saying, particularly; the ultimate triumph of Austen's art in this work is to suppress all really difficult questions about Emma's development so repeatedly, and to award her (actually in defiance of probability) so continual a series of personal rescues from each of her blunders, that we come to feel it as immitigable law that Emma *has* a charmed life; that in any material matter—like her relationship to Highbury and its townsfolk, or the quality and felicity of any marriage she may make—happiness will be a *donnée* of her situation, a given thing, over all but the shortest term assured.

> 'Do you dare say this?' cried Mr. Knightley. 'Do you dare to suppose me so great a blockhead, as not to know what a man is talking of?—What do you deserve?'
>
> 'Oh! I always deserve the best treatment, because I never put up with any other. . . .' (LIV, 474)

This can beguile other readers as it may. All of us have elements in us which would like to join Austen's wonderfully realized pink dream. It *would* seem nice if we could live under a dispensation such that, whatever we chose to do, the Universe would bestow upon us the treatment we should like ('because we never put up with any other'). And it seems fairly evident to me that the book has been written to indulge, via identification with its heroine, exactly this ugly fantasy, this craving for (after all, pretty base kinds of) acceptance and support by which all selves are assailed. Perhaps the novel's popularity derives from its entertaining the aspirations of egotism so fundamental, with far more subtlety than any lesser artist could contrive. But this has nothing to do either with reality or decency.

Yet what is the point of reasoning more on this subject? What is the point, indeed, of saying so much? These faults surely stand out very clearly; but an universal *ukase* has gone forth to disregard them. Introducing his 1971 edition of the novel David Lodge enunciates the only expectable view:[20]

> *Emma* was the last completely finished product of [Austen's] maturity; and in the opinion of most modern judges it is, of all her novels, the one which most perfectly represents her genius.

NOTES

1. *Letters*, No. 77, p. 299.
2. Here I trip up over that stumbling-block which perhaps sends every student sprawling once in a while. I know and have cherished this phrase of Hood's for a long time but in seeking to lay my hands on its provenance cannot trace this. I have the same difficulty with the Forster comment on Fanny Price (please see my chapter on *Mansfield Park*, p. 124). Can any reader of better information, more retentive memory or simply more alert powers in the diligence of research help me to these utterances' location (which doubtless will prove in the event to be discoverable printed in capitals at some such obvious spot as page 1 of their respective authors' Collected Works)?
3. See Frank W. Bradbrook, *Jane Austen and Her Predecessors* (Cambridge, 1967), pp. 124–36 (especially 134–36).
4. Sigmund Freud, *Jokes and Their Relation to the Unconscious*, transl. J. Strachey (Harmondsworth: Penguin, 1976), p. 302.
5. *JA: Irony as Defense and Discovery*, the very opening of ch. IV, which is also to be found in *Collection of Essays*, p. 76.
6. D. W. Harding, 'Regulated Hatred: An Aspect of the Work of Jane Austen' (originally in *Scrutiny*, VIII: 1940, reprinted) in *Collection of Essays*, p. 170.
7. George Whalley, 'Jane Austen: Poet', in *JA's Achievement*, pp. 121–22.
8. *The Notebooks of Henry James*, ed. F. O. Matthiessen and K. B. Murdock (New York, 1947) p. 111. This phrase comes from an entry James made, apostrophizing his own spirit, in October 1891.
9. *Pride and Prejudice*, ed. Tony Tanner (Harmondsworth, 1972), p. 397.
10. *Critical Quarterly*, Vol. 19, Number 4 (Winter 1977), 3–19.
11. *JA: Irony as Defense and Discovery*, p. 194; also to be found in *'Emma'—A Selection of Critical Essays* (in the Macmillan 'Casebook' series), ed. David Lodge (London, 1968), p. 117. I refer whenever possible to this volume (as 'E Casebook') like its companion on *'Northanger Abbey' and 'Persuasion'*.
12. See G. E. Mingay, *English Landed Society in the Eighteenth Century* (London, 1963), ch. II passim and especially p. 26.
13. *Memoir*, pp. 375–76.
14. F. R. Leavis, *The Great Tradition* (London, 1960), p. 161.
15. *Letters*, No. 120, p. 443.
16. *Critical Essays on Jane Austen*, p. 65 (Robert Garis, 'Learning Experience And Change').

17. Ibid., p. 76.
18. *E Casebook*, p. 127.
19. Ibid., p. 120.
20. *Emma* (Oxford English Novels Series), ed. D. Lodge (Oxford, 1971), p. vii.

3

The Great Tragedy of Social Life: *Sense and Sensibility*

Yasmine Gooneratne offers almost the mildest in the range of critical opinions by which the first published of Austen's novels is saluted in print:

> Of *Sense and Sensibility* alone, perhaps, can the word 'immaturity' be used with any real meaning, . . . it bears many marks of its author's inexperience—notably a certain crudeness in characterisation and an unevenness of texture that betrays uncertainty and a flagging interest. And yet, even here, so unified does the novel seem that such weaknesses appear only when we compare it with her later work.[1]

Reginald Farrer was much more dismissive:

> With *Sense and Sensibility* we approach the maturing Jane Austen. But it has the almost inevitable frigidity of a reconstruction, besides an equally inevitable uncertainty in the author's use of her weapons. There are *longueurs* and clumsinesses; its conviction lacks fire; its development lacks movement; its major figures are rather incarnate qualities than qualitied incarnations. Never again does the writer introduce a character so entirely irrelevant as Margaret Dashwood, or marry a heroine to a man so remote in the story as Colonel Brandon. This is not, however, to say that *Sense and Sensibility*, standing sole, would not be itself enough to establish an author's reputation. . . . But its tremendous successors set up a standard beside which *Sense and Sensibility* is bound to appear grey and cool;

nobody will choose this as his favourite Jane Austen, whereas each one of the others has its fanatics who prefer it above all the rest.[2]

Most twentieth-century views are to be found at various points along the spectrum bounded by such evaluations, confident in their very qualified applause. The three essays which have become established as the weightiest appreciations of the novel in our time: Marvin Mudrick's chapter on it, and introductions of 1961 and 1969 by Ian Watt and Tony Tanner respectively to reprints of the text; even these concur in believing that part of the time here Austen is being dishonest. 'Marianne, the life and center of the novel, has been betrayed; and not by Willoughby' (Mudrick);[3] '. . . there is certainly an unconvincing quality about Brandon, especially when he tells all to Elinor; and the final marriage to Marianne is hurriedly presented and psychologically unconvincing' (Watt);[4] '. . . Looking back through the book one can see that very often the validity of Marianne's responses is subtly undermined by giving them an edge of caricature—as though Jane Austen were defending herself against her own creation' (Tanner).[5]

One thing we can be sure of, however, is that the author's opinion of this book was drastically higher. There is not only the telling reference to it in her letter of 25 April 1811, when she was correcting the proofs:

No indeed, I am never too busy to think of S & S. I can no more forget it, than a mother can forget her sucking child . . . (*Letters*, No. 70, p. 272)

There is the hard fact that, alone of the work she had achieved by 1809–10, this was the fiction she elected to present to the public on what might well have proved the first and last occasion of her having any such opportunity. It is worth recalling the history, by no means really felicitous, of Austen's dealings with publishers (and it is well summarized by Jane Aiken Hodge in a bicentennial article[6]) to make this point quite clear.

The very first attempt to get her work into print of which we have any evidence is her father's, the Revd. Mr. George Austen's, when he wrote on 1 November 1797 to the major London publisher Thomas Cadell seeking to interest him in a manuscript novel, comprising 3 vols., about the length of Miss Burney's 'Evelina'. As I am well aware of what consequence it is that a work of this sort sh^d make its appearance under a respectable name, I apply to you. I shall be much obliged therefore if you will inform me whether you choose to be concerned in it, what will be the expense of publishing at the author's risk, and what you will venture to advance for the property of it, if on perusal it is approved of. Should you give any encouragement, I will send you the work.[7]

No encouragement was given, perhaps unsurprisingly—publishers have a hard enough time finding anything to like amongst what they are sent, let alone angling for reproducible matter from the amorphous sea of the unknown—yet Miss Lascelles properly deduces,

> The Austens, however, continued to think well of *First Impressions* [which almost certainly, given the date of George Austen's letter and from Cassandra Austen's 'Note of the date of composition of her sister's novels'[8] this was]; there are references to readings and re-readings of it in Jane's letters, and in its later form [*Pride and Prejudice*] it remained a favourite among them,

and 'She . . . seems to have recovered her confidence in it without waiting for encouragement'[9]—in as much (we should qualify this by remarking) as that allegedly 'by April 1811 *Sense and Sensibility* was in the printers' hands [i.e. had not yet received the verdict of its public reception], and *Pride and Prejudice* far advanced.'[10]

We know of no other attempt till 1803 when the author's brother Henry, through his agent Mr. Seymour, approached Richard Crosby and Co. (of Stationers' Hall Court) who agreed to pay £10 for the copyright of *Susan*, the original version of *Northanger Abbey*. Yet now something very bizarre developed. This book was actually once advertised by this publisher—in *Flowers of Literature* for 1801–2 (published 1803)—and that is as far as its promulgation went. Crosby monopolized but did not issue it and when in 1809 Austen wrote to him under the pseudonym Mrs. Ashton Dennis (=MAD?) suggesting she should send another copy if the original 'by some carelessness' had been lost, and threatening to find another home for it should she not hear from him, with no less inconsistency than his behaviour had shown hitherto he sent an immediate reply to her *poste restante* at the Post Office, Southampton (in which city she now lived) admitting the novel's purchase, pointing out that no date had been agreed for its publication, in his turn threatening proceedings if she published elsewhere, and offering her the ms. and its copyright back for the money he had paid for it. In the event he continued to engross *Susan* till 1816, when Henry Austen redeemed this pledge and 'When the bargain was concluded and the money paid, but not till then, . . . had the satisfaction of informing him that the work which had been so lightly esteemed was by the author of "Pride and Prejudice".'[11]

Austen's domestic fortunes looked up in 1809 with the bestowal of a grace-and-favour cottage in Chawton upon her mother, sister and herself by her prosperous brother Edward Austen Knight, inheritor of the great house to this Hampshire village where she now went to live. Whether or not the event was an exhilaration or stimulus, certainly at this time she appears to have decided on one more determined effort at reaching a wider audience; for though no letters survive for the period 26 July 1809–18 April 1811, at that latter date we find her revising the proofs of *Sense and Sensibility*, which appeared at the year's end. That at last near her thirty-seventh anniversary and after two-and-a-half decades of writing she achieved 'the muffled majesty of authorship' was not owing to this ermine's being thrust upon her shoulders by any bookseller's acclaiming insistence but because she contracted with Thomas Egerton of the Military Library, Whitehall (not a major publisher) on what for him was a 'can't lose—may win' basis, issuing the work on commission. For the author

> This meant that she paid the expenses of printing the book and took the receipts, subject to a commission paid to the publisher for his handling of it. This was not the most hopeful method of publication. A publisher who was confident of a book preferred to buy the copyright outright, or, perhaps, to pay all expenses and then share the final profit with the author (the basis of the modern royalty system).[12]

In his *Biographical Notice of the Author* Henry Austen, who again acted for her on this and subsequent occasions tells us that so persuaded was she that its sale would not repay the expense of publication, that she actually made a reserve from her very moderate income to meet the expected loss.[13]

But since it cost between £100 and £200 in those days to produce an average edition of a three-volume book (like *Sense and Sensibility*) and since the total stipend of the Chawton ladies was £460 per annum—'The greater part of George Austen's income had died with him'[14]—one or other of her brothers, probably Henry, must have helped Jane Austen fund the venture. All we know of her strictly scrupulous and honourable character makes it inevitable that if this first publication had lost money, she would not have permitted her relatives or anyone else to assist her a second time in risking capital; even if she and they had been inclined so to do.

In short what took place was a single desperate throw of the dice. After her previous series of hiatus and disappointment she was to establish herself as a publishable, a financially and critically endorsable, novelist on this occasion or never. Blessedly in fact the scheme was successful.

> She could scarcely believe what she termed her great good fortune when 'Sense and Sensibility' produced a clear profit of about £150.[15]

though even thereafter the chances of her authorial career seemed uncertain enough to her own imagination for her to part with the copyright of *Pride and Prejudice* for £110.

> Egerton got a good bargain. The first edition, probably of about 1,500 copies at 18 shillings, came out in January 1813 and was sold out by July. Once again there were good notices in the *British Critic* and the *Critical Review*, and Egerton printed a second edition in November, presumably without telling Jane Austen, who might have asked for more money and would certainly have corrected the errors she had pointed out in the text.[16]

Yet that lay in the future, and her biographers have puzzled over why, circa 1809–10, it was *Sense and Sensibility* on which she chose to stake her first appearance (and in my view what must have seemed to her her only chance) and not *Pride and Prejudice*; or for that matter *Northanger Abbey* and ' "Lady

Susan" '—all four of which were now completed, albeit in other than their final avatars.

There is one sole possible inference from all of this; and that is that, whether or not she thought it the most likely to succeed, *Sense and Sensibility* was the book which Austen most wished to preserve and disseminate. It may well have been an agonizing choice. We know that *Pride and Prejudice* was also 'my own darling child'[17] and her opinion of Elizabeth Bennet has been felt with a thrill by all the world—

> I must confess that I think her as delightful a creature as ever appeared in print, and how I shall be able to tolerate those who do not like *her* at least I do not know. (*Letters*, No. 76, p. 297)

But indigence, like being about to be hanged in the morning, wonderfully concentrates the mind; and what could Jane Austen do, in the last analysis (which all her difficulties of getting published had brought her to), but literally put her money on the work she valued as the deepest and most representative of what she had accomplished to date. Certainly she cannot have thought it, as her critics do, weaker—in parts more wooden, less convincing and less honest—than these other productions. If she were to be once again unfortunate, and that looked a strong possibility at the time, she would surely choose to 'be hanged for a sheep and not a lamb'. Of all that had been accomplished hitherto *Sense and Sensibility* was the novel she determined to secure to posterity.[18]

For those who are intelligent, sensitive and just, is human society worth the pains they have to take to live with it? That is the question at the heart of *Sense and Sensibility*; and this is one of the great tragic novels because it answers 'No' with a very fine calibration of the complexities of social life.

The tale particularly concerns two sisters. Upon Mr. Henry Dashwood's death his widow has to leave Norland, her home and that of her three daughters, which falls by inheritance to John Dashwood, her late husband's son by a former marriage. Far from giving them substantial help as pledged to his dying father, the new owner and his wife, 'a strong caricature of himself;—more narrow-minded and selfish', consider these four women well enough provided in having their own five hundred pounds a year; and the latter remove far away indeed—from this Sussex estate to a cottage in Devon—when Mrs. John Dashwood insults her stepmother-in-law by intimating that an engagement between Elinor, the eldest of that lady's daughters and Edward Ferrars, her (Mrs. J. Dashwood's) brother would be highly unpleasing to his family. Edward and Elinor have been mutually attracted, during his recent sojourns in his sister's new home, but it is some little while after the Dashwood ladies' establishment in the purlieus of Barton Park, the estate of their kinsman and landlord Sir John Middleton, before he takes up their offer of hospitality and comes to visit.

Meanwhile Marianne, the second daughter, has encountered a very good-looking and lively young man John Willoughby— her 'preserver, as Margaret', the youngest of the girls, 'with more elegance than precision' styles him; for the meeting derives through her spraining her ankle on a nearby hillside and Willoughby's assistance carrying her back to her new home. The impetuosity which caused the accident in the first place governs their attitudes towards each other and very soon, though no formal declaration of engagement is made, the young couple are so evidently wrapped up in one another that all their acquaintance suppose just such an understanding to exist between them. (Prudent discretion is alien to Marianne's temper, as to her mother and younger sister.) Nevertheless Willoughby comes one day to inform them that he has to leave the district and without a guarantee of returning there in any brief period. The others assume this may be due to snobbish meanness on the part of the old rich relative in his life, Mrs. Smith of Allenham Court not very far away, whose heir Willoughby hopes to be and who may have vetoed both his contracting so modest an alliance as one with the ill-dowered Marianne and his remaining in her neighbourhood.

All are abashed after he has departed to London, but Marianne's hopes glow again when she has the opportunity of following him there. This is in company with her elder sister and Mrs. Jennings, a good-natured, somewhat vulgarly cheerful woman who is mother-in-law to Sir John Middleton. Mrs.

Jennings is a widow amply left with a fashionable town house and she takes the two Dashwood sisters to the capital for the late winter and spring season by way of providing outlets for them (she is something of a matchmaker) and company for herself.

Written at her new abode near Portman-square Marianne's notes to Willoughby, however, produce no visit from him and at an evening party, in 'a room splendidly lit up, quite full of company, and insufferably hot', when they do see him at last and he offers merely a hasty acknowledgement, Elinor Dashwood only with difficulty avoids a hysterical scene, quickly getting her sister home. The morrow brings a letter from the erewhile sweetheart disclaiming any relationship between them more than a polite friendliness of past date—somewhat inconsistently with the lock of hair he had formerly begged of Marianne and which he now returns as well as the letters she has sent him.

His marriage to a wealthy heiress Miss Sophia Grey is soon publicized and Marianne with wretched sleeplessness indulges all her emotional misery and the bodily disturbance she allows it to create. Yet she appears to have avoided an unhappy fate after all when Colonel Brandon—a fellow-visitor with the Dashwoods at Barton Park during the previous autumn, and now newly again in London—reveals to her sister his knowledge of John Willougby's previous history. This, like Wickham's in *Pride and Prejudice*, features the debauch of a young ward, Eliza Williams, herself an illegitimate child left to the Colonel's guardianship by her mother, whom he had adored and lost in time gone by (he is now 36–37 years old). Brandon and Willoughby have fought a duel over the issue, but neither was hurt, and the Colonel presently awaits his unhappy protégée's lying-in.

During all this time Elinor has secretly endured a heartache of her own from an equal and analogous cause. At Barton in the autumn two other kinsfolk of the Middletons have been staying, the Misses Steele, and Lucy, the younger of this pair of not particularly refined ladies, has notified Elinor that Edward Ferrars's affections are bespoke, in having paid vows of affiance to *her*. He and his partner in this secret engagement are of the same age, and four years previously, when he was 19 and not yet entered at Oxford but still staying with her uncle Mr. Pratt the tutor in Exeter, they had contracted their alliance which his mother's mean-spirited financial snobbery would inevitably reprobate, should it ever be discovered to the world.

It is pretty clear that Lucy Steele holds Edward Ferrars to this consequence of the early infatuation on his side, long after he has wearied of her company, purely for worldly gain; not least because she indefinitely defers their wedding (thus much of relief is afforded him) which could lead to his almost complete disinheritance. She wants to be sure of the money, not the man, and is only confiding her secret to Elinor so as to establish squatter's rights and to torment her rival. Elinor's hopes seem as inevitably exasperate by Edward's honour as her griefs are by her own, since Edward must hold to his betrothal, and she, having pledged absolute silence about this information and the other barbed remarks offered her in the matter from Lucy, cannot relieve her misery in confidential communications of her own—any more indeed than she wants to, given the mere emotional turmoil such confidences would unhelpfully invoke from her family.

Mrs. John Dashwood responds warmly to the sycophancy of the Steele girls when she meets them in London, for they too have come up to town, and she invites them to stay at her residence there, pointedly thus snubbing her sisters-in-law. But she finds these pains ill-bestowed when Anne Steele 'pops it all out' about Lucy and Edward, and with violent hysterics she has the visitors bundled out of her house. Mrs. Jennings and the rest of their acquaintance are shocked at this ill-treatment of what they suppose is innocent love; and Colonel Brandon generously offers what he can, the (albeit not very well-endowed) living of Delaford ('the late incumbent, I believe, did not make more than 200l. per annum') in his gift as patron and local squire in that Dorset village, once it is learned that Mrs. Ferrars has cast off her eldest son for this offence of his engagement to a portionless and unprestigious girl and has promised furthermore that ' "if he were to enter into any profession with a view of better support, she would do all in her power to prevent his advancing in it" ' (XXXVII, 267). To Elinor falls the further painful plight of having to inform Edward about his 'good' fortune.

Then the Dashwood young ladies leave the capital, and in

their way home to Barton visit Cleveland, the home of Mrs. Jennings's younger daughter Charlotte Palmer, newly delivered of a son. Marianne, in spite of now having learned of her sister's unhappiness and observed the very different fortitude with which it has been borne, continues to give scope to the expression of her wretchedness and a walk in the wet uphill woodlands of their new abode following upon the weeks of poor feeding and scant sleep with which she has rioted her feelings now produces a really serious illness from which she nearly dies. Her mother is sent for but, two hours before she can arrive, Elinor hears a carriage pull up, sees a different one in the drive from Colonel Brandon's who has gone to fetch Mrs. Dashwood and, on rushing downstairs to break the news of a new improvement in her patient, finds only Willoughby in the drawing-room. He has travelled almost ceaselessly from London that morning, full of anguish lest Marianne should die and die without his motives in the treatment accorded her by him having been ameliorated in her sight. He has a passionate conversation with Elinor seeking, not unsuccessfully, to exculpate his behaviour in some degree, before plunging back to the city and his loveless match of convenience there. It appears he would have asked Marianne to marry him but that Mrs. Smith discovered his villainy in the matter of Eliza Williams and cast him off. With his expensive tastes and extravagant career of accumulated debts, he deemed it essential now to wed for money; hence his execrable conduct immediately before and since he last left Barton.

Marianne recovers, chastened in body and spirit, and when she has removed with her mother and sister back to their Devonshire home and Elinor finds an appropriate opening for the subject, she is informed of what Willoughby has said. She is now resolved upon the life as of a well-regulatedly studious anchoress, but her mother and elder sister anyway cherish the likelihood of her coming to recognize the quiet earnest love Colonel Brandon has felt for her all along and agreeing to his marriage proposals when they are made.

All remission in matters of the heart seems to be foreclosed for a long while in Elinor's case, when they are told by their servant over dinner one day that in Exeter he has seen Lucy Steele that morning in her new character as 'Mrs. Ferrars'; but it turns out that the Mr. Ferrars Lucy has ultimately married is not Edward—rather, his silly coxcomb of a younger brother Robert, upon whom their mean rich mother has settled an inalienable fortune at the time of Edward's fall from grace. The latter is now a free man and can come post-haste, as he does, to Barton Cottage to pay at last his proper addresses to the woman he really cares for. The story concludes with this young couple settled in Delaford Parsonage by Michaelmas of that year, sufficiently reconciled with Mrs. Ferrars senior for them to have received a donative which permits their married life on terms modest but not penurious, and with Marianne's hand bestowed on Colonel Brandon and his patient devotion.

The novel is written in such a fashion as to be readable two ways—like the lives upon which it centres; and the aptest reception of it consists in holding to both modes of attention simultaneously. Both are sufficiently solicited.

In one aspect it is a subtle cautionary tale on the theme of emotional restraint and self-indulgence. Broadly speaking the two sisters embody different outlooks. Marianne adheres to the Romantic ideals of spontaneous feeling and 'the holiness of the heart's affections'. To a large degree she acts out the basic Rousseau-istic premises about the native benevolence of Man and his instinctual wholesomeness as a social being when he is not oppressed by cruel circumstances and his speech and conduct are not perverted into dishonest forms by worldly considerations. This makes her in fact an alarming and mischievous liability. In the earlier phase of the story, until the visit to London is well under way, one actually flinches at her participation in any social scene, so likely is she to worsen matters for herself and those associated with her by her free expression of inward feelings. It is not only that the actual morality of her behaviour's laws has itself not been thought through very hard:

> 'What a sweet woman Lady Middleton is!' said Lucy Steele.
> Marianne was silent; it was impossible for her to say what she did not feel, however trivial the occasion; and upon Elinor therefore the whole task of telling lies when politeness required it, always fell. (XXI, 122)

To that as to most instances of divergence between these sisters' rules of conduct we have, or should have, a complex response.

It is also that a commitment to 'immediacy'—whether of utterance or action—under an apparently guiding belief in honesty, sincerity etc., can in fact be as good a way as any other of muffling the real nature of what it is one does. When Willoughby and Marianne, during his courtship of her in Devon, whirl off for a visit on their own to Mrs. Smith's house at Allenham and look all over her property in uninvited secrecy, they are guilty of cheap bad manners and should know it. But the most alarming thing of all is that when her sister remonstrates with her to this effect, the younger Dashwood lady cannot see her objection:

> 'I am afraid,' replied Elinor, 'that the pleasantness of an employment does not always evince its propriety.'
> 'On the contrary, nothing can be a stronger proof of it, Elinor; for if there had been any real impropriety in what I did, I should have been sensible of it at the time, for we always know when we are acting wrong, and with such a conviction I could have had no pleasure.' (XIII, 68)

That there is irony in the episode as well as shame, is to be noted. Later Marianne's disappointment in losing Willoughby will be heightened by their having undertaken an expedition so speaking in the intimacy it implied; she will be able to visualize the house she would have occupied before long as Mrs. Willoughby, the domestic haunts that would have become dear to her and her husband; and Elinor's appeal that the trip has already exposed her sister to 'some very impertinent remarks' (ibid.) is equally of application in refuting the fallacy with which Marianne has defended herself.

But these are lesser matters beside the snake in the grass which this little colloquy highlights; how the moral sense itself soon begins to dissolve in the warm self-endorsing bath of such a belief in Sentiment as Marianne, after the pattern of leading eighteenth-century philosophers, exalts. Her wilfulness, in this earlier part of the story, is egoistic and can be very irritating.

Elinor's line of attitudes however is also a fraught one. She espouses the virtues of restraint and in the same earlier phase of the novel comes regularly before us as a welcome relief, sane and necessary amongst the three other females who make up her household (for Margaret the 13-year-old youngest of the sisters is also nowise enamoured of moderation in anything). Elinor dissuades the family from extravagant expenditure upon needless developments to their new home which they cannot afford, and her demand that Mrs. Dashwood should get clarification of Marianne and Willoughby's relationship according to social usage and in defiance of their 'romantic delicacy', their disregard of such conventions, is fully justified by the collapse of their *un*spoken, *un*official engagement. (Indeed, if we bother to note what is later revealed, we may reflect that had Mrs. Dashwood so provoked an earlier declaration from Willoughby, either Marianne would have been spared some of her pain— that of having plunged further into a trustful regard for this visitor—or their marriage would actually have taken place. He would have been a pledged committed being in the eyes of all society—and we are further to remember that his wedding a respectable woman would have released Mrs. Smith's bounty upon him after all.)

When Elinor nevertheless, talking with Colonel Brandon at Barton, says of her impulsive sister such things as ' "A few years however will settle her opinions on the reasonable basis of common sense and observation" ' and ' "a better acquaintance with the world is what I look forward to as her greatest possible advantage" ' (XI, 56), we smile as well as being in essential accord. Adult life and conversation did begin earlier at that period (as is observable from the book as a whole; for one thing people tended to expect shorter lives); yet this *is* the voice of inexperienced 19 confidently criticizing, out of the false dawn of a supposedly ripe maturity, a sibling who is only two years younger than herself.

The hopes Elinor expresses are pertinent, Marianne *has* a lot of 'sense' to learn; but we come to perceive also how the belief in worldly wisdom has alienated Youth itself from her sister's life. Elinor has not completed her second decade of existence when Mrs. Jennings aptly fails to think of her as 'one of the young ladies' (XIII, 66). Moreover, 'when the means are autonomous they are deadly'; 'sense' elevated into a social principle can prove every bit as destructive as uncontrolled 'sensibility'. Restraint, moderation of one's utterance is inevitably of a piece with keeping a secret, and confidentiality as such relies on that. But the very ideal of honour has got out of hand when, according to the codes of this time, it is proper and expectable in Colonel Brandon that he should fight a duel with John Willoughby but cannot reveal what he knows about Marianne's apparent suitor till all her woe has encumbered her; or that Lucy Steele can hold Edward Ferrars to his engagement when each of them is not in love with the other. We have reached a situation where the villainous can and do imprison the virtuous by the shackles of the latter's own integrity; Lucy's secret behaviour with Robert Ferrars (which leads to *their* engagement) attends on no such laws and simply has an eye to the main chance.

Elinor is committed to making her peace with the world by living as much as possible on its terms. But the attempt to do so without compromising one's principles is dangerous as well as difficult. A heightened respect for the social codes can produce a courtesy which, as Marvin Mudrick has remarked, 'is liable to contract on occasion into a cold hypocrisy hardly distinguishable from its object'.[19] The scenes between Lucy and Elinor not only establish the former as a thoroughly nasty piece of work, they show us the pervertedness of her character—its dishonesty and dissimulation—transferring to her companion because not opposed by outright reproof, whether of contemptuous silence (Marianne's response to Lucy's conversational gambits) or denunciation. When consenting to accommodate herself—in outward forms—to Lucy's strategems, Elinor effectually is sucked into the Mrs. Ferrars type of morality. After all, the penalities of speaking with Lucy being severe, the unholy compensations inevitably become the more indulged:

> 'With almost every other man in the world, it would be an alarming prospect; but Edward's affection and constancy nothing can deprive me of, I know.'
> 'That conviction must be every thing to you; and he is undoubtedly supported by the same trust in your's. If the strength of your reciprocal attachment had failed, as between many people and under many circumstances it naturally would

during a four years' engagement, your situation would have been pitiable indeed.'

Lucy here looked up; but Elinor was careful in guarding her countenance from every expression that could give her words a suspicious tendency. (XXIV, 147)

As Mudrick comments on this

> . . . the point is not so much that Elinor must learn these things by some method or other, as that she exploits Lucy's own method without hesitation, even with eagerness; that dissimulation, no longer distinguishable from courtesy, becomes a positive pleasure, sanctified by custom and most useful in social emergencies.[20]

And of course such immersion in the witches' brew does not rub in and out at our heroine's mere good pleasure. The habit of prudential social intercourse imposes itself even on some of the utterances she gives vent to in the bosom of her trustworthy family. When Edward has paid a call on the two Dashwood sisters in their London accommodation and Lucy Steele, having come round before him, sits out this visit of someone she must know to be an old friend of theirs, a kinsman by marriage who has not seen them for a considerable period, Marianne, though still as yet unenlightened about this trio's tangled relations, is properly vexed at her bad manners:

> 'What can bring her here so often!' said Marianne, on her leaving them. 'Could she not see that we wanted her gone!— how teazing to Edward!'
>
> 'Why so?—we were all his friends, and Lucy has been the longest known to him of any. It is but natural that he should like to see her as well as ourselves.'
>
> Marianne looked at her steadily, and said, 'You know, Elinor, that this is a kind of talking which I cannot bear. If you only hope to have your own assertion contradicted, as I must suppose to be the case, you ought to recollect that I am the last person in the world to do it. I cannot descend to be tricked out of assurances, that are not really wanted.' She then left the room. . . . (XXXV, 244).

At this miniature climacteric Elinor has delivered herself neither of what she knows to be the truth, nor of a charitable, really necessary lie, nor of something accurate but non-committal. Such language of un-meaning (and in the most active sense of that word—it constitutes a raid on the principle of meaningfulness itself that is here being performed), which long persisted-in would wither any relationship to the roots, is well within hailing-distance of the verbal blur where the John Dashwoods choose to spend their whole lives. To sup with the Devil you need a very long spoon.

Nevertheless Elinor is not of his party. As I have argued we are given to see, she and Marianne are not unfaulted *exempla* of human nature. (And welcome; Austen's own remark about fictional characterization, 'pictures of perfection as you know make me sick & wicked',[21] will surely find an echo in most readers.) But they are very attractive personalities, being seriously committed to truth and justice, and most of the time discriminatively withal. They are, indeed, refreshing oases of virtue and living-mindedness in a fairly desert zone where these qualities are too often seen to deliquesce and lapse.

Mrs. Ferrars and the John Dashwoods are odious without a redeeming feature. Egotism is the beginning and end of their characters, and it impinges on their associates with particular unpleasantness in the form which consists in living vicariously through kindred thoroughly dominated. This can show them for contemptibly funny as well as alarming:

> But [Edward Ferrars] was neither fitted by abilities nor disposition to answer the wishes of his mother and sister, who longed to see him distinguished—as—they hardly knew what. They wanted him to make a fine figure in the world in some manner or other. His mother wished to interest him in political concerns, to get him into parliament, or to see him connected with some of the great men of the day. Mrs John Dashwood wished it likewise; but in the mean while, till one of these superior blessings could be attained, it would have quieted her ambition to see him driving a barouche. But Edward had no turn for great men or barouches. All his wishes centered in domestic comfort and the quiet of private life. Fortunately he had a younger brother who was more promising. (III, 15–16)

Yet what they principally inspire us with is hatred and fear. The greed and miserliness of the John Dashwoods, the

irrational tyranny of Mrs. Ferrars (her stupid younger son
Robert ends by committing a still greater marital offence
than Edward has done, but she is better reconciled to him
and his wife, Lucy Steele, and provides for them more generously, because the silly-nasty pair are willing flatterers)—
these embody the rapacities of exploitation which are to be
met with in certain individuals everywhere and who make
life a much more troublous, incarcerative experience for
others than it need be.

The supreme irritation of such beings' existences, which
again and again has with difficulty to be coped with by the
virtuous, Austen vividly evokes throughout. The conversation between Mr. and Mrs. John Dashwood in Chapter 2,
where, from doing something material for their bereaved
mother-in-law and her children—as promised to his father
on his death-bed—they reason each other out of any charitable act at all, is justly famous; for the way it exemplifies
this possibility in human nature, Austen's knowledge of that
abyss and people's capacity for deliberate self-deception, her
skill in dialogue, in economically presenting given characters, their anterior history, the very rhythm of their thought
and idiosyncratic tricks of their speech. But this is only one of
many such instances in the novel, and the cumulative impact
of them is pithily to realize for the reader the dark moral
environment in which the intelligently generous-spirited have
to lead their lives.

When Elinor meets John Dashwood at Gray's shop in
Sackville-street and he rejoices to find ways of speaking of his
much greater wealth as less than hers, not inviting his half-
sisters to stay with him and his wife either in London or back
at their own old home in Sussex, and on top of all this, by way
of compensation, bestows upon himself an immaculate conscience by hopefully estimating Elinor's and her sister's values
in the marriage-market, it is very hard not to wish that a large
celestial boot would just descend from on high and utterly
squash the repositories of hypocritical, exploitive, greedy
unkindness which are this particular human insect and its
equally horrid allies.

Insensitivity and insolence made powerful by worldly fortune the whole work shows as very prevalent in the social

scene and this intuition even provokes in the author two utterances (to my sense) slightly hysterical:

> Lady Middleton was equally pleased with Mrs. Dashwood. There was a kind of cold hearted selfishness on both sides, which mutually attracted them; and they sympathised with each other in an insipid propriety of demeanour, and a general want of understanding. (XXXIV, 229)

> Mrs. Ferrars was a little, thin woman, upright, even to formality, in her figure, and serious, even to sourness, in her aspect. Her complexion was sallow; and her features small, without beauty, and naturally without expression; but a lucky contraction of the brow had rescued her countenance from the disgrace of insipidity, by giving it the strong characters of pride and ill nature. (Ibid., 232)

A bitter desperation seems to dwell in the relative heavy-handedness of such commentary. The remarks are accurate enough on one level, there *is* a mutual attraction between the cold-heartedly selfish (when their interests do not diverge), but it is not expressed with such open crudity as to stand self-exposed and condemned before the human majority. In these instances it is as if Austen is trying to turn into rhetoric as of a public response to the three women some punitive insights which will compensate for her feeling of impotence in respect of such types' successful predominance in the world. But that response is not general, this is not how Mrs. Jennings, Sir John Middleton, Lord Morton *etcetera* see these ladies; the manner of perceiving them here given vent is limited to a few, the awareness of the morally observant. If the narrator could truthfully claim instead that personalities of this kind invariably fell downstairs and gave both their legs compound and irreparable fractures, the tone of sarcastic contempt—'a *lucky* contraction of the brow'—would not be requisitioned. It is after all something fairly crude, at least in respect of this author's expressional compass, and one feels it is chafed out of her by the felt meagreness of such utterances', of any utterances', revenge.

Of course there are other kinds of people as well, and an element in this novel's great achievement is that it exhibits a full range of human types—within the representatively

delimited sphere of acquaintance available to its main characters; a sphere every bit as ample—in terms *of* its range—not
only as anything Austen and *her* sister could have known, but
also as most of her readers will have acquaintance with in their
own lives. Introducing a valuable collection of essays, B. C.
Southam addresses himself to what he sees, it would appear,
as *the* Austen critical problem:

> . . . reconciling the notion of literary 'greatness' with the
> modesty of Jane Austen's achievement. Modesty, with its
> personal ring, is the very word, because it draws attention to
> the author's self-imposed and self-declared limitations (which
> we can find in her correspondence, particularly with the Prince
> Regent's Librarian, the Rev. W. Clark). It also draws attention
> to the author's presence in the novels, a personal stance in the
> grace and charm of her narration, in the quietness of style, and
> in the affected incompleteness of the author's knowledge and
> control over her characters' destinies. These are the tactics of
> irony. There is modesty, too, in the limited range of subject-
> matter and treatment. And any critic convinced of Jane
> Austen's greatness, of her claim to be considered alongside
> such writers as George Eliot, James, Conrad or Lawrence, in
> the English tradition, or Tolstoy, Fontane, Stendhal, Kafka or
> Proust in the wider European scene, bears the responsibility of
> explaining the remarkable phenomenon of such 'limited'
> greatness.[22]

The reasons why Austen's work is as important and of as wide
an application as that of these other novelists my whole study
addresses itself to intimating, but in respect of the *dramatis
personae* of *Sense and Sensibility*, we need to avoid being
bamboozled, here more than ever, by the clichés of un-
examined rhetoric about 'real life' in relation to the fictionist's
purview. For how many of us know well or at any one time
have much to do with as many as fifty people in our actual
existences—or twenty? For that matter, unless they marry
early, how many women, even in modern mobile fluid
emancipated society, easily find a spouse after the age, say, of
30? If you are really looking for realism, you have as much of it
in this story-teller's booth as anywhere.

Sir John Middleton is by no means all bad. He is free
equally with the things of his table and good wishes towards all

his acquaintance. The difficulty is that, like Mr. Weston in *Emma*, his inanity makes him not really worth knowing. Relationship depends upon discrimination, which includes being willing (though not happy) to sift and reject this person and that from one's best opinion. How can the Misses Dashwood feel that conversation with Sir John has any value when he is as delighted with the Miss Steeles' company as their own, as anybody else's, and when he cannot distinguish between matters of the chase and of psychology itself?

> 'And what sort of a young man is he [Willoughby]?'
> 'As good a kind of fellow as ever lived, I assure you. A very decent shot, and there is not a bolder rider in England.'
> 'And is *that* all you can say for him?' cried Marianne, indignantly. 'But what are his manners on more intimate acquaintance? What his pursuits, his talents and genius?'
> Sir John was rather puzzled.
> 'Upon my soul,' said he, 'I do not know much about him as to all *that*. But he is a pleasant, good humoured fellow, and has got the nicest little black bitch of a pointer I ever saw. Was she out with him to-day?' (IX, 43–4)

His sister-in-law Mrs. Palmer and her husband also afford conversation and society which is pointless. Charlotte is simply fatuous—whether or not in nervous reaction to her husband's taciturnity—and laughs at everything as well as being entirely self-contradictory:

> Mrs Palmer, in her way, was equally angry. 'She was determined to drop his acquaintance immediately, and she was very thankful that she had never been acquainted with him at all. She wished with all her heart Combe Magna was not so near Cleveland; but it did not signify, for it was a great deal too far off to visit; she hated him so much that she was resolved never to mention his name again, and she should tell everybody she saw, how good-for-nothing he was.' (XXXII, 215)

Mr. Palmer sins by being excessively the opposite of his spouse.

> Elinor was not inclined, after a little observation, to give him credit for being so genuinely and unaffectedly ill-natured or ill-bred as he wished to appear. His temper might perhaps be a little soured by finding, like many others of his sex, that

99

through some unaccountable bias in favour of beauty, he was the husband of a very silly woman,—but she knew that this kind of blunder was too common for any sensible man to be lastingly hurt by it.—It was rather the wish of distinction she believed, which produced his contemptuous treatment of every body, and his general abuse of every thing before him. It was the desire of appearing superior to other people. The motive was too common to be wondered at; but the means, however they might succeed by establishing his superiority in ill-breeding, were not likely to attach any one to him except his wife. (XX, 112)

Both Austen and her Elinor are too intelligent to under-value the negative virtues of these people. Marianne's desperate exclamation ' "The Middletons and Palmers—how am I to bear their pity?" ' is an apt reflection upon them but it really does matter that Sir John is a friendly, albeit oppress-ively hospitable, landlord; that the Palmers are essentially civil to their visitors and everything well-intentioned and helpful when Marianne falls ill while staying at their home; even, that Lady Middleton is so much a devotee of 'good breeding', however insipid and nothing else, that when requested to take the sisters home from the London party where Marianne's meeting with Willoughby has proved so painful, she

> was too polite to object for a moment to her wish of going away, and making over her cards to a friend, they departed as soon as the carriage could be found. (XXVIII, 178)

When one considers the sorts of brutality which are to be met with in this world, which distinguish Lucy Steele's treat-ment of Elinor or Mrs. John Dashwood's of Lucy herself—turning out the Steele sisters bag and baggage at a moment's notice with scarcely any money to get anywhere—the rela-tively considerate and good behaviour of Mrs. Jennings, her two daughters and their husbands is no trivial item in the social sum.

Indeed Mrs. Jennings proves an object lesson, especially to the impatient Marianne. Both she and the reader have to learn—as Elizabeth Bennet does with Darcy—that not all character reveals itself immediately. The self-confident vul-

100

garity of Sir John Middleton's mother-in-law *is* an imposition
to begin with. Like him she intrudes without a qualm upon the
innermost privacies of other people's lives, picks up and
brandishes misconceptions which could reasonably be very
much resented, and is an irrepressibly cheerful gossip—always
a dangerous function. Her breezily declaring to the company
seated over breakfast at Barton Park (Chapter 13) that
Colonel Brandon has a natural daughter—which he has not,
this is another of her frequent misprisions—could be very
hurtful in its effects, though blessedly here it does not happen
so to prove. But if there is a salient difference between this
episode and the heroine of *Emma* jumping at the suspicion
that Jane Fairfax has had a disappointed love affair with a Mr.
Dixon then it is because Mrs. Jennings is less malicious than
Miss Woodhouse. As we get to know her over a longer period
we find her goodheartedness not only authentic but an article
of considerably more worth than her relatives' better aspects.

For one thing she is shown to be no trimmer. Rating love
higher than money or status, she is shocked at Mrs. Ferrars
and the John Dashwoods' attitude to Lucy Steele and
Edward, whose sincere attachment (as she supposes it) they
are out to thwart, and she so declares herself to one of the
opposition's most interested parties:

> 'Nothing should prevail on him to give up his engagement. He
> would stand to it, cost him what it might.'
> 'Then,' cried Mrs. Jennings with blunt sincerity, no longer
> able to be silent, 'he has acted like an honest man! I beg your
> pardon, Mr. Dashwood, but if he had done otherwise, I should
> have thought him a rascal. I have some little concern in the
> business, as well as yourself, for Lucy Steele is my cousin, and I
> believe there is not a better kind of girl in the world, nor one
> who more deserves a good husband.' (XXXVII, 267)

Here much of Mrs. Jennings is expressed. Her foolish belief
in everyone's good nature, her capacity for misreading
human behaviour (which her younger daughter has inherited)
are almost boundless; but some of her values are sterling in
quality, and they are not kept in camphor; she acts and speaks
upon them.

We may at first deem it *simply* fatuous of her to hope that a

glass of Constantia wine will possess 'healing powers on a
disappointed heart', that it can be of material comfort to
Marianne when the loss of Willoughby is very new and her
grief at its freshest, but what else can the rest of society
essentially after all offer the stricken girl? Another ideal
husband cannot be procured. Mrs. Jennings's wish expressed
in this scene (XXX, 197–98) that her younger guest will
knock back a fortifying drink, set her face against the past and
turn her thoughts to making a marriage less passionate and
fulfilling but comfortable, convenient, respectable (in the full
Austenian sense of that word) and which does offer the ideal
spouse at least to someone else—Colonel Brandon—is what
the novel as a whole has to endorse in fact as her best
alternative course in life.

Marianne's London hostess, whom we may have suspected
of bringing the Dashwood sisters to the capital to minister to
her great yen for company, *her* satisfaction, is in the event
seen really putting herself out for these charges. It is certainly
wrong and of a piece with what is blunderingly insensitive in
Mrs. Jennings, when her daughter's boy-child is born there,
and she is absent in attendance upon Charlotte Palmer to
conspire, out of her impercipient goodwill and fixation upon
the idea of company, any company as the ultimate human
necessity and blessing, to oblige Elinor and her sister to spend
the whole of every day in Conduit-street:

> For their own comfort, they would much rather have remained,
> at least all the morning, in Mrs. Jennings's house; but it was not
> a thing to be urged against the wishes of everybody. Their
> hours were therefore made over to Lady Middleton and the
> two Miss Steeles, by whom their company was in fact as little
> valued, as it was professedly sought. (XXXVI, 246)

But when Marianne becomes seriously ill, Mrs. Jennings is
quite ready to turn her own and her family's world upside
down in this visitor's interest. The Palmers leave their very
home to Charlotte's mother and the Dashwood sisters rather
than requiring the invalid guest to do the travelling away
from their tiny infant, and

> Mrs. Jennings, . . . with a kindness of heart which made
> Elinor really love her, declared her resolution of not stirring

102

from Cleveland as long as Marianne remained ill, and of
endeavouring, by her own attentive care, to supply to her the
place of the mother she had taken her from; and Elinor found
her on every occasion a most willing and active help-mate
desirous to share in all her fatigues and often by her better
experience in nursing, of material use. (XLIII, 308)

This is not only kind, it is also courageous. Not only Mr.
Woodhouse but very many of the Austen characters read
like raving hypochondriacs on such subjects as the weather,
catching colds, wrapping up etc. Ronald Blythe has some
(largely delighted and amused) notes on this in his edition of
Emma:

> . . . Winter turns them into moles. Snow makes them panic.
> The weather is never ignored or forgotten. . . . Carriage
> gossip nearly gives away Jane Fairfax's secret. But walking is
> worse. Emma has only once walked to Randalls, which is only
> half a mile away, 'but it was not pleasant'. Both Frank
> Churchill and Mr Elton become hot and upset by walking.
> Jane Fairfax walks in the meadows and to the post office and
> causes consternation (many of the things she does seem to
> anticipate the emancipated woman). Harriet goes for a walk
> and meets some gipsies, and is frightened out of her wits. All
> these young people are unusually strong and healthy. It is the
> great period of the interior, with the garden recognised as an
> extension of the interior, beyond which is chaos.[23]

But the key fact is that Austen's society exists on the other
side of *the* great divide of the modern era—life before and
after The Medical Revolution. If it is almost impossible now
to imagine ourselves back into a world without anaesthesia
(the empathy is too painful), it is scarcely less difficult to
conceive a state of existence without antibiotics. Yet up until
the third decade of the present century, if you caught a cold,
and, turning to influenza or pneumonia, it produced a high
temperature—a fever—you stood quite a chance of dying,
and quickly. Infectious ailments (which Marianne's is diag-
nosed as being [XLIII, 307]) therefore carried this risk to the
patient's attendants too. Breaking a limb was serious for the
same reason: complications might set in. That is why Emma
on a walk can stoop down, schemingly tear off her shoelace
and solicit Mr. Elton's assistance at Highbury Vicarage with-

out being deemed a ridiculously demanding fusspot. (And unfortunately—like all her other delinquent experiments—this one does not backfire on her. It is vain to wish that, hobbling towards the help thus artificially necessitated, she should give herself a real sprain; the aggravating creature enjoys the devil's own luck.)

Folly, innocence and good-nature are blended not only in Mrs. Jennings's character, but that of Mrs. Henry Dashwood as well—and even arguably in that of Anne Steele. Elinor and Marianne's mother partakes of their virtues and her younger daughters' faults. She is true, sincere, loving and good; but also, like Marianne and Margaret, impractical, wayward, wilful—generally immoderate in her attitudes. She *will not* be counselled into demanding an *éclaircissement* from Marianne and Willoughby about their relationship in the days when it is overdue and could help. She has encouraged, has indeed brought up her younger girls to give the emotions free rein, regardless of the expediency of doing so—and one piece of her handiwork here is Marianne's nearly fatal illness. When she hears of Willoughby's treachery in London,

> Long letters from her, quickly succeeding each other, arrived to tell all that she suffered and thought; to express her anxious solicitude for Marianne, and entreat she would bear up with fortitude under this misfortune. Bad indeed must the nature of Marianne's affliction be, when her mother could talk of fortitude! mortifying and humiliating must be the origin of those regrets, which *she* could wish her not to indulge! (XXXII, 212–13)

And she has not that coherence, that attentive memory of what has been—not least in the matter of attitudes and utterances—which distinguishes the real right sort in this novelist's fiction from the others, the less than truly adequate. She falsifies the past just as in future she will falsify what is now the present; and Austen's major theme in all her work is that the beloved republic—of reason, good behaviour and fulfilment—cannot be erected, can only be hurt thereby. The dreadful burden of their past acts and speeches is what the virtuous acknowledge and deliberatively carry in her world; because only with these dusty bricks can the civil estate of the valid life be built.

'My partiality does not blind me; he is certainly not so handsome as Willoughby—but at the same time, there is something
much more pleasing in his countenance.—There was always a
something,—if you remember,—in Willoughby's eyes at times,
which I did not like.'

Elinor could *not* remember it;—but her mother, without
waiting for her assent, continued,

'And his manners, the Colonel's manners are not only more
pleasing to me than Willoughby's ever were, but they are of a
kind I well know to be more solidly attaching to Marianne.
Their gentleness, their genuine attention to other people, and
their manly unstudied simplicity is much more accordant with
her real disposition, than the liveliness—often artificial, and
often ill-timed of the other. I am very sure myself, that had
Willoughby turned out as really amiable, as he has proved
himself the contrary, Marianne would yet never have been so
happy with *him*, as she will be with Colonel Brandon.'

She paused.—Her daughter could not quite agree with her,
but her dissent was not heard, and therefore gave no offence.
(XLV, 338)

The treatment of Lucy Steele's sister, like that of several
other characters, mellows as the novel progresses—aptly,
since Marianne and the reader both are learning to accommodate themselves to the only available sphere of existence,
which they inhabit. 'Not being the worst/Stands in some
rank of praise', and with the silly Nancy, whose impertinence,
sycophantic flattery of the important, and compliment-
fishing with regard to her own female powers of attraction,
are principally in focus in the first half of the tale, the reader
gains a little sympathy as he comes to realize how compara-
tively valuable her artless incompetence in selfishness and
exploitation is, beside the hypocrisy of true adepts.

Lucy, who was hardly less anxious to please one parent than
the other, thought the boys were both remarkably tall for their
age, and could not conceive that there could be the smallest
difference in the world between them; and Miss Steele, with
yet greater address gave it, as fast as she could, in favour of
each. [XXXIV, 234)

We are actually made to feel her pathos, and the poignancy
of her condition as a woman destined to be an unwilling old
maid. (Of Elinor and Marianne in relation to her the narrator

says 'An effort even yet lighter might have made her their friend. Would they only have laughed at her about the Doctor!' [XXXVI, 247].) And her innocent and pathetic aspects remain perhaps uppermost in our consciousness from the day she goes to sojourn with the John Dashwoods. She is so ungifted a dealer in insincerity, she misconstrues that of her hostess and blurts out the fact of her sister and Edward Ferrars's secret engagement. The scene, even at third-hand but revived in the lively narration of Mrs. Jennings—all vivid, unconsciously actualizing presentment—makes very amusing reading (XXXVII, 258–59).

Lucy's discomfiture is cheering. That that artful minx should have spent endless pains ingratiating herself with foes to decent feeling and all for the ugly upset which immediately ensues comes at this very point as a timely welcome relief in a novel where the grasping cold-hearted would otherwise seem too successful, too much carrying all before them and unfairly ensconced under the protection of the fates. *Sense and Sensibility* is not allowed to stray, Hardy-esque or otherwise, into a grim determinism, an embittered pessimism unsupported by the variety of life's accidents. Such consolation is *also* denied its good characters.

But to the treatment of 'poor Nancy' on the occasion we have a more complex response, I think. 'No conjurer', and having 'popt it all out', she 'fell upon her knees, and cried bitterly . . .'. It is a hard reward, as well as comic, for trusting in Lucy's popularity with her hosts; and a still severer is what she gains from having relied upon her sister's good will. When Mrs. Jennings learns of Lucy's marriage to *Robert* Ferrars, she writes thus to Elinor from town:

> Not a soul suspected anything of the matter, not even Nancy, who, poor soul! came crying to me the day after, in a great fright for fear of Mrs. Ferrars, as well as not knowing how to get to Plymouth; for Lucy it seems borrowed all her money before she went off to be married, on purpose we suppose to make a shew with, and poor Nancy had not seven shillings in the world;—so I was very glad to give her five guineas to take her down to Exeter, where she thinks of staying three or four weeks with Mrs. Burgess, in hopes, as I tell her, to fall in with the Doctor again. (XLIX, 270–71)

The forlorn note of an aimless peripatetic future counterpoints the verily funny elements here in her portrayed dimminded strandedness.

Other human elements exist and are more fugitively scanned in the societal arena of middle-class country and town life, parties in the capital and rural quietudes, which *Sense and Sensibility* exhibits. Robert Ferrars is so arrantly foolish a knave, his insolence gives less offence than that of the other villains of the piece. Elinor probably does well to keep silence during his boasting of how he would have retrieved his brother Edward from the engagement with Lucy Steele and to agree to all his posturing and self-preening on the equipment of cottages and the rest of it, 'for she did not think he deserved the compliment of rational opposition' (XXXVI, 252). D. W. Harding has well observed in his essay 'Character and Caricature in Jane Austen', that this character's behaviour at the jewellers' shop earlier

> constitutes a performance in front of the sisters, as well as in front of us, without the mitigation of any personal contact, leaving him a ridiculous object rather than a person entitled to the consideration of equals.[24]

But this is not a matter of authorial technique alone—of Austen having decided that she will present Robert Ferrars by a different method from the Dashwood sisters, essentially for architectonic reasons (of narrative rhythm, shaded tones, pace); any more than the differences in her representation of Mrs. Elton and Harriet Smith in *Emma* derive from so purely technical a motive. The whole point about people like Mrs. Elton, Robert Ferrars, or Mrs. Norris in *Mansfield Park* is that they can and must be 'caricaturized' as portraits because their egotism, which is extreme, takes the form of an essential blindness and deafness in human company. They do all the talking and no real listening, are incapable of genuine attention to what another person says or relationship with them, because they are only self-aware. Other people's individual outlook upon things, and possible attitudes to different issues, are just so many grains of dust dropped into the churning hopper of their absolute preoccupation with their own social role.

Evidently Miss Sophia Grey has not only got £50,000 but the kind of sad hard foolish wilfulness which characterizes Maria Bertram in *Mansfield Park*. She is cruel to Marianne in forcing Willoughby to write the callous letter he sends from Bond Street repudiating their connection (XXIX, 183) but it is still more cruel to Willoughby and herself that she should insist on going ahead with their wedding now she has discovered the nature of his relationship to this other young lady. It is a desperately self-defeating remedy, obdurately to proceed with a marriage which on one partner's side has been shown to be loveless. Presumably Lord Morton's daughter, given the chance, would have been a similar sort of obstinate clutching harridan with regard to Edward Ferrars, and youthful only in her tale of numbered years.

Mr. Donovan, probably an apothecary, comes across as a cringing gossip; and Mrs. Smith of Allenham as an upright old lady whom we should like to have met (and would have done, had Willoughby had integrity enough and the courage of his real love?).

There are other fleeting human presences and references upon this canvas; the fierce passions and miseries of Eliza Williams the older and the younger, the aloofness of Dr. Davies D.D. in the West Country, and so on; Elinor and Marianne cannot complain of having been dealt an acquaintance unusually thin or in which there is a rare overplus of the mean-spirited, the selfish and the foolish—not least because they have each other, and in each other intimate friendship with a blood-relation who is intellectually alert, morally sensitive, conversationally lively; who can be very pleasant company and is *good*. Nevertheless with regard to forms of satisfying human mutuality, it is an organum of seriously limited resources, and Elinor Dashwood appears to have 'faced up to' this feature of life's scene from early on. She realizes, as it were has realized from before the action begins, how very difficult it is for the scrupulous and intelligent female to make in the actual world even a decent tolerable marriage—especially when she is practically dowerless; let alone one which offers brilliant nourishment. And this sustained perception is, I think, the motive of her ardent devotion to the dull Edward Ferrars.

Now a big case can of course be made against *Sense and Sensibility*. Professors Mudrick and Garis put it better than most—and most put it—in their essays, 'Irony and Convention versus Feeling' and 'Learning Experience and Change'[25] respectively upon this author. Here the regular complaints appear, well-honed; against the novel as having a priggish outlook and utterance and offering strained forced inert moralizing; against its alleged weaknesses in characterization—'If Edward Ferrars is dull, Colonel Brandon is a vacuum';[26] not least against the entire role of Elinor Dashwood:

> One can accept the possibility of an *initial* conflict between Edward's love for Elinor and the sense of honour that forbids him either to break his engagement with Lucy or to tell Elinor about it. But one can't accept this conflict as an abiding and insoluble dilemma without falling into one or the other of two mutually exclusive conclusions which are both fatal to Jane Austen's scheme. One is the suspicion that Marianne voices: though caution, propriety and protocol matter more to us than they do to Marianne, even we can see that Elinor's and Edward's love must be a very poor business, hardly worth the name of love, if it can't give them any help whatsoever toward clearing up misunderstandings, doubts and depressions of such magnitude. . . . [and alternatively] Since even Elinor's unparalleled prudence cannot save her from such misery, then prudence seems in the major concerns of life to lack just the *practical* value that Jane Austen claims for it successfully in the minor concerns. . . . Marianne's indecorous directness would have done very well here, and would have amounted to very good sense indeed.[27]

Yet a principal weakness in all such criticism is that to credit it you have to believe that in writing this novel its creator was—and in a highly *intermittent* manner—all-perceptibly, crashingly stupid.

I shall not oppose the argument that perhaps in most great *oeuvres* we can find big mistakes and inadvertencies. But can we say the same of Jane Austen? Her brother tells us of *her* endeavours:

> Some of these novels had been the gradual performances of her previous life. For though in composition she was equally

rapid and correct, yet an invincible distrust of her own judgement induced her to withhold her works from the public, till
time and many perusals had satisfied her that the charm of
recent composition was dissolved.[28]

This statement seems very literally borne out by what is
known of the composition history of the works. Furthermore
she strikes me as being quite the sternest of her critics among
those basically sympathetic towards the *données* of her art.
Whether or not *Northanger Abbey* seemed to her the unfocused work I have argued it to be, the fact is that, though
she revised it again in 1816–17, she was doubtful enough
about it to withhold publication: 'Miss Catherine is put upon
the Shelve for the present [March 1817], and I do not know
that she will ever come out.[29] It appeared posthumously,
according to the initiative of her legatee and literary execu-
tor. *Persuasion* she did consider 'ready for Publication'
(same letter) but she says to Fanny Knight, 'You will not like
it, so you need not be impatient. You may *perhaps* like the
Heroine, as she is almost too good for me.'[30] And this, like
her comment on *Pride and Prejudice*, however bantering—
'The work is rather too light, and bright, and sparkling'[31]—
surely expresses artistic-critical wakefulness in a high degree
and of an ultra-perfectionist sort.

The will to self-asserting self-endorsement and a general
irresponsibility at root undiscomfited is deliberately so enter-
tained in *Emma*. No more there than in her other works are
we dealing with a writer whose capacity for judgement is
asleep with regard to her own creative acts.

Yet we are asked to believe that the portraits of Edward
Ferrars and Colonel Brandon, whose dullness and 'vacuity'
are leading hallmarks of the personalities achieved for them
by their author, for that matter artistically emphatic, are an
oversight or miscalculation. Is that congruent even with the
tonal control operating in the rest of this narrative? Elinor *can*
decline into priggishness occasionally; that is one of her
shown character traits. But of the values she embodies in the
Sense and Sensibility spectrum is her at times something
starched rectitude a quality which has the author's imagination in hand? It is surely the other way about. When she and

110

Marianne go to stay with Mrs. Jennings's younger daughter, we are given the following:

> Nothing was wanting on Mrs. Palmer's side that constant and friendly good-humour could do, to make them feel themselves welcome. The openness and heartiness of her manner, more than atoned for that want of recollection and elegance, which made her often deficient in the forms of politeness; her kindness, recommended by so pretty a face, was engaging; her folly, though evident, was not disgusting, because it was not conceited; and Elinor could have forgiven her every thing but her laugh. (XLII, 304)

This, with its sudden final, absolutely apt, tonal jump is characteristic and presents us with what in fact is the largest element in Miss Dashwood's outlook on the world; its continuous attempt at a charitable comprehensive view of other people and its (in the last analysis) drastic sanity, its inability to be beguiled even by its own needs and wishes as to the satisfactoriness of inadequate psychologies.

That passage does not stand alone, as such, or at odds with the rest of the text; it is part of an ongoing constatation. Elinor is regularly and deftly witty, witty with a live intelligence—e.g. the conversation in Chapter 17. She is as alert and aware—in all important respects—as her sister, but she has chosen to make her peace with herself-in-society by, as much as possible, suppressing the feelings which probably cannot be satisfied there and being tactful. If her love for Edward Ferrars seems insufficiently motivated by its object, that I think is Austen's point. She is a young woman a lot older than her years in many ways because she has been brought up in a relatively improvident household; whatever his opportunities were or could have been, the fact is that Mr. Henry Dashwood has not made splendid provision for his relicts by the time he dies. Her natural propensity for self-control (and a mordant *quiet* form of wit as distinguished from her sister's more exclamatory sort) has been the more elicited to compensate for the tendency to little restraint among her immediate family. She appears before us, from the very beginning of the book's action, as one who has measured the way of the world with a clear and undeluded—but highly principled—eye:

111

No, Marianne, never. My doctrine has never aimed at the subjection of the understanding. All I have ever attempted to influence has been the behaviour. You must not confound my meaning. I am guilty, I confess, of having often wished you to treat our acquaintance in general with greater attention; but when have I advised you to adopt their sentiments or conform to their judgment in serious matters? (XVII, 94)

Such a woman must obviously have come already to a very realistic view of her nuptial chances and of the range of satisfactions society is likely to offer generally. She well knows that the odds are heavily stacked against the following: (a) that she will ever meet more than a very limited number of marriageable males; (b) that a high proportion of this tiny few will be sympathetic types, morally, intellectually and physically speaking; (c) that, given her financial position, she will receive any proposal of marriage at all (with neither wealth nor brilliant looks *Pride and Prejudice*'s Charlotte Lucas decides at 27 to close upon the only offer likely to come her way and accepts the awful William Collins).

Now the matter is not explicit between author and reader, any more than within Elinor herself, but it is as if when meeting Edward Ferrars and finding him an attentive admirer, she has staked the very real wealth of her emotional life upon his suit because though no great catch as a personality, he is likely to be the best by far and away with whom she can ever hope for espousal. Such discriminations are not conscious within her, I repeat. How could they be, unless she were to be represented as guilty, which she is not, of Charlotte Lucas's unlikeable (though not unjustified) cynical calculation? The sense of Edward's serious limitedness is repressed in her, is never allowed to rise to the point where it would challenge, as Marianne is often bristlingly moved to do, the validity of her choice and affections in the first place. She 'makes the service greater than the god' so as to have a focus for her various potentialities better than her only other option—to be a lonely and increasingly poor spinster. This is the best chance she will ever have—so our experience in the novel, and her experience of society already no doubt, equally affirm—and she *makes* it a grand passion by bringing a grand passion to the relationship. Edward's virtues are too important and rare to be otherwise responded to, she has decided:

> [He] was not recommended to their good opinion by any peculiar graces of person or address. He was not handsome, and his manners required intimacy to make them pleasing. He was too diffident to do justice to himself; but when his natural shyness was overcome, his behaviour gave every indication of an open affectionate heart. His understanding was good, and his education had given it solid improvement. (III, 15)

But, as that introduction of himself indicates, Austen is wide awake to his serious deficiencies as a lover and as a man. She is the one who deliberately so establishes him as deficient. He can in fact be quite talkative and witty in his turn:

> But, in return, your sister must allow me to feel no more than I profess. I like a fine prospect, but not on picturesque principles. I do not like crooked, twisted, blasted trees. I admire them much more if they are tall, straight and flourishing. I do not like ruined, tattered cottages. I am not fond of nettles, or thistles, or heath blossoms. I have more pleasure in a snug farm-house than a watch-tower—and a troop of tidy, happy villagers please me better than the finest banditti in the world. (XVIII, 98)

Yet on the whole he is indeed too dispirited, lifeless, unoriginal, ungallant, too little interesting simply, to make a gratifying hero. The novelist goes out of her way to emphasize his gaucheness, his resourceless lack of address and inferiority of parts in every scene where he figures, and to deny him the opportunity of redeeming himself by an initiative—whether of action; or of conversation in the more lively vein which her fairness has admitted the possibility of in the instance quoted immediately above.

The same, *mutatis mutandis*, is to be said of Colonel Brandon, and it is a brilliant stroke by which Charlotte Palmer's volubility of silliness, her speech-mode of gabbling self-contradiction, hits out the leading duality of his nature and social presence: 'He is such a charming man, that it is quite a pity he should be so grave and so dull' (XX, 115). To find a spouse who is worthy, well-behaved, *respectable* (again, in the full sense)—who is a lot better than the Middletons or the Palmers—is as difficult as to receive a marriage proposal

113

anyway, if you are a portionless young woman at this period and in this social sphere. John Dashwood's obsession with purely mercenary values in the matrimonial bazaar is vicious but it also nakedly reflects one of their world's leading characteristics. Whether financially or in terms of status the Dashwood sisters are not an impressive alliance—whereas 'Miss Morton is Lord Morton's daughter' (XXXIV, 236)—and what Austen is portraying in their wedding Edward Ferrars and Colonel Brandon is their acceptance of the best of likeliest futures—worthwhile but unexhilarating—for the intelligent, just and unimportant females of her age.

Indeed so emphatic is the portrayal of their fiancés' colourlessness, these matches seem to me, especially in the case of Brandon, an authorial turning of the screw. In Henry James's *Washington Square* (1880) the betrayed Catherine Sloper survives her father, wealthy and embittered: 'From her own point of view the great facts of her career were that Morris Townsend had trifled with her affection, and that her father had broken its spring' (Chapter 32). She expresses this bitterness in one way only. Amidst 'forming habits, regulating her days upon a system of her own, interesting herself in charitable institutions, asylums, hospitals, and aid societies; and going generally, with an even and noiseless step, about the rigid business of her life' (ibid., adapted), she chooses to remain single, when in her remaining years of youth and in her middle age other men court her for her hand. She refuses even those who do genuinely love her for herself and are lovable in their turn. It is the final consquence of the breaking of those affections' spring in which Dr. Sloper and Mr. Townsend have so cruelly indulged. After many years the latter revisits her in the hope of reviving his fortunes, the blackguard, but to no avail:

> 'She doesn't care a button for me—with her confounded little dry manner.'
> 'Was it very dry?' pursued Mrs Penniman, with solicitude.
> Morris took no notice of her question; he stood musing an instant, with his hat on. 'But why the deuce, then, would she never marry?'
> 'Yes—why indeed?' sighed Mrs Penniman. And then, as if

from a sense of the inadequacy of this explanation, 'But you will not despair—you will come back?'

'Come back? Damnation!' And Morris Townsend strode out of the house, leaving Mrs Penniman staring.

Catherine, meanwhile, in the parlour, picking up her morsel of fancy-work, had seated herself with it again—for life, as it were.

Thus the tale concludes.

This is only one degree less of self-abnegation than suicide—which in most instances is the ultimate, and self-defeating, protest of the individual either against himself or the terms upon which he has to hold his life. But at least it can be said to have a similar 'gratification'; that of rejecting the world and its reign of hope and possibility.

Even such consolation as this Austen denies to the heroines of her novel. The marriages they make are almost metaphors of celibate solitude—but without the 'comfort' of the expression of resentment at the dispensation of things which would inhere in their being able to choose actual spinster-hood. Even that quasi-heroic response (albeit sentimental and egoistic, merely negative), even *that* defiance of the gods, they do not 'enjoy'.

For of course what they have had a glimpse of, in Willoughby's intrusion into their fairly dull round—as Catherine Sloper has had with the adventurer in *her* life—is a very different reality. The kind of relation which seems offering during Willoughby's courtship of Marianne at Barton—this would justify the gift of consciousness and the burden of the rest of the world's delinquency. So powerful are his good looks and lively address that Elinor herself strays into being half in love with him when, his conduct having proved execrable, he comes to Cleveland and seeks to vindicate himself, with explanations which really extenuate little (Chapters 44–5). Marvin Mudrick writes about this episode almost pruriently, as if lighting upon some hidden element in Austen's thought which is inadvertent and ought to give us a slightly lurid shock, outside the scope of her conscious intentions:

When Willoughby leaves at last, sped by Elinor's good wishes, he leaves Elinor to a 'crowd of ideas', (p. 333) most of them

115

astonishingly imprudent for a protagonist of sense: 'She felt that his influence over his mind was heightened by circumstances which ought not in reason to have weight. . . . But she felt that it was so, long, long before she could feel his influence less' (p. 333). Even the arrival of her anguished mother at Marianne's bedside hardly diverts these musings. Elinor, in a state of agitation as much erotic as compassionate, cannot drive 'Willoughby, "poor Willoughby", as she now allowed herself to call him' from her thoughts long enough to fall asleep (pp. 334 ff. cited).[32]

But the matter is as open between author and reader, as acknowledged, as this critic's own textual references specify; that is to say, compatibly with the turbidity of Elinor's motives and the confusion of her ideas on the occasion. This extended scene has its place in achieving the work's whole meaning. What John Willoughby represents for the sisters is the possibility of a perfect relation, an ideal reciprocity, with participants deeply satisfied in a mutuality which is energic and stimulating. This is counterpoised against the insufficiency of the human world at large; and the fact of its however remote and infrequent possibility (further substantiated by having been realized in Mrs. Henry Dashwood's case) is what adds such poignancy to the two girl's experience.

Correspondent to its rarity and difficulty of accomplishment, the ideal social experience has proved clay-footed in the present instance. But it remains no less appealing for that. Willoughby's featuring in the novel, with his lively mind, good looks and bounding spirits, 'implies and projects the possible other case, the case rich and edifying where the actuality is pretentious and vain',[33] amidst the otherwise disappointing realm of social relations at large.

Sense and Sensibility, then, can and *should* be read as a moral tale. Indeed it was probably so conceived by the author, and from first to last, at the level of fully deliberated enterprise—the point can be waived. As such, it is rich and subtle. The necessity of taking sensible positions—on one's self-expression, social obligations and acts—is rationally enforced, while the dangers and weaknesses of such a commit-

116

ment are dramatized in the flaws of the elder Miss Dashwood's outlook and deeds.

We are shown the real outer world and its brutality in the very first two intimations of the novel—the inconsiderate self-indulgence of the old Mr. Dashwood, expressed in his testamentary dispositions which reward his grand-nephew's

> imperfect articulation, an earnest desire of having his own way, many cunning tricks, and a great deal of noise, [so] as to outweigh all the value of all the attention which, for years, he had received from his niece and her daughters. (I, 4)

and the meanness of the John Dashwoods towards this family of vulnerable females who are at the centre of the novel's focus. Given that life is like this, it does behove the individual to be politic; yet caution and self-restraint, subjugation of one's behaviour to outward standards, can soon have the judgement imprisoned too; this is what Elinor overlooks in enforcing her view of the issue during the conversation between her, Marianne and Willoughby already cited (Chapter 17). It is silly that, in being the messenger of Colonel Brandon's offer of Delaford Parsonage, she should be doing for Edward Ferrars what is misery-making for herself and doom to him and that the pair of them should be consenting to it, in a rigmarole of insincerity, pretending to want this development which at that stage in their story seems to increase the likelihood of his marriage to Lucy Steele. Elinor is even betrayed by her respect for the conventions into radical hypocrisy, of a kind quite unnecessary— which implies 'the subjection of the understanding' with a vengeance—when she tries to make out that Lucy is capable of being a good wife to Edward (XXXVII, 263).

On her side Marianne Dashwood represents her belief in strong feelings, their strong expression; and the self-indulgence, blindness and mischief-making of this commitment are fully exposed. The almost punitive scorn of the early chapters towards such 'romantic delicacy' valuably counterweighs, in recollection, our growing sympathy, equally meant at the creative levels of Austen's enterprise, for Marianne's precepts and practice as we confront more and more of a morally reprehensible society—the only kind of society that these characters, or we, shall ever know in this life.

There is everything to be said for the general upshot of both sisters' careers and conduct. It *is* the case that within the ordinary meanings of 'happiness' and 'dignity' the two young ladies and their connections do well. In a sense which really matters—that of accommodating oneself to the real world— the novel which is visible on the upper side of this fictional palimpsest (*Sense and Sensibility* 'Mark 1' we may term it) ends happily. And it is in the spirit of *this* book's important intuitions that the whole second half of the work is more humorous than the first. Such is a triumph of art. The novel is wrenched back into the mode of social comedy just when it has overwhelmed us with a grim presentment. Willoughby defects, and in fact of all that portends, the narrative returns to find satiric mirth:

> At last the affair was decided. The ivory, the gold, and the pearls, all received their appointment, and the gentleman having named the last day on which his existence could be continued without the possession of the toothpick-case, drew on his gloves with leisurely care. . . . (XXXIII, 221)

> Within a few days after this meeting, the newspapers announced to the world, that the Lady of Thomas Palmer, Esq. was safely delivered of a son and heir; a very interesting and satisfactory paragraph, at least to all those intimate connections who knew it before. (XXXVI, 246)

> Here he stopped to be thanked; which being done, he went on. (XXXVII, 266)

Near the conclusion we have indeed one of the liveliest single paragraphs in the whole of Austen, which I will not scruple to quote in full:

> The whole of Lucy's behaviour in the affair, and the prosperity which crowned it, therefore, may be held forth as a most encouraging instance of what an earnest, an unceasing attention to self-interest, however its progress may be apparently obstructed, will do in securing every advantage of fortune, with no other sacrifice than that of time and conscience. When

118

Robert first sought her acquaintance, and privately visited her in Bartlett's Buildings, it was only with the view imputed to him by his brother. He merely meant to persuade her to give up the engagement; and as there could be nothing to overcome but the affection of both, he naturally expected that one or two interviews would settle the matter. In that point, however, and that only, he erred;—for though Lucy soon gave him hopes that his eloquence would convince her in *time*, another visit, another conversation, was always wanted to produce this conviction. Some doubts always lingered in her mind when they parted, which could only be removed by another half hour's discourse with himself. His attendance was by this means secured, and the rest followed in course. Instead of talking of Edward, they came gradually to talk only of Robert,—a subject on which he had always more to say than on any other, and in which she soon betrayed an interest even equal to his own; and in short, it became speedily evident to both, that he had entirely supplanted his brother. He was proud of his conquest, proud of tricking Edward, and very proud of marrying privately without his mother's consent. What immediately followed is known. They passed some months in great happiness at Dawlish; for she had many relations and old acquaintance to cut—and he drew several plans for magnificent cottages;—and from thence returning to town, procured the forgiveness of Mrs. Ferrars, by the simple expedient of asking it, which, at Lucy's instigation, was adopted. The forgiveness at first, indeed, as was reasonable, comprehended only Robert; and Lucy, who had owed his mother no duty, and therefore could have transgressed none, still remained some weeks longer unpardoned. But perseverance in humility of conduct and messages, in self-condemnation for Robert's offence, and gratitude for the unkindness she was treated with, procured her in time the haughty notice which overcame her by its graciousness, and led soon afterwards, by rapid degrees, to the highest state of affection and influence. Lucy became as necessary to Mrs. Ferrars, as either Robert or Fanny; and while Edward was never cordially forgiven for having once intended to marry her, and Elinor, though superior to her in fortune and birth, was spoken of as an intruder, *she* was in every thing considered, and always openly acknowledged, to be a favourite child. They settled in town, received very liberal assistance from Mrs. Ferrars, were on the best terms imaginable with the Dashwoods; and setting aside the jealousies and ill-will continually subsisting between Fanny and Lucy, in which their husbands of course took a part, as well as the frequent domestic disagreements between Robert and Lucy themselves, nothing could exceed the harmony in which they all lived together.

(L, 376–77)

These instances only sample the business but what they do indicate I believe is how fully deployed Jane Austen's range of comic perception here is; in consequence of which we vibrate with the renewed sense of a positive value in social life: it is variously amusing, and while so comprehensive an intelligence as our author's is possible in relation to it the game cannot be condemned as wholly unworthy of the candle.

This same emphasis is appropriate because of a principal issue of the second half of the book is that of going on living, coping with existence, in the wake of essential defeat. But such insights cannot redeem the loss implicit in the Dashwood sisters' failure to make exhilarating marriages, just as being assured of Willoughby's deep guilt is of little real use to Marianne. She needs transfiguration, not philosophy. So that the other 'point', or pointedness, in Austen's incorporating so much of her humour into the later part of her tale is ultimately its own inadequacy as a resource. Its function is equally to embody a truth T. S. Eliot has remarked: 'People change, and smile: but the agony abides.'[34]

Not that the heroines are sentimentally protected by their author:

> 'When I see him again,' said Elinor to herself, as the door shut him out, 'I shall see him the husband of Lucy.'
>
> And with this pleasing anticipation, she sat down to reconsider the past, recal the words and endeavour to comprehend all the feelings of Edward; and, of course, to reflect on her own with discontent. (XL, 291)

That invites a response only a little less complex. Once again the novelist's authority very perceptibly 'backs' our subtle admixture of feelings about Elinor's attitudes here—without unfairly betraying her impressive quality, or imposing a detached cynical view. It is a part of Austen's absolute moral realism on all occasions (except *Emma*) about the make-up

120

of people's impulses and their images of themselves. Reading this book we continually have the thrill of experiencing a mind (the least patronizing of intelligences) indefatigably unfooled which never compromises along the finest edge of discrimination.

Such elements only substantiate the more the other novel—the novel below the immediate surface, as it were—which this is. *Sense and Sensibility* '*Mark 2*' is deeply tragic. It gives us a glimpse of one of the transforming sorts of human dealing amid a powerful portrayal of society's frustrating character, and convincingly suggests how rarely real fulfilment is realized in the lives of the intelligently, appreciatively deserving. The fruits of the kind of attitude which opposes Marianne's tactlessness are not enough to justify the fact of human consciousness; only to create a *modus vivendi* in the disappointing world we all share.

To have 'spent' my essay's tale of words making this emphasis is merely to have attempted to resist the novel's depreciation as a whole, as not being a provident account of a major theme. But there is vastly more to note in discriminative praise for its treatment of the ancillary social and personal considerations through which this theme is drawn. Every sentence practically adds a new insight to the sum total of its view of the individual in society, the complex of ligatures which are there in question. Bloomsbury's foolish *snobbisme* about the nineteenth-century Russians being the greatest of all novelists is, one would happily suppose, quite dead and buried by now. Yet I do obviously mean it for the highest kind of esteem when I say that *Sense and Sensibility* seems to me as good as *Anna Karenina*.

NOTES

1. Gooneratne, op. cit., p. 12.
2. '*Sense and Sensibility*', '*Pride and Prejudice*' and '*Mansfield Park*'—A *Selection of Critical Essays* (in the Macmillan 'Casebook' series), ed. B. C. Southam (London, 1976) p. 88. I refer whenever possible to this

volume (as 'SS Casebook') like its companions on *'Northanger Abbey' and 'Persuasion'*, and *'Emma'*.

3. *JA: Irony as Defense and Discovery*, p. 93; p. 115 of *SS Casebook*.
4. *SS Casebook*, p. 128.
5. Ibid., pp. 143–44.
6. *JA: Bicentenary essays*, pp. 75–85.
7. See *Memoir*, p. 362.
8. See note 11 to Chapter 1.
9. *JA and her Art*, p. 14.
10. *The Life and Letters of Jane Austen* (see note 1 to Chapter 1), p. 243.
11. *Memoir*, p. 363.
12. *JA: Bicentenary essays*, p. 81.
13. *NA and P*, p. 7.
14. David Cecil, *A Portrait of Jane Austen* (London, 1978), p. 109, which gives the details of Mrs. Austen's economic situation from 1805, after the death of her husband.
15. *NA and P*, p. 7.
16. *JA: Bicentenary essays*, p. 81.
17. From the same letter as is immediately quoted below in my text.
18. R. W. Chapman says 'But *Sense and Sensibility*, in the form in which it left Steventon, was the later work; and she may have feared that *First Impressions* would be thought frivolous' (*JA: Facts and Problems*, Oxford, 1948, pp. 76–7). Arguably. Much is arguable on the issue. But nothing can weaken the significance of the fact that SS was for all *she* knew at that time the only one of her works which she *could* secure to posterity, once it had been chosen by her for printing, since it was possible she would have only this one throw of the publishing dice.
19. *SS Casebook*, p. 99.
20. Ibid., p. 100.
21. *Letters*, No. 142 (23 March, 1817), pp. 486–87.
22. *Critical Essays on JA*, p. xii.
23. *Emma*, ed. R. Blythe (Harmondsworth: Penguin, 1966) pp. 470–71.
24. *Critical Essays on JA*, p. 88.
25. Chapter 3 of Mudrick's study of Jane Austen's work already cited. Robert Garis's essay can be found in *Critical Essays on JA*, pp. 60–82.
26. *SS Casebook*, p. 111.
27. *Critical Essays on JA*, p. 64.
28. *NA and P*, p. 4.
29. *Letters*, No. 141, p. 484.
30. Ibid., No. 142, p. 487.
31. Ibid., No. 77, p. 299.
32. *SS Casebook*, p. 108.
33. Henry James's phrase about the appropriate role of 'operative irony' in fiction: *The Art of the Novel* (New York, 1934), p. 222.
34. *The Dry Salvages*, l. 114.

4

A Flawless Masterpiece: *Mansfield Park*

'My Mother—not liked it so well as P. & P.—Thought Fanny insipid.—Enjoyed Mrs. Norris.'[1]

Many and various are the opinions of *Mansfield Park* which the author herself collected just after its first publication, but we can now look back upon Mrs. Austen's reactions as prophetic of the majority view in most of the 167 years which since have passed. Even committed Austenians have shaken their heads over this book. It was indeed Lord Macaulay's favourite, but he is an exception which proves the rule. Reginald Farrer calls it 'Jane Austen's *gran rifiuto*. . . . alone of her books . . . vitiated throughout by a radical dishonesty, that was certainly not in its author's own nature.'[2] D. W. Harding speaks of 'The priggishness of *Mansfield Park*' which 'is the inevitable result of the curiously abortive attempt at humility that the novel represents.'[3] C. S. Lewis, who might be supposed to welcome the Evangelical elements and four-square commitment to a very strict, even 'narrow' interpretation of traditional morality, himself says of its heroine,

> But into Fanny, Jane Austen, to counterbalance her apparent insignificance, has put really nothing except rectitude of mind; neither passion, nor physical courage, nor wit, nor resource. Her very love is only calf love—a schoolgirl's hero-worship for a man who has been kind to her when they were both children, and who, incidentally, is the least attractive of all Jane Austen's heroes.[4]

123

It is Fanny of course who is the heart of the problem; E. M. Forster (that warm admirer of Austen's art) was taking a swipe back at the whole book with his *bon mot*: 'I always thought Fanny Price of *Mansfield Park* a mouse-trap, and that in Edmund Bertram she caught a nice fat mouse.'[5] In making this young woman, who is much the least lively, most introverted, censorious and self-pi.ying of her heroines, the *speculum* and focus of her novel's debate, Austen can easily be felt to have placed this in a very restricted and imprisoning compass.

In my own view the novel is as perfect as need be and there is not enough space here to canvass all its beauties and merits; so I fix upon three major cruxes as a way of opening out what I take to be the issues of the work and in vindication of the author's treatment of them: the theatricals at Mansfield, the Henry Crawford–Fanny Price relationship, and the ending. There are other things in this text which have disturbed and divided the critics, but these sequences have all been deemed the most perplexing or annoying.

Firstly, however, a recapitulation of the story.

Fanny Price, the daughter of a penurious Portsmouth-based Lieutenant of Marines, is introduced at Mansfield Park and brought up, from her tenth year, in this Northamptonshire house of her uncle-in-law and her younger aunt, Sir Thomas and Lady Bertram, through the officious charity of her mother's older sister Mrs. Norris, who is soon left the widow of Mansfield's vicar and who spends most of her time at the manorial Bertram home. Quietly despised by her two female cousins Maria and Julia Bertram, and teased by the heir to the baronetcy, Tom, Fanny is lonely until befriended by Edmund, the younger of the two boys of the family (then 16 and on holiday from Eton), for whom ordination and the livings of Mansfield and Thornton Lacey, in his father's patronage, are designed. Fanny is the Cinderella of the family. Mrs. Norris turns out to have recruited her only to persecute her with perpetual bad temper, reproofs and aspersions upon her dependent status as a poor relation. In her accommodation and her role she is neither really a servant at the hall, nor a full member of the family. When the other girls, as the years move on, go to dances, Fanny is left behind as a companion to the supine and almost mindless Lady Bertram. But this retired and quiet life she prefers to any other.

Sir Thomas's estate in Antigua giving cause for concern (for this—1805 presumably—was the time of slave-riots and abolitionist legislation in the British West Indies) he and Tom sail there personally to supervise their holdings. During his absence Maria, now in her twenty-first year, contracts a mercenary engagement to a neighbouring squire whom she does not love or respect, Mr. Rushworth, and of whom Edmund rightly remarks 'If this man had not twelve thousand a year, he would be a very stupid fellow.' But matters become much livelier with the return of Tom Bertram, a spendthrift playboy, and the visit of Henry and Mary Crawford, the brother and sister of Mrs. Grant, the wife of the new vicar of Mansfield, Mr. Norris's successor. The Crawfords are witty, handsome, gay young Londoners of property who soon have developed a busy social life with the siblings of the Park. Both the Bertram girls encourage Crawford to flirt with them—even on an expedition to Sotherton Court, the country mansion of Maria's husband-to-be; and Mary Crawford begins to reciprocate a growing attachment to her on Edmund's side. As they progress through the final summer before Sir Thomas's greatly delayed but now actually promised return in November (1807 on this estimate), Tom and a visiting friend, the Hon. John Yates (who 'had not much to recommend him beyond habits of fashion and expense') propose that they recreate with a play. After much squabbling over a choice of vehicle in which each may shine the best, *Lovers' Vows*, a 'hit' of the period, is fixed upon, and even Edmund's warmly urged scruples being ultimately overcome, the only thing which intermits the project's entire prosecution to a public performance is Sir Thomas's premature return home.

The theatricals episode has given trouble to every reader. We all know that the teenage Jane Austen herself, her family (a clerical household) and friends performed plays in the barn at her home—and some of them plays no less 'dubious' than *Lovers' Vows*; she even indeed wrote some for such exhibition. Yet Fanny who at first 'looked on and listened, not unamused to observe the selfishness, which, more or less disguised, seemed to govern them all' (MP, XIV, 131) in the matter of the choice of text, moves from feeling that 'For her own gratification she could have wished that something might be acted, for she had never seen even half a play, but everything of higher consequence was against it' (ibid.) to a revulsion of sick indignation at the very idea of this amateur show.

Are her reactions hysterical, are *Austen's* out of scale? Is the author advocating a supremely punctilious decorum for young people of the upper middle class such as hardly existed in her own life; and if so, why with such passion?

To this problem Lionel Trilling returned several times during his career. He deemed *Mansfield Park* one of the works of imaginative literature most seminal to a true understanding of the whole current Occidental cultural phase (the Romantic Era of the eighteenth century to our present day) and yet his defence of Austen's handling of the theatricals has a note of strain. As late as 1970 he speaks of 'the unequivocal judgement the novel makes that the enterprise is to be deplored,'[6] reiterating the argument of his famous 1954 paper 'Jane Austen and Mansfield Park':

> What is decisive is a traditional, almost primitive, feeling about dramatic impersonation. We know of this, of course, from Plato, and it is one of the points on which almost everyone feels superior to Plato, but it may have more basis in actuality than we commonly allow. It is the fear that the impersonation of a bad or inferior character will have a harmful effect upon the impersonator; that, indeed, the impersonation of any other self will diminish the integrity of the real self.[7]

Yet this is wire-drawn by way of defence, for what the reader meets in this text is a repugnance towards the scheme which seems out of scale with what is proposed. Beginning the episode, Austen specifies that 'a love of the theatre is so general, an itch for acting so strong among young people' (XIII, 121), yet what they are meditating at the Park might, from the attitudes and language of the opposition, be a robbery or a murder. Edmund, who 'begins to listen with alarm' to the scheme and, 'determined to prevent it' (XIII, 124), says ' "I think it would be very wrong" ' (125) speaks of it to Fanny as 'a great evil' (adapted from 128). Fanny, conning the chosen text for the first time, is astonished 'that it could be proposed

126

and accepted in a private theatre!' with its two main female roles 'so totally improper for home representation' (XV, 137). Yet the only version of this German play (1791, of which the original title means 'The Love-Child') which Austen and the Mansfield personages know and use is Mrs. Inchbald's heavily bowdlerized translation of 1798.[8]

Kingsley Amis is not irrelevant when he reminds us that 'a cursory reading will show *Lovers' Vows* is in fact innocuous rubbish',[9] and as R. W. Chapman remarks in the Note prefatorial to his useful reprinting of the version in question, it 'had a great vogue and was frequently reprinted; a twelfth edition is recorded of 1799' (MP, 474). If it was so much accepted in Society generally, if 'the Right Hon. Lord Ravenshaw' and his family could have undertaken it at Ecclesford, that peer's Cornish seat and in a company which comprised 'a large party assembled for gaiety', not simply the closest blood-relations of his house, it adds to our giddying sense, characteristic of the whole episode, of participating in a moral debate of which some of the terms of reference are occluded, when we are told 'Lord Ravenshaw . . . is one of the most correct men in England' (XIII, 122).[10] It is as though one were to step into another country where, for example, the marriage of first cousins were deemed a disgraceful perversion, like incest—but only by one-sixth of the population (Edmund and, much more tenaciously, Fanny are here effectually opposed against the three other Bertram siblings, Lady Bertram, Mrs. Norris, Mrs. Grant, the Crawfords and Mr. Yates), and where these objectors do not sufficiently amplify and substantiate their case. Faced by Fanny's paroxysms of wretchedness at being pushed into undertaking the small part of Cottager's wife makes one recall T. S. Eliot's remark about *Hamlet*: 'Hamlet (the man) is dominated by an emotion which is inexpressible, because it is in *excess* of the facts as they appear.'[11]

Of course, just as Queen Gertrude's suspected murderous adultery *is* very horrible (our problem is that 'the guilt of a mother' does not seem to account for all of Hamlet's motivating psychology), so there is a real case against this enterprise. Edmund states it early:

In a *general* light, private theatricals are open to some objections,

127

but as *we* are circumstanced, I must think it would be highly injudicious, and more than injudicious, to attempt any thing of the kind. It would show great want of feeling on my father's account, absent as he is, and in some degree of constant danger; and it would be imprudent, I think, with regard to Maria, whose situation is a very delicate one, considering every thing, extremely delicate. (XIII, 125)

The modern reader must remember the danger of a sea-voyage in those days and across an ocean divided by maritime powers, Britain and France, then at war. It will take the head of the family several weeks to make the crossing and if he meet with mishap, the news of it can arrive no faster. So there is the bad taste of holding high festivity in his home at such a time. (However would they live down the scandal, let alone digest their self-reproach, at having been acting a play, without his known permission, the very day their father was later reported to have died at sea?)

Then the choice of play is provocative, and Austen's skill in selecting this particular drama—which is, with all her usual marvellous *naturalness*, the unforced easy likelihood of her realism, one of the recent successes of the London stage 1798–99—has a motive which ramifies. Kotzebue, its author (1761–1819) was a Romantic, one of the early Socialists and a free-thinker. He believed in free love and was only a Deist in religion, if not an atheist outright. Trivial as the play artistically is, therefore, it is unthinkingly treacherous on the part of these young people to the codes by which they are supposed to live, to have chosen it, and that they can be so easily, *thoughtlessly* disloyal, as Fanny is not, is also part of the author's meaning. How much *Mansfield Park* is, at the deepest level, in agreement with the politico-economic basis of the Bertrams' way of life, is a nice question; but Kotzebue's *ethics*, in this play, and still more in his life and other writings, were directly opposed to those Austen—*at* the deepest level—is concerned to vindicate with her novel. One can glance forward to the exchange on Romantic poetry between Charlotte Heywood and Sir Edward Denham in 'Sanditon':

I have read several of Burn's [*sic*] Poems with great delight, said Charlotte as soon as she had time to speak, but I am not poetic

128

enough to separate a Man's Poetry entirely from his Character;—& poor Burns's known Irregularities, greatly interrupt my
enjoyment of his Lines.—I have difficulty in depending on the
Truth of his Feelings as a Lover. I have not faith in the *sincerity* of
the affections of a Man of his Description. He felt & he wrote &
he forgot. (MW, 397–98)

The fault in the choice of text is much compounded by the way
its four major *dramatis personae* use the play as a means of being
dishonest with each other in the real world, of developing
covert feelings and entering upon relationships without being
properly committed to them. It is again of the excellence of
Austen's art, her so presenting the episode that no reader
misses anything greatly material by not being acquainted with
Lovers' Vows. Yet many among her contemporaries did know it.
That it had been a best-seller in polite society as a printed text
and a great success among fashionable theatre audiences not
so very long before, made *her* book all the more necessary in
opposition to the values it mediates. And many readers would
quickly see how badly compromised are Maria and Edmund
Bertram, Mary and Henry Crawford by their respective roles
of Agatha, Anhalt, Amelia and Frederick.

Fanny's misgivings about this are justified. The play, in
prolonged rehearsal, carries forward these principals considerably farther in the process of deceit—of themselves and of each
other. 'Frederick'—Crawford meeting 'Agatha'—Maria, does
a lot of warm embracing with her in their extended first scene
(hence its being undertaken 'so needlessly often' between
them: XVIII, 165). He speaks to her as her natural child; and
there is a fine sad irony in the fact that Maria, enjoying herself
in the role of 'Agatha', will in the end also be a 'ruined
woman'. She addresses him as his poverty-stricken mother;
but lines like 'I cannot speak, dear son! [Rising and embracing
him.] My dear Frederick! The joy is too great—' (MP, 483), or
Frederick's 'Ill, and I was not with you? I will, now, never
leave you more. Look, mother, how tall and strong I am
grown. These arms can now afford you support.' (484), and
such accompanying actions as '[Frederick with his eyes cast
down, takes her hand, and puts it to his heart.]' (487) are being
used by this woman who is engaged to marry another man and
this man who is only trifling with her affection, for purposes of

self-indulgence quite other than the merely Thespian.

In their more advanced degree, then, and under a correspondingly 'better' cover, the *Lovers' Vows* rehearsals, like the day-trip to Sotherton earlier (Chapters 8–10), take Maria's feelings so much the further towards a mad passion, while no more compelling an honest proposal from Crawford than self-knowledge in his acting partner; who 'in all the important preparations of the mind' is shortly to be 'complete; being prepared for matrimony by an hatred of home, restraint, and tranquillity; by the misery of disappointed affection, and contempt of the man she was to marry. The rest might wait.' (XXI, 202).

A similar criticism is to be made of Mary's and Edmund's participation in the stage-piece. As Amelia and Anhalt they too can play at being in love, in this case can both fall more deeply for each other, without being obliged rigorously to examine where these feelings are leading them—what real possibility they have of making a happy marriage. The matter is more complex here, since neither is simply trifling with the other, and the role of Amelia in the play, that of a woman who is forward in expressing her feelings and herself proposes to the man she loves, might seem one proper to Austen's sympathy. Mrs. Leavis well remarks that she behaves

> in defiance of the Richardsonian canon that a lady cannot with propriety entertain a sentiment for a man until he has made her an offer. . . . the distress of Edmund at finding that the lady he wishes to marry is willing to make Amelia's shameless avowals is well grounded in conventional notions of decorum. We should be resigned to this in Fanny Burney, but Miss Austen is elsewhere noticeably in advance of the conventions—not of course 'advanced' like a novelist-*philosophe* such as Bage, but compared with novelists within the pale—and likes to represent such features of the age as cant or unwholesome affectation, as she had in *Pride and Prejudice*.[12]

Yet though it may be one of the brightnesses of Mary Crawford that she is willing to take the initiative in this courtship, she does not after all want to be married to a clergyman—upon which career Edmund is resolved. With the *tendresses* her theatre-role permits, Mary prosecutes all the more her basic attempt to seduce Edmund from his chosen profession and into a life entirely on her terms; which is dishonest. So that in this case too all the divisions of ethos and ambition between the partners are not aired and resolved by these rehearsals, but rather inspissated under the development of infatuation which the theatricals promote.

In all four main *actors*, in short, this recreation does *not* provoke 'lovers' *vows*'.

The worst eventually befalls: Maria Bertram is carried off on the wave of one more dalliance, sudden and temporary, on the part of Henry Crawford, into complete and permanent wretchedness; Mary and Edmund achieve only each other's hurt. But that lies in the unknown future as yet, and therefore by no means fully accounts for the almost morbid detestation with which Fanny reacts to the project as it unfolds at the time. She is 'most frightened' (XV, 145) when the others ask her to participate as Cottager's wife. 'To be called into notice in such a manner' is bad enough, yet this has been 'but the prelude to something so infinitely worse, to be told that she must do what was so impossible as to act' (XVI, 150)—and this reaction is not represented solely as a function of her shyness, her *social* embarrassment. After Edmund has capitulated and, taking on the part of Anhalt, has left her in lone opposition, in 'a scheme which . . . she must condemn altogether' (XVII, 160), 'it was all misery *now*' (XVI, 157).

She has a new motive for feeling so, at this later time, which is not absolutely virtuous—her jealousy of Mary Crawford's opportunities for increasing Edmund's attachment in their acting together. But Fanny's—and Edmund's—general objections were so ardent even before he joined the cast, we may indeed feel there was an element of 'scrupulousness run mad' in them, as the Bertram sisters expressed it, remonstrating with their brother then.—'There could be no harm in what had been done in so many respectable families, and by so many women of the first consideration . . .' (XIII, 128).

In fact the concessionary pledges given by Maria, Julia and Tom are not honoured. The project does not ultimately 'comprehend only brothers and sisters, and intimate friends' (adapted, ibid.), the alterations and expense to which they put their father's house are not conducted 'on the simplest plan' or within a budget of 'twenty pounds' (127), and Edmund's earlier

131

remonstrances—'I am convinced that my father would totally disapprove it. . . . His sense of decorum is strict.' (126–27)—are proved as totally correct as all inwardly anticipate. Sir Thomas is angered and hurt in his discovery of the venture when he comes home.

Yet what is the value of this disapproval and strict decorum, intrinsically?

> Sir Thomas's return made a striking change in the ways of the family, independent of Lovers' Vows. Under his government, Mansfield was an altered place. Some members of their society sent away and the spirits of many others saddened, it was all sameness and gloom, compared with the past; a sombre family-party rarely enlivened. There was little intercourse with the Parsonage. Sir Thomas drawing back from intimacies in general, was particularly disinclined, at this time, for any engagements but in one quarter. The Rushworths were the only addition to his own domestic circle which he could solicit. (XXI, 196)

This is pretty damning of itself, but that such sobriety does not feed back into social health we are immediately made to observe in Austen's account of the conference now following between Maria Bertram and her father on the subject of her forthcoming marriage to Rushworth. Faced with the imbecility of his prospective son-in-law and 'little observation being necessary to tell him that indifference was the most favourable state her feelings could be in' towards this man (adapted, XXI, 200), Sir Thomas does remonstrate with his daughter; yet he is quickly satisfied by her reassurances; 'too glad to be satisfied perhaps to urge the matter quite so far as his judgment might have dictated to others' (201). The return of the head of the house, in sum, does not make for 'a striking change' in the calibre of Mansfield Park's moral life. It is now once again much more dull and gloomy than under the influence of the Crawfords' lively spirits and the play-acting, but ethical compensations do not come forward. The restored baronet presides over one of the saddest pieces of self-delusion in which a parent and child could indulge. The girl persists in, and her father endorses her engagement, on each side from motives very unworthy. Generally Sir Thomas knows himself, by the end of the Rushworth marriage, an almost complete paternal failure:

. . . the anguish arising from the conviction of his own errors in the education of his daughters, was never to be entirely done away.

Too late he became aware how unfavourable to the character of any young people, must be the totally opposite treatment which Maria and Julia had been always experiencing at home, where the excessive indulgence and flattery of their aunt had been continually contrasted with his own severity. He saw how ill he had judged, in expecting to counteract what was wrong in Mrs. Norris, by its reverse in himself, clearly saw that he had but increased the evil, by teaching them to repress their spirits in his presence, as to make their real disposition unknown to him, and sending them for all their indulgences to a person who had been able to attach them only by the blindness of her affection, and the excess of her praise. (XLVIII, 463)

What greater instance of this 'stop-go' policy do we find in the whole story but the project of the theatricals during Sir Thomas's absence, and his inability to tolerate them on his return? The suppression of the scheme itself is not the consequence of communicated sentiments between father and children, the reasoned debate of people who open their hearts to each other, but another cold fiat in a relationship where so much is outward show.

Our feelings towards the theatre-enterprise should be mixed, therefore; and Fanny's rejection of it, by the same token, also needs a fluctuating response. Indeed that is of the essence of the book, it seems to me. The whole work is a series of complex intuitions—albeit not mediating a paralysed or merely hobbling sense of life's alternatives—and we do not pick up more than a fraction of what it has to offer unless we are willing so to ponder its movement. In Fanny's reaction to the stage-venture at the Park we see yet another function of her dividedness—as partly the most consciant character in this community, partly a personality considerably crippled. But Austen's point is—and it is at least semi-tragic: these are two aspects of one unitary competence; you only find responsibility growing beside or out of disablement.

Why is Fanny at Mansfield Park at all? We may share the slight surprise of Mrs. Price, early in the tale, at her domestic economy being relieved by the choice of a girl and not a boy-child to go and live with their highly-placed and well-to-do Northamptonshire relations (I, 11). After all a boy can rise, as does Fanny's brother William, by native talent, some little influence and hard work to a very respectable and well-provided way of life on, as it were, his own devices (in such a manner two of Austen's own brothers became admirals); but as Sir Thomas conscientiously reflects—'a girl so brought up must be ade-quately provided for, or there would be cruelty, instead of kindness in taking her from her family' (I, 6). Unless in the coming years, with no name or fortune comparable to that of the Bertram sisters, this woman is lucky enough to make a good marriage during the brief period of female eligibility *de rigueur* in that epoch (we see how in *Persuasion* Anne Elliot at 27 and her sister two years older are practically 'on the shelf', will they, nill they) her uncle will have to lay aside a small fortune to provide her with such an annuity as will afford her a life less harrowing than that of the poor or a governess. That is why she is encouraged to seize her lucky offer from Henry Crawford. One can glance forward to Austen's next novel *Emma* and the predicament of Miss Bates, whose 'youth had passed without distinction, and her middle of life was devoted to the care of a failing mother, and the endeavour to make a small income go as far as possible' (E, III, 21); or worse still, to that of Jane Fairfax:

> 'When I am quite determined as to the time, I am not at all afraid of being long unemployed. There are places in town, offices, where inquiry would soon produce something—Offices for the sale—not quite of human flesh—but of human intellect.'
>
> 'Oh! my dear, human flesh! You quite shock me; if you mean a fling at the slave-trade, I assure you Mr. Suckling was always rather a friend to the abolition.'
>
> 'I did not mean, I was not thinking of the slave-trade,' replied Jane; 'governess-trade, I assure you, was all that I had in view; widely different certainly as to the guilt of those who carry it on; but as to the greater misery of the victims, I do not know where it lies.' (XXXV, 300–1)

By being brought to Mansfield Park Fanny has been rescued not only from the real squalor and meanness of her childhood home but also from a probably quite grim future, by her benefactors' generosity. Her debt to Sir Thomas Bertram and his household, therefore, is immense. Yet this household is, like any other human group (and here we have the universality of Austen's subject-matter) a society of 'the bossers and the bossed'.[13] Mrs. Norris as another poor relation and dependant has brought Fanny in, we can see, to be one notch lower than herself in the pecking-order of this domestic sphere. The whole novel is organized around showing us the radical cruelty inherent in a social organism where status and rank exist to make some feel dominant and others dependent; namely, one of the great wounds at the heart of the only world we know. So the aunt's perfect victim in turn is a girl who is neither a fully-fledged member of the family nor of the servants' hall. Fanny is crippled by her lack of standing in this ménage. Afflicted with insult or injury from any other inhabitant or visitor, she has little right to react, as with open hostility and criticism, that is recognized either by society or by her own moral sense. She is just too lucky to be there in the first place. When Mrs. Norris attacks her head-on with

> I am not going to urge her . . . but I shall think her a very obstinate, ungrateful girl, if she does not do what her aunt and cousins wish her—very ungrateful indeed, considering who and what she is. (XV, 147),

she is, though unfairly, touching upon a bond of obligation which cannot be simply waived away as *totally* irrelevant.

So Fanny then, and always, is thrown back in upon herself and retreats once more to her cold East Room to think out the episode, to digest it, assimilate and in that, the only method open to her, mitigate its hurt. In so doing over the years she has become the conscientious member of the family aware, as her fellows are not, of many essential features of their relation to their world; all her intellectual power and emotional energy have been directed into thinking out conduct—the others', her own—on every side. But this same process which makes her the only really perceptive person in her social group is also an invidious one. It can, it must, too easily fall over into a mode of revenge, vindication which is also vindictiveness, of defining her own identity always at the expense of others.

This is the inescapable dilemma not only for Fanny Price but for Everyman. We regularly see re-surfacing Austen's

135

theme of how suffering, gainsaying, deprivation develops the
personality in creative ways. This shows for true even of Julia
Bertram's as against her sister Maria's fate. Denied her chance
of acting with Crawford in the theatricals and of developing a
flirtation with him at her sister's cost, *her* elopement and future
(with Yates) can be patched up for her far better than the
younger Mrs. Rushworth's.

> There was comfort also in Tom, who gradually regained his
> health, without regaining the thoughtlessness and selfishness of
> his previous habits. He was the better for ever for his illness. He
> had suffered, and he had learnt to think, two advantages that he
> had never known before . . . (XLVIII, 462)

In the significantly named 'wilderness' at Sotherton, as one
deluded couple after another circumambulate the stationary
and central Fanny, she alone observes, weighs, estimates,
scruples over their behaviour—partly out of her impotence to
do anything else, to have any social role of her own which
permits delinquency. This gives her an ethical gravity which
the others badly lack, yet her physical debility derives from it
too, I think; all of which is represented as early as the horse-
riding episode. That whole scene (Chapter 7) compresses
Fanny's loneliness; the importance to one powerless as herself,
in all human relations, of the conduct of people who disregard
her, the honing of her moral judgement which fascinated
dependence upon their deeds achieves and which itself is also
morbid; the censorship which is accurate and just, yet adds to
the habit of ungenerousness. Jealousy—even her simple sexual
jealousy of Mary Crawford, significantly the better horse-
woman—becomes inseparably one thing with appropriate
censure:

> The houses, though scarcely half a mile apart, were not within
> sight of each other; but by walking fifty yards from the hall
> door, she could look down the park, and command a view of the
> parsonage and all its demesnes. . . . A happy party it appeared
> to her—all interested in one object—cheerful beyond a doubt,
> for the sound of merriment ascended even to her. It was a sound
> which did not maker *her* cheerful; she wondered that Edmund
> should forget her, and felt a pang. . . . After a few minutes, they
> stopt entirely, Edmund was close to [Mary Crawford], he was

speaking to her, he was evidently directing her management of the bridle, he had hold of her hand. . . . She could not but think indeed that Mr. Crawford might as well have saved him the trouble; that it would have been particularly proper and becoming in a brother to have done it himself; but Mr. Crawford, with all his boasted good-nature, and all his coachmanship, probably knew nothing of the matter, and had no active kindness in comparison of Edmund. She began to think it rather hard upon the mare to have such double duty; if she were forgotten the poor mare should be remembered. (VII, 67–8)

All her objections are fair; but her solicitude for 'the poor mare' (which it is anyway a privilege and kindness from Edmund, unique among his family, to let her ride daily for exercise) is inextricably interwoven with an enforced meanness of spirit. She has to be out of doors watching them in case they are waiting for her to appear for her 'turn' on the horse; but this very looking-on is demoralizing and destructive.

Being the most aware person here and throughout the story, yet the most 'politically', socially constrained makes an ever-developed tension to which I attribute her shown weakness of body and spirit. She does not know how to (because she cannot wholly, legitimately) answer back, and when we compare the very natural *spontaneous* little girl who first arrived at the Park and who openly cried, quite normally, that first day from bewilderment, fear and fatigue, we see someone behaving with an immediacy and innocence which this same Fanny never has again.

Immediacy-and-innocence of that kind is one thing. Spontaneity for its own sake—*the* arch, essential virtue of the Romantic philosophers and of their whole age in the 'Western' world, is another. That as the leading value in living this novel thoroughly exposes and damns, but it acknowledges as much as any image of life the need for *an* immediacy and innocence as the central core and bloom of vitality, wit, social grace, livingness—and it does so *in* the contrasted characterizations of Fanny Price and Mary Crawford, for neither of them has it. Marvin Mudrick in his valuable book has railed upon Fanny and against her author for the treatment of Mary. He quotes from Austen's own letters several times, aptly pointing out— 'This is Mary as we know her in the novel, unmasking cant in

others, free of it herself, driven to no false system: very like
Elizabeth Bennet. . . . And we come finally to be convinced
that both Mary and Jane make such continual demands upon
their wit in order to protect a certain depth of privacy, to avoid
a full commitment.'[14] He lambasts Fanny's cattiness towards
her rival and Jane Austen's falsifying—as it seems to him—
Mary Crawford's role at times in order to blacken it.

> Tom has become ill, and Fanny concludes at once that Mary
> will wish him dead so that Edmund may succeed to the
> baronetcy:
>
>> '. . . Miss Crawford gave her the idea of being the child of
>> good luck, and to her selfishness and vanity it would be
>> good luck to have Edmund the only son.' (XLV, 430) . . .
>
>> '. . . I put it to your conscience, whether "Sir Edmund"
>> would not do more good with all the Bertram property, than
>> any other possible "Sir. . . ."' (434)
>
> We are asked to believe, therefore, that a worldly, intelligent
> girl—even if excited by the not uncommon selfishness that
> comes with the anticipation of a windfall—would confide her
> feelings unreservedly to a stiff moral object, an obsessed par-
> tisan of the Bertram code, like Fanny.[15]

He puts the case against this characterization as well as it
can be stated—vividly and with an element of truth. Austen's
book is great precisely because she is not writing about lay-
figures, devils swathed in green lights to be comfortably hissed
and easily rejected out of hand, but dramatizing complex
alternatives of which her own nature lives all the different
attractions and justifications. Yet his argument is a perfect
statement of the dominant modern view of human psychology
which *Mansfield Park* exists to confute.

The Crawfords are all spontaneity; and it makes them
infinitely more pleasing, some of the time, than Fanny; in
them are embodied powers and energies which life is sadly
grey without. We see Edmund's, let alone Fanny's, stolidness
of mind by comparison, in the conversation on the Church
between him and Mary Crawford during their Sotherton day-
visit. All his sentiments show for perhaps worthy but certainly

ponderous beside Mary's witty and relevant comment on their morning at Mr. Rushworth's home:

> That [Miss Price] should be tired now, however, gives me no surprise; for there is nothing in the course of one's duties so fatiguing as what we have been doing this morning—seeing a great house, dawdling from one room to another—straining one's eyes and one's attention—hearing what one does not understand—admiring what one does not care for.—It is generally allowed to be the greatest bore in the world, and Miss Price has found it so, though she did not know it. (IX, 95–6)

Yet the Crawfords have their kind of liveliness as a consequence of not having been suppressed or gainsaid from childhood upward; they have been so much 'the children of good luck', they are spontaneous in the extreme, erratic. Mary's conversation is to be pondered not in particular parts but as a whole across the book. There is the excellent kindness of her treatment of Fanny when it is proposed she should play Cottager's wife and, not wanting to, is attacked by Aunt Norris (Chapter 15). Here Mary shows herself far more sensitive and actively, almost courageously, helpful than any other member of the Bertram circle. Yet we are given the extravagant vulgarity of her 'Rears and Vices' pun on the admirals she has known at her uncle's (VII, 60). There is the clever, and considerate, drollery of the remark just quoted about people being fatigued by sightseeing; yet the easy cheapness of her 'Every generation has its improvements,' to Edmund when they are told in the Chapel at Sotherton, 'Prayers were always read in it by the domestic chaplain, within the memory of many. But the late Mr. Rushworth left it off' (IX, 86).[16]

By letting themselves be carried about on each gust of their psychic energy, by speaking to every impulse; in not having been disciplined into reflection and restraint by denials and thwartings, the Crawfords have become people each without, really, a personality at all. They are chameleons, non-existent in the sense of having identifiable centre to and from which loyalties can be made—which are the very staple of relationship as of identity. Thus it is that sister and brother both can be enthusiastically well-disposed towards Fanny Price, yet are willing to exploit her trust with their imposition of the necklace to be worn, on a false understanding, at the Mansfield ball (Chapter 26). As far as any feeling can be said to be sincere in natures so unfixed and wandering, both authentically care for her and both practise cheerfully upon her a (not delicate) fraud.

Fanny interests Henry Crawford at first as the one and only woman he is unable flirtatiously to attach in this Mansfield scene. But drawn in, he becomes sincerely attracted to her, and as deeply as in his nature it is possible for him to be. By comparison with his rakish handling of the trip to Sotherton and his caddish performances with the Miss Bertrams, his treatment of the Prices at Portsmouth is a marvel of sustained fine tact (Chapters 41 and 42). Fanny notices a 'wonderful improvement in Mr. Crawford' (end of Chapter 42) and actually moves well within the orbit of accepting his marriage-proposal:

> Poor Susan was very little better fitted for home than her elder sister; and as Fanny grew thoroughly to understand this, she began to feel that when her own release from Portsmouth came, her happiness would have a material drawback in leaving Susan behind. That a girl so capable of being made, every thing good, should be left in such hands, distressed her more and more. Were *she* likely to have a home to invite her to, what a blessing it would be!—And had it been possible for her to return Mr. Crawford's regard, the probability of his being very far from objecting to such a measure, would have been the greatest increase of all her own comforts. She thought he was really good-tempered, and could fancy his entering into a plan of that sort, most pleasantly. (XLIII, 419)

Her suitor is so much genuinely influenced by her, as well as anxious to please, that his new schemes of improvement for his tenants at Everingham (his Norfolk estate) are earnest of a possible fine future for them both. Yet what we are is the consequence of what we have been drilled into being, or trained ourselves to be, over many years. Fanny's long career of hurts, insults and denials at Mansfield Park has forced upon her self-definition, the creation and maintenance of a *consistent coherent identity*; and this Crawford lacks.

The weakness in Plato's original argument in the *Republic* against dramatic art is that it has too simple-minded a notion of deception. When we adopt any social role or *persona* off the stage (this I think is Austen's theme), *that* then constitutes or assails our selfhood radically, according as it is persisted in or varied. But a man dressing up as Frederick in the Kotzebue play, or reading the part of Henry VIII in Shakespeare's drama at a family entertainment, is deluding neither himself nor other people into really believing he is either of those gentlemen. Though a fine skill in such representations *may* betoken a self which is dangerously fluid or unfixed, great acting is not to be hoped for only from men and women with weak personalities. Nevertheless it is artistically significant that

> in Mr. Crawford's reading there was a variety of excellence beyond what [Fanny] had ever met with. The King, the Queen, Buckingham, Wolsey, Cromwell, all were given in turn . . . and whether it were dignity or pride, or tenderness or remorse, or whatever were to be expressed, he could do it with equal beauty. (XXXIV, 337)

and there is also dramatic irony in this choice of play. What was Henry VIII but, supremely, a man incapable of a sustained relationship with a woman?

Carried off by the next strong impulse, Crawford's very recent habits, his creation of that new consistent self which has been oriented towards Fanny, are still too weak, and the possible marriage between them tragically lapses. I say tragically, because we cannot but feel how much better it would be if to respective espousals the partners from Mansfield Park brought their steadying influence, their sobriety, and the Crawford siblings their vitality and free-flowing bright spirits. The best possible marriages—those of Edmund and Mary, Henry and Fanny—are frustrated, and in their place we see the kind of wedding people make in the real world often enough where matters, following the vagrancy of so many human identities, have to be patched up.

We may well feel wistful at such an outcome. That, it seems to me, is an underlying creative intention of the work, as some attempt to falsify Mary Crawford and her brother into simple

141

villains at the last, to retreat into a starchy prudery, certainly is not. All along, Austen's handling of these characters with whom, in the most crucial analysis, her response to life is at odds, has an empathetic sacrifice of all fixed preconceptions to realizing them from within and giving them the fullest and fairest possible representation, which leaves most other fictionists' efforts at equitable portraiture far behind.

Take for instance the scene where, over a card game at Mansfield Parsonage during William Price's visit, the Crawfords and Edmund Bertram converse on the subject of 'improving' the clergyman's house and its demesnes at Thornton Lacey.

> 'And I have two or three ideas also,' said Edmund, 'and one of them is that very little of your plan for Thornton Lacey will ever be put in practice. I must be satisfied with rather less ornament and beauty. I think the house and premises may be made comfortable, and given the air of a gentleman's residence without any very heavy expense, and that must suffice me; and I hope may suffice all who care about me.'
>
> Miss Crawford, a little suspicious and resentful of a certain tone of voice and a certain half-look attending the last expression of his hope, made a hasty finish of her dealings with William Price, and securing his knave at an exorbitant rate, exclaimed, 'There, I will stake my last like a woman of spirit. No cold prudence for me. I am not born to sit still and do nothing. If I lose the game, it shall not be from not striving for it.' (XXV, 242–43)

Christopher Gillie rightly highlights the significance of this last utterance:

> Mary Crawford, in other words, is determined to get Edmund, but determined to get him at his full social value, with no nonsense about moderate expense, or duties to his parishioners, or making minimum changes in an established building on the grounds that it is adequate as it is.[17]

But the whole episode, like practically every event and conversation in Austen's novels, has a resonance over and above the face value of the topics mentioned. That is one of the two reasons why Austen strikes me as the Dante of the Novel: as a form. The other is her relentless 'essential secularity' within this, as perhaps it may be termed. Just as the character itself of

Poetry is best congruent with a religious outlook upon life—for to believe in incantation, which poetry is, is of itself to entertain a supernaturalist sense of existence's phenomena; so prose fiction has its nature best honoured, finds its highest fulfilment in a this-worldly vision. More than any other great novelist Austen does not permit into her frame the spiritual concern, the beyond-the-grave reference or the ghostly—even as a convention (as the ghostly is in Henry James). These issues get the minimal passing allusions in her work compatible with its being a satisfactorily convincing picture of life in an age of established religious belief and practice. This discipline on her part, this perfect adaptation of form and matter—by which is meant the life-view she was concerned to offer as an artist, not the whole of her cosmography as a private person—seems to me uniquely to parallel Dante's.

As in the great Florentine's ravishing cantos, there are at least three levels of meaning operating analogously in her work at any one time and cross-fertilizing one another; yet each embodied for its own sake and given its own absolute value.

(1) Here at the simplest 'level' of meaning we see Mary Crawford speaking to William Price from the stimulus of a particular moment over cards; and both behave entirely in character.

(2) But the fact that she is at a game of chance and skill, one with stakes, and it is called 'speculation'; the fact that she is at play when she responds to Edmund's challenge (there is an element of the unserious, the not committed in her courtship); that she buys, of all the court cards, a *knave* (machination?) and 'at an exorbitant rate' from her opponent at this juncture: these things equally chime with and illuminate her role elsewhere in the story.

(3) The whole situation is emblematic. Edmund's challenge is uttered with only a little circuitousness of address. But the woman he favours answers back more indirectly, utilizing her position *vis-à-vis* one of his junior relatives for this purpose. (Is not this Mary's activity towards William's sister also in the tale?) Furthermore, any contest is spoilt for all the participants if one of them defends his side in it with less than full committedness of talent and concentration. Concluding her dealings with Price so recklessly as she does must mar the sport

143

for him as well as herself. Near the end of *Mansfield Park*—with her characteristic extravagant lapse over her brother's conduct with Maria Rushworth—does she not damage things not only in her own interest, but Edmund's and Fanny's also? Is there not a sense in which the *matrimonial* game between these three is (likewise abruptly) concluded, with Edmund and Fanny being conceded to at too high a cost—getting the wrong exchange, getting the 'exorbitant rate' with which they don't ideally deserve to be paid off and inflicted? 'The game was her's', we are next told, 'and only did not pay her for what she had given to secure it' (ibid., 243).

The 'surface' and the anagogic significance in Austen are like the writing through a stick of Brighton rock. You cannot separate one off from another any more than in Dante; they are unitary, and our consciousness of one part of a given episode's indications inter-animates our sense of the others, just as the literal and immediate intentions of her characters' speeches and deeds are as important as their tralatitious implications. It is of moment that at its simple face value Mary's utterance in this scene inevitably also pleases us. There is 'cold prudence' enough at Mansfield Park (particularly in Fanny) for us to weary of; we are already somewhat fatigued with the heroine's role of 'sitting still and doing nothing'—enforced (we wincingly will admit) as that is. There is essential generosity and warmth in Miss Crawford's remark as well as the very real delinquencies Mr. Gillie brings to notice.

Likewise with her brother, if we look back half a page to the terms in which he prescribes alteration for the parsonage at Thornton Lacey:

> The farm-yard must be cleared away entirely, and planted up to shut out the blacksmith's shop. The house must be turned to front the east instead of the north—the entrance and principal rooms, I mean, must be on that side, where the view is really very pretty; I am sure it may be done. And *there* must be your approach—through what is at present the garden. You must make you a new garden at what is now the back of the house; which will be giving it the best aspect in the world—sloping to the south-east. . . . (ibid., 242)

This kind of utterance should by rights raise up a steamy irritation in the reader, just as the comparable outpourings of Lady Catherine de Burgh's bossy patronage and uninvited interferingness made Elizabeth Bennet's indignation seethe. But Henry Crawford has not the reputation of one of the Austen bullies; and the reason why is an achievement of her subtlety. Crawford is indeed speaking out of turn on this occasion; we feel that; but it is a function, we also sense, of his really quite acute lack of self-confidence. He is richer and freer, with respect to choice of action, than any other person presently in company. Yet, for all that he is a landowner in another county, as a town-bred male he lacks the social role and traditions of someone (like the Bertram brothers) with an established squirearchical place and history in a community; something he must feel the more where he is now, in their kind of territory, rural England. Nor has he, like Edmund Bertram, been trained to a career, and his family and its social record have not been such as to give him self-assurance ready-made. The 600 words which he offers of lengthy commentary on Edmund's parish-to-be, its present and future possibilities, and which would be well-nigh insupportable from the lips of Mrs. Norris at this juncture, we do considerably tolerate not simply because his speeches are modified, to our perception of their importunity, by the whole context already established, our knowledge of his redeeming features and positive graces, but because most forms of social insecurity tend to be appealing. There is something essentially humble and non-egoistic in at least certain kinds of vulnerability; and Crawford suffers from one of these kinds.

That this boldness attempts to compensate for an uneasiness of social orientation, he himself gives a clue to in the substance of his narrative. Talking of his journey the previous day, which had brought him to the village in question, he says: 'I lost my way after passing that old farm house, with the yew trees, because I can never bear to ask. . . .' (p. 241). But the general and engaging nervousness is there in slighter indications, no less artistically deft; his words for instance of horticultural advice—'*You must make you* a new garden. . . .'

It is none of his business to elaborate schemes for another man's dwelling and way of life; but what is nice about the self-conscious archaism I have there italicized is that, not merely does it betoken nervousness; Crawford is trying so to dispose his ill-assurance as to put his auditors at their ease. His insecurity can pay attention to others' concurrent needs. (Some of the time therefore, he has an altruism and charm of address—as in the Portsmouth scenes later—to which the other *jeunes premiers* of the story never attain.)

It is by touches so slight but wholly achieved that Austen equally individuates this personage and is far more fair to him than some of the critics of his portrayal have been to her.

Just as Crawford's anxiety to please, as expressed in the generally unsatisfactory harangue he permits himself on the subject of Edmund's future residence, is pleasing, so Fanny's recourses often leave us disgruntled. Much of the time she is such a stick, so calculating and ungenerous, that however much we allow her responses as forced upon her, inevitably we ask ourselves what the social health and virtue amounts to after all, into which her kind of responses feed; and whether there isn't the possibility of a better, a more cheerful and liberal spirit in the individual oppressed and meritorious.

The answer is 'Yes of course; being a Henry Crawford or a Fanny Price are by no means the solely available human alternatives', and Austen substantiates this in two ways. One is her arch *coup de reine* executed in the later stages of the novel with the introduction of Fanny's sister Susan, who has as many disadvantages as her Mansfield-reared sibling and who yet is undaunted, blithe and capable. At the end, we are told, she is established in Fanny's former place beside Lady Bertram, and it is clear she will know how to manage that succubus better.

'With quickness in understanding the tempers of those she had to deal with, and no natural timidity to restrain any consequent wishes' (XLVIII, 472), her future there looks a happier one than Fanny's past. But if she has a 'more fearless disposition and happier nerves' (ibid.), is that not due to her Portsmouth upbringing? Her disadvantages have been different ones; and that these too have exacted their toll we have already been made aware. Fanny's resolution to educate her sister while she takes that sojourn by the sea in her place of origin has its very questionable aspects. It is as much a relief to herself in a situation where she is unhappy and wants distraction as a task dedicated, with open eyes, wholly to Susan's improvement. What is more, Austen is willing to set a different evaluation on the younger girl's kind of aptitudes than the artless, stuffy (and also very young) one which is evidently Fanny's:

> Susan was growing very fond of her, and though without any of the early delight in books, which had been so strong in Fanny, with a disposition much less inclined to sedentary pursuits, or to information for information's sake, she had so strong a desire of not *appearing* ignorant, as with a good clear understanding, made her a most attentive, profitable, thankful pupil. Fanny was her oracle. Fanny's explanations and remarks were a most important addition to every essay, or every chapter of history. What Fanny told her of former times, dwelt more on her mind than the pages of Goldsmith; and she paid her sister the compliment of preferring her style to that of any printed author. The early habit of reading was wanting. (XLIII, 418–19)

There is more than a dash of *erlebte Rede* here; this is partly Fanny's indirect reported thought; and one cannot but chuckle at the unction of that 'most attentive, profitable, thankful'.

Nevertheless, 'the early habit of reading was wanting'. Yes, the above certainly is ponderous and priggish but it equally signifies a real limitedness, that educational *manque* in the younger girl, a contractedness of intellectual and therefore emotional and moral dimension which does matter.

Moreover we are given to infer *why* Susan is a more positive, less grimacing personality than her visitor. *Something* is allowed to innate temperament as other than just environmentally produced. The younger relative's mind indeed possesses a 'natural light' (XL, 395). The novel is not committed to enforcing a ruthless determinism. Yet that Susan's 'general manners' are of a 'determined character' so that in her home she 'was only acting on the same truths, and pursuing the same system, which [Fanny's] own judgment acknowledged, but . . . where *she* [Fanny] could only have gone away and cried' (ibid.), surely derives from the fact that in poor Susan's case 'never was there any maternal tenderness to buy her off' (ibid., 396)? We are told of Mrs. Price how Fanny's

> Every flattering scheme of being of consequence to her soon fell to the ground. . . . Her heart and her time were already quite

full; she had neither leisure nor affection to bestow on Fanny. Her daughters had never been much to her. She was fond of her sons, especially of William, but Betsey was the first of her girls whom she had ever much regarded. (XXXIX, 389)

Likewise—

> Her days were spent in a kind of slow bustle; always busy without getting on, always behindhand and lamenting it, without altering her ways; wishing to be an economist, without contrivance or regularity; dissatisfied with her servants, without skill to make them better, and whether helping, or reprimanding, or indulging them, without any power of engaging their respect. (Ibid., 389–90)

Just as Austen is so poignantly damning about the Ward sister who has become a miserly widow—'She had never been able to attach even those she loved best' (XLVIII, 466)—so we have the perfect equity of her sympathetic-severe judgement on them both:

> She might have made just as good a woman of consequence as Lady Bertram, but Mrs. Norris would have been a more respectable mother of nine children, on a small income. (XXXIX, 390)

In this wise it has followed for Susan that 'The blind fondness which was for ever producing evil around her, *she* had never known' (XL, 396), while Lady Bertram's kind of torpid dependence over the years, and the whole set-up at the Park, have forced Fanny neither into real sanctity nor her sibling's robustness.

The other element which bodies forth a different response to the world's invidiousnesses from Fanny's prudence and censure is the author's own presence in her tale. Her sanity is a major feature, constituting as it does her sly humour; and you have to have a spleen of brick not to heave with that quiet rich inward mirth which her art signally inspires:

> [Dr. Grant] had a wife about fifteen years his junior, but no children, and they entered the neighbourhood with the usual fair report of being very respectable, agreeable people. (III, 24)

> It was some months before Sir Thomas's consent could be received [to the marriage of his daughter Maria with Mr.

Rushworth]; but in the mean while, as no one felt a doubt of his most cordial pleasure in the connection, the intercourse of the two families was carried on without restraint, and no other attempt made at secrecy, than Mrs. Norris's talking of it every where as a matter not to be talked of at present. (IV, 39)

Sir Thomas was most cordially anxious for the perfection of Mr. Crawford's character in that point. He wished him to be a model of constancy; and fancied the best means of effecting it would be by not trying him too long. (XXV, 345)

[Speaking of Lady Bertram, Mrs. Norris and Tom Bertram, left behind at Mansfield after the catastrophes which overwhelm the family towards the end of the story.] It had been a miserable party, each of the three believing themselves most miserable. (XLVII, 448)

There is not so much of this characteristic humorous commentary in *Mansfield Park* as in Austen's other works; nonetheless while her almost festal energy of ironic perception can recurrently be brought to bear, it is too partial to speak of the tale as offering only tragic intimations. Yet if the author has found a way of answering back at life which is more wholesome and pleasing than Fanny's, which is balanced and cheerful where this heroine's is fairly crabbed and vindictive, that is because Jane Austen can comment as a detached arbitress outside the situation she is dealing with. (Doubtless D. W. Harding's remark is again appropriate here: 'Her object is not missionary; it is the more desperate one of merely finding some mode of existence for her critical attitudes.'[18]) The storyteller's disablements and competences have been formed in another sphere—that of *her* personal history, not Miss Price's.

What is shown us compressed, but artistically achieved and convincing, in the Portsmouth scenes, the book as a whole writes large. We are importantly what our frustrations, or lack of them, have made us. Our outlook on life is so shaped. Susan's greater resource of inward happiness, her better ability to cope with Mansfield existence when she gets there than Fanny had in the past, her general capability of more open, positive (and no doubt more generous) attitudes than her predecessor's, have been vouchsafed her with the penalties denoted in these glimpses of *her* childhood and youth.

The theme operates on every hand; but we see it spelled out in the case of Julia Bertram, as of other characters, in the winding-up commentary of the conclusion:

> That Julia escaped better than Maria was owing, in some measure, to a favourable difference of disposition and circumstance, but in a greater to her having been less the darling of that very aunt, less flattered, and less spoilt. Her beauty and acquirements had held but a second place. She had been always used to think herself a little inferior to Maria. Her temper was naturally the easiest of the two, her feelings, though quick, were more controulable; and education had not given her so very hurtful a degree of self-consequence. (XLVIII, 466)

Yes, there is such a thing as 'disposition', we are to note. The novel is nowhere in the grip of an obsessed behavourist view. But the crucial factor is, what has happened to us. ('Julia's folly' has been saved from being as bad as 'Maria's guilt'— ibid., 467—not least by the rebuff her hopes suffered during the early stages of the theatricals, as I remarked before.)

Austen sums up the matter herself—her continuous treatment throughout the book of this principal perception—at the end:

> In *her* [Susan's] usefulness, in Fanny's excellence, in William's continued good conduct, and rising fame, and in the general well-doing and success of the other members of the family, all assisting to advance each other, and doing credit to his countenance and aid, Sir Thomas saw repeated, and for ever repeated reason to rejoice in what he had done for them all, and acknowledge *the advantages of early hardship and discipline, and the consciousness of being born to struggle and endure.* (Ibid., 473; emphasis added)

All individuals the author sees as potential developers, even though her heroine does not. Fanny's jealous grief of Mary Crawford's success with Edmund Bertram earlier, which finds vent in acid despair about that rival's character, the novelist repudiates. Edmund's cousin may be forgiven by older sages, for looking on the chance of Miss Crawford's future improvement as nearly desperate, for thinking that if Edmund's influence in this season of love, had already done so little in clearing her judgment, and regulating her notions, his worth would be finally wasted on her even in years of matrimony. (XXXVII, 367)

But the narrator herself stipulates otherwise:

Experience might have hoped more for any young people, so circumstanced, and impartiality would not have denied to Miss Crawford's nature, that participation of the general nature of women, which would lead her to adopt the opinions of the man she loved and respected, as her own. (Ibid.)

And the later scenes of Henry Crawford's visit to Fanny in her seaport 'home' introduced a new mood into the tale—a mellow warmth:

The day was uncommonly lovely. It was really March; but it was April in its mild air, brisk soft wind, and bright sun, occasionally clouded for a minute; and every thing looked so beautiful under the influence of such a sky. . . . (XLII, 409)

With good cause may the season be so vernal and smiling (though the dappled, not wholly certain benignity of the light and weather which this lovely paragraph conveys reflects not only a particular observed physical scene but also the present phase in its principals' relation). This courtship is becoming a sensitive happy thing imbrued with generosities of human feeling and real altruism which have been too frequently lacking in the story hitherto.

For what is one's leading, even one's overwhelming sensation in reading this novel?—That of a world of selfishness. Austen's characteristic preoccupation with peculiarly close scrutiny of people's motives comes in here. Nearly every speech and act we are shown derives from in fact quite ruthless self-regard on the part of the drama's personages.

Instance: Fanny is determined to make a hero out of Edmund Bertram, and he has indeed extended to her many passing kindnesses over the years. Almost alone he has shown her consideration at Mansfield in the past and he is still pre-eminent for this during the main action of the story. But these charitable attentions seem to occur when nothing else is particularly pressing on his attention. We may think it pretty natural in him to forget his cousin's need of riding-exercise when Mary Crawford appears and exhibits an interest in the same; but it cannot be lost on us that once Fanny, under her paternal roof, is out of sight and mind, Edmund takes seven whole weeks to write her a letter; and for all that he does not at that stage know he is the individual around whom she builds her emotional life, this is still, in their acknowledged relation, as casual and churlish as anything in the book. He writes her, we ought to notice, only when once again he can use Fanny as on most of the occasions we have seen him bothering with her since the appearance of the Grants' relations: as a means of being more closely linked with the Crawford siblings (hoping that Fanny will accept Henry's proposal) or as a confidant, the sole confidant he can turn to in his perplexity of mind about Mary. His letter, when it does come, is one long soliloquy on that theme and little else. The real active concern in it for how Fanny may be, in health, spirits and occupations, is effectually zero.

Much of the way of life Austen portrays is typified in the episode where, at the scratch Mansfield dance given before the head of the family's return from Antigua, Fanny, 'longing for the re-entrance of her elder cousin, on whom all her own hopes of a partner then depended' (XII, 117), finds that he does not want to oblige her:

> When he had told of his horse, he took a newspaper from the table, and looking over it said in a languid way, 'If you want to dance, Fanny, I will stand up with you.'—With more than equal civility the offer was declined;—she did not want to dance.—'I am glad of it,' said he in a much brisker tone, and throwing down the newspaper again—'for I am tired to death.' (Ibid., 118)

Yet when Mrs. Norris interposes with her own attempt at enforcing compliance to what is only nominally a request—in this case that Tom will join her, Dr. Grant and Mrs. Rushworth to make up a quartet for a rubber of whist—Tom wants this even less than the other entertainment offering, is indignant at the manner as well as the substance of his aunt's plea; and

avoids such penitential duty by using Fanny's wish for dancing
after all:

> *That* is what I dislike most particularly. It raises my spleen more
> than any thing, to have the pretence of being asked, of being
> given a choice, and at the same time addressed in such a way as
> to oblige one to do the very thing—whatever it be! If I had not
> luckily thought of standing up with you, I could not have got out
> of it. (Ibid. 120)

The double standard reigns supreme; and Fanny's own
participation in it accounts for the dislike she has raised in so
many readers. Worked upon as we are here by a rhetoric and
narrative scheme which continually elicit from us keen attention to the springs and implications of conduct, we cannot but
be aware of Fanny's share in the comprehensive taint of
egoism—with the added aggravation of her being offered to us
as the heroine of the tale. We can see both the process of the
pressures under which she lives and her way of replying to
them in almost the worst instance of its kind, that of Chapter
47 where she and Edmund indulge to its utmost their very
unendearing habit of dissecting Mary Crawford's character
together, concluding thus:

> Fanny, now at liberty to speak openly, felt more than justified
> in adding to his knowledge of her real character, by some hint of
> what share his brother's state of health might be supposed to
> have in her wish for a complete reconciliation [*etc*]. (p. 459)

This spiteful dig at her vanquished rival is of course *necessary*:
since Edmund has irretrievably lost his beloved sweetheart, it
may palliate the hurt and grief somewhat for him to learn of
that element in Mary which was represented in the letter she
sent to Fanny at Portsmouth (XLV, 433–35). Facts are facts
and the whole truth is only to be obscured with possible consequent danger to individuals later on. Yet we cannot feel
Fanny is hitting back with grit—to have seen her do some
open fighting earlier would have been a relief—because this is
underhand now, Mary is absent and *hors concours*.

In short and throughout, we resent Fanny's lack of initiatives, and the egotistic priggishness which fills their place. But
then we ourselves have not been deprived in the manner she
has known deprivation—of the possibility of independent

153

action. It is interesting to compare her hobbled role in Sir Thomas Bertram's household with the decisive critical act of Anne Elliot in *Persuasion* when Frederick Wentworth appears before her father and sister at a party in Bath, and she turns her back on them to offer him a real welcome. She is more polite than they to this visitor, but the very fact that she can have the courage of her conviction of doing 'everything which she believed right to be done' (P, XX, 181) derives from her different status in her familial group. Though unimportant with her kindred she is one of Sir Walter Elliot's daughters, not accountable to him for her upbringing and comforts in the same way that Fanny Price is in Sir Thomas Bertram's debt and therefore his hopelessly compromised dependant guest.

As such over long years Fanny has neither had the right nor been allowed the privilege of taking an independent line on any occasion at the Park; protest, opposition, open censure has really not been a legitimate response:

> Mrs. Norris fetched breath and went on again.
>
> 'The nonsense and folly of people's stepping out of their rank and trying to appear above themselves, makes me think it right to give *you* a hint, Fanny, now that you are going into company without any of us; and I do beseech and intreat you not to be putting yourself forward, and talking and giving your opinion as if you were one of your cousins—as if you were dear Mrs. Rushworth or Julia. *That* will never do, believe me. Remember, wherever you are, you must be the lowest and last; and though Miss Crawford is in a manner at home, at the Parsonage, you are not to be taking place of her. And as to coming away at night, you are to stay just as long as Edmund chuses. Leave him to settle *that*.' (XXIII, 221)

Thus we come back to the novel's principal insight. We are fashioned by our sufferings and deprivations (or lack of them); but being significantly deprived, while it may confer important virtues and strengths, will also seriously cramp the personality. What gives Fanny a supreme virtue—'constancy', consistency of outlook and behaviour, and thereby *the possession of an identity itself*—is the bullied role which makes her a stick. Her attention to moral issues is likewise most important; there is a wounding ethical somnambulism in the other characters of which we get heartily and properly tired. But Fanny's alertness to issues of behaviour and responsibility at Mansfield evolves from the humiliated nature of the part she has to play there, a depressed, devalued function upon which she revenges herself by becoming physically feeble, quickly ill, self-righteously censorious and conventional in her value-judgements.

Her exclamations upon Nature illustrate this.

> Fanny agreed to it, and had the pleasure of seeing him continue at the window with her, in spite of the expected glee; and of having his eyes soon turned like hers towards the scene without, where all that was solemn and soothing, and lovely, appeared in the brilliancy of an unclouded night, and the contrast of the deep shade of the woods. Fanny spoke her feelings. 'Here's harmony!' said she. 'Here's repose! Here's what may leave all painting and all music behind, and what poetry only can attempt to describe. Here's what may tranquillize every care, and lift the heart to rapture! When I look out on such a night as this, I feel as if there could be neither wickedness nor sorrow in the world; and there certainly would be less of both if the sublimity of Nature were more attended to, and people were carried more out of themselves by contemplating such a scene.' (XI, 112–13)

This invites a complicated response. It does signalize a superiority of outlook that she almost alone in Mansfield society is awake to 'the choir of heaven and all the furniture of earth'. The way the others, with the partial exception of Edmund, conceive of man's environment only as a setting for social life is part of their aforesaid sleep-walking. But Fanny's attitude to the non-human world, like the rest of her attitudes, does not constitute a sufficiently resourceful dynamic of its own. Her feelings are sincere but clichéd. 'Here's . . . what poetry only can attempt to describe', i.e. the experience itself she filters via the Nature-poets of her reading and assumes at second-hand. And that all this is rather limp second-hand thinking we ironically may perceive by noting that immediately after this, when Edmund turns back to the other young people at song beside their pianoforte and in particular to the charms of Mary Crawford, Fanny is not 'carried out of herself', for all her 'attention to the sublimity of Nature', nor is *her* 'sorrow' palliated. 'Fanny sighed alone at the window till scolded away by Mrs. Norris's threats of catching cold' (ibid.). She does not in fact make of her relation to the outer scene a

sanctuary for the spirit—as it is in Wordsworth; a vitalizing
refuge into *an independent and different mode of consciousness* athwart
that of the social frustrations by which she is begirt.

Austen is aware of all this and regularly teases her heroine.

> 'I suppose I am graver than other people,' said Fanny. 'The
> evenings do not appear long to me. I love to hear my uncle talk
> of the West Indies. I could listen to him for an hour together. It
> entertains *me* more than many other things have done—but
> then I am unlike other people I dare say.'
>
> 'Why should you dare say *that*? (smiling)—Do you want to be
> told that you are only unlike other people in being more wise
> and discreet?' (XXI, 197)

> [Mrs. Norris] was regretted by no one at Mansfield. She had
> never been able to attach even those she loved best, and since
> Mrs. Rushworth's elopement, her temper had been in a state of
> such irritation, as to make her every where tormenting. Not
> even Fanny had tears for aunt Norris—not even when she was
> gone for ever. (XLVIII, 466)

These are only two of many 'digs', and in various ironic
modes, at her principal character which the novelist wittingly
affords. But it is right nevertheless that Fanny Price is the
tale's heroine and the observer through whom almost all of its
action is mediated to us. And for two reasons.

The first is so obvious, it could only need spelling out in an
age like our own, besotted with the Crawford-type commitment to 'spontaneity'. Fanny is head and shoulders above the
other characters because she is conscious that life is a moral
debate—even if herself all-unlikeable (and that is putting it
strongly) she has a developed ethical sense continually at
work. This permits improvement within her own personality
and social 'space' in a way that Maria Bertram cannot afford.
She can be challenged—as Edmund challenged her in the
extract just given above—and reproved. In a Day of Judgement Fanny, her faults glaringly ranged all against her, would
hang her head. The others, wheeled off to their fates, would
wonder what all the fuss was about; as Mary Crawford does
near the end.

The other reason is more subtle though no less continuously
operating upon us in every line of the book as we read.

Rather like *The Iliad*, though by a different *procédé*, the theme of *Mansfield Park* is expressed in the sum total of what it represents, and only there: namely the very nature of social living, the character, feel and 'trick' of human experience. To Fanny's changing attitudes as she goes to Portsmouth and thence back to Northamptonshire—on each occasion unfairly idealizing her destination—we have a more complex response than she, the essence of which catches up what has been shown through the rest of the novel. We come to acknowledge, something against our will, Mansfield's superiority to the Price home, but with that the larger realization that in fact there are no perfect ambits or achieved sanctuaries of the spirit—though as leading values their idealization is not unworthy for that.

No, in the actual world, the only one we shall know here under this sun, environments and people come flawed; and if not with these faults which this particular tale has detailed, then with others.

So likewise as to the heroine of the piece and her whole function. It is probable, I will cheerfully concede, that Jane Austen did not have such a purpose deliberately in mind with her thorny characterization as it strikes me is accomplished. Very likely she did think she was writing the story of a reliable moral agent versus a lapsing social group, more simply, and dramatized it through Fanny's consciousness because that kind of artistic process—showing the world through the eyes of an unmarried and fairly powerless young woman who ultimately 'triumphs'—is congenial to her. But what is effectually wrought seems to me the most rigorous, honest, indeed courageous expression of the novel's central apprehension which its author can offer.

Here, in Fanny Price, is a particular psychology as all psychologies are particular, and a human being who would have been greatly more pleasing if she had been 'dealt a different hand of cards' as it were. Being made to experience the action of *Mansfield Park* principally, though not exclusively, through this heroine, all avenues to a kind of moral escapism on our side are closed. We are shut up, in Fanny, with the same truth which the rest of the book enforces—that there is no human mentality which can cheeringly stand outside its origins and upbringing, the penalties and freedoms it has known. If we resent this and reject her for not being delightful or at least gutsy, we are left skating about on the thin ice of the alternative plea—that people somehow *can* avoid being shaped by their past, their thwartings and liberties. Were this young lady half as splendid as we wish ('My Mother. . . . Thought Fanny insipid') all that the novel exists to show would be stood on its head; Fanny her individual self would somehow have broken out of the very laws of human determination it exhibits, and we should comfort ourselves with a proved dreamy untruth.

This is the book's subtlest aptness, its enforcing the recognition that no individual, not even a heroine, not even a reader, can opt out of the syndrome of competence-and-disablement which the novel as a whole demonstrates. Here is the ultimate point in its being presented through Fanny, and of that personage having her special status (acknowledged with the 'My Fanny' of Chapter 48, authorially so expressed).

Yet it is not Fanny's story simply as such. We look through her eyes rather than other characters', but *Mansfield Park* is about life within the social group as a whole; hence the novel's being so entitled and not 'Fanny' (*or* 'Ordination': on this please see p. 203 below). Just as its very method obliges to know that grand options like being marvellous and perfect, standing outside all the major possible alternatives of human inadequacy, scarcely exist, so *Mansfield Park* demonstrates how people are ever thus in societal relation. There are no escape hatches; and you have to make the best of an always unsatisfactory human world. We can be discriminative and responsible, if we will, as—in significant respects—Fanny is; let us hope so! But that too will have been bought at a 'Price'.

It is appropriate therefore that the end should read relatively so scamped as it does. Austen cannot, though she approves the match as well enough, make of Edmund's and Fanny's union a grand matrix of the kind of liveliness which *should* be there. All along her intuitions have tended to this tragi-comic constatation in which the novel concludes but the tragedy in them is not to be underplayed. The concluding tableau expresses, like what has gone before, the mingled yarn of existence in Middle Earth. At the close of it all Fanny is once again a dependant at Mansfield, this time in Mrs. Norris's former position (as vicar's wife; and though she occupies it doubtless very differently, the role of hanger-on at a great house we have been shown is not a healthy one). Edmund has in fact accepted two livings—Mansfield as well as Thornton Lacey—after having spoken earlier, and well, against plurality; concessions and compromises continue.

Certain important kinds of awareness however have been restored which had lapsed when the tale began and authority is in the hands of people who have a coherent identity, faulty as they are: Fanny, the two Thomas Bertrams (somewhat reformed characters now), Edmund, Susan.

These things are valuable and matter. But they have come at a high cost.

NOTES

1. *MW*, p. 432.
2. In *The Quarterly Review*, vol. 228 (July 1917), reprinted in *SS Casebook*, p. 209.
3. *SS Casebook*, p. 214.
4. *Collection of Essays*, p. 31.
5. See note 2 to Chapter 2 above.
6. L. Trilling, *Sincerity and Authenticity* (London, 1972), p. 75.
7. In B. Ford (ed.), *The Pelican Guide to English Literature* (Harmondsworth: Penguin, 1957; 1969 reprinting, revised), p. 121.
8. Reproduced from its fifth edition, with Mrs. Inchbald's Preface, etc., in the text of *Mansfield Park* used here. My quotations from this material give the page numbers in this volume of Chapman's.
9. *SS Casebook*, p. 245.
10. This is a difficult one, but difficult with the problematic nature of the issue itself here under discussion. The tribute to Lord Ravenshaw is made (resentfully) by the giddy Mr. Yates, who may be supposed not to have the highest standard of 'correctness'; he is aggrieved that the Ecclesford theatricals should have been terminated merely by a 'poor old dowager' who 'could not have died at a worse time; and it is impossible to help wishing, that the news could have been suppressed for just the three days we wanted. It was but three days; and being only a grand-mother, and all happening two hundred miles off, I think there would have been no great harm, and it *was* suggested, I know . . .' (loc. id.). But the point is that the play was called off, that his close relative's demise and the sobriety due to such an event *was* respected by the

master of that house. We therefore cannot say that Yates has been holidaying under the aegis of an aristocratic wastrel in this Cornish establishment; the evidence is otherwise, and his tribute to Lord Ravenshaw's character tends to show for, perhaps exaggerated but, sufficiently valid.

11. T. S. Eliot, *The Sacred Wood* (London, 1950), p. 101. The phrase almost immediately following—'the guilt of a mother'—comes from the same essay (pp. 99, 100).
12. *SS Casebook*, p. 237.
13. E. M. Forster, *Two Cheers for Democracy*, ed. O. Stallybrass (London, 1972), p. 67.
14. *JA: Irony as Defense and Discovery*, pp. 169, 170.
15. Ibid., p. 167.
16. As with her choice of Kotzebue's play for the text of the Mansfield theatricals, here again the totality of this author's representation of her themes and world may be remarked. We are told that 'This chapel was fitted up as you see it, in James the Second's time' (loc. id.). That it should have been refurbished in that very brief of all English reigns suggests that it was so in opposition to the assault upon Anglicanism which, rightly or wrongly, most English Protestants then believed their monarch to be making. This led to his enforced flight and abdication in 1688; but not before seven senior bishops had chosen to go to the Tower rather than be party to his new ecclesiastical policies and other leading individuals had taken the path of defiance rather than preferment. Austen's implication as I read it is that the present, her contemporary age, is also an epoch in which valid traditions at the heart of English life are under attack. Ranks should be closing, accordingly, around the (highest ideals of the) English Church and British polity as understood by rural Toryism. That prayers have been left off by the late Mr. Rushworth, and the chapel at Sotherton is not now again new furnished, because not again the focal centre and 'power-house' of that community's self-orientation, is of a piece with the decayed morality among the landed gentry which the novel treats of at large.
17. Christopher Gillie, *A Preface to Jane Austen* (London, 1974), p. 83.
18. See note 6 to Chapter 2.

5

Ripeness is All: *Persuasion*

Now let us stint all this and speak of mirth. We have observed Austen engaging with themes about the individual coping with society in such a way as to divulge insights that are comic and tragic together. Her last complete work is deeply and resonantly celebrative. The tragic, defeating elements in our human experience are not ignored or tidied aside; they are incorporated and transcended in the vision which is *Persuasion*. For this novel, with *Sense and Sensibility*, like *The Winter's Tale* and *King Lear*, are the works wherein their authors lay all cards on the table, expressing respectively the comic and tragic potentialities of existence as they see it. Indeed the theme and upshot of *Persuasion* is much the same as that of *The Winter's Tale*; the validity of a certain order of consciousness set over against the ravages of Society and despite those of Time.

Sir Walter Elliot, 'a foolish spendthrift baronet' who is vain both of his rank and his good looks, has incurred so much debt through extravagant living that he is obliged to let his home, Kellynch-hall, to an Admiral Croft, lately come ashore with the outbreak of Peace—for this is the summer of 1814. Sir Walter is a widower with three daughters; the eldest, Elizabeth, as proud and empty as he; the youngest, Mary, a querulous sharer in 'the Elliot pride'; and the other, Anne, the heroine of the tale, '. . . with an elegance of mind and sweetness of character, which must have placed her high with any people of real understanding,' is 'nobody with either father or sister' (I, 5).

161

Admiral Croft and she have once nearly become relatives by marriage; though this is known only to her father, her elder sister, and her closest friend and confidant Lady Russell, their near neighbour and tenant at Kellynch Lodge, who has supplied the place of her mother since Lady Elliot's death thirteen years ago when Anne was 14. One of the Admiral's two brothers-in-law by his marriage has been a curate in the district, and the other, Frederick Wentworth, visiting him during the summer of 1806 and encountering Anne Elliot, this young couple have been 'gradually acquainted, and when acquainted, rapidly and deeply in love'.

They entered into an engagement at that time but it was broken off; not so much from its being considered 'a very degrading alliance' by her father, as upon the advice—the Persuasion—of Lady Russell, who remonstrated against her favourite's being united to 'a young man, who had nothing but himself to recommend him, and no hopes of attaining affluence, but in the chances of a most uncertain profession, and no connexions to secure even his farther rise in that profession'.

> Anne Elliot, so young; known to so few, to be snatched off by a stranger without alliance or fortune; or rather sunk by him into a state of most wearing, anxious, youth-killing dependance! It must not be, if by any fair interference of friendship, any representations from one who had almost a mother's love, and mother's rights, it would be prevented. (IV, 26–7)

Anne renounces the match, to her own and her lover's misery and his disgust; and since the rupture Wentworth has prospered even beyond his own most sanguine hopes. Commanding one leaky but fortunate old boat he has taken excellent prizes from pirates and the enemy alike, has since been made a Captain, given a better vessel and increased his fortune.

Reappearing on this Somerset scene he is now a very eligible suitor and indeed seems to be looking about for a young bride; for when he stays with his sister Mrs. Croft, and visits the neighbouring Musgrove family, the attentive interest of their two daughters he evidently reciprocates.

Mary Elliot has married Charles Musgrove, the son and heir of that particular Great House and to this sister Anne goes, on the removal to Bath of her father and Elizabeth, pursuant to his plan for retrenchment and the vacation of Kellynch-hall in time for its new lessees. The relation Wentworth offers the secretly still devoted Anne is one of cool formality, but he is greatly popular with all the Musgrove clan—except Charles Hayter, who is the eldest nephew of that name to Mrs. Musgrove senior. On his return to Uppercross Hayter discovers his beloved cousin Henrietta enchanted by the new naval hero and his own understanding with her apparently at an end. He retires therefore from the lists but this provokes a happy clarification between them, a restoration and improvement of their tie, and the portion of a conversation between Louisa Musgrove and Captain Wentworth which Anne Elliot overhears seems also to show the marriage of *this* pair as simply a matter of time.

> 'What!—would I be turned back from doing a thing that I had determined to do, and that I knew to be right, by the airs and interference of such a person?—or, of any person I may say. No,—I have no idea of being so easily persuaded. When I have made up my mind, I have made it up. . . .
>
> 'Your sister is an amiable creature; but *yours* is the character of decision and firmness, I see. If you value her conduct or happiness, infuse as much of your own spirit into her, as you can. But this, no doubt, you have always been doing. It is the worst evil of too yielding and indecisive a character, that no influence over it can be depended on.—You are never sure of a good impression being durable. Every body may sway it; let those who would be happy be firm. . . . If Louisa Musgrove would be beautiful and happy in her November of life, she will cherish all her present powers of mind.' (X, 87–8)

The whole party, however, makes a trip to Lyme Regis, to visit its sights and some of his friends—Captain and Mrs. Harville and a Captain Benwick; and near the proposed conclusion of the outing, Louisa, headstrong and unrestrainable, insists on being 'jumped' by Wentworth down the steps of the Cobb there.

> He advised her against it, thought the jar too great; but no, he reasoned and talked in vain; she smiled and said, 'I am determined I will:' he put out his hands; she was too precipitate by half a second, she fell on the pavement on the Lower Cobb, and was taken up lifeless! (XII, 109)

163

Only Anne has presence of mind to rally the others to good measures at this crisis; her sister Mary is hysterical, Henrietta has fainted, the three men of the party are paralysed by the event. A surgeon being gone for, the victim is lodged in the Harvilles' little house, and during her long convalescence from what proves to have been a severe but not fatal concussion, remains there, excellently nursed by Mrs. Harville, encumbered by Mary, and attended by Captain Benwick, hitherto the Harvilles' lodger.

After a spell staying with Lady Russell, Anne moves on as planned to Bath where her father and elder sister now glory in all the consequence of their Camden-place lodging and its possession of two drawing-rooms. This self-flattery is ably abetted by the attentions of Mrs. Clay, the widowed friend of Elizabeth who has frequently been ensconced at Kellynch-hall in the past and now has come to be her guest in Bath, much to the discontent of Lady Russell, since it is fairly evident that Mrs. Clay is a minx who, albeit working under the disadvantages of a protruding tooth and freckles, has designs upon Sir Walter. He is also gratified by the revival of interest shown towards his family in their cousin, and heir to the baronetcy, William Walter Elliot. In former years this young man has snubbed their overtures, but Elizabeth's hopes of marrying him (and thereby maintaining not only caste but the all-superior Elliot name and home, along with the status of a baronet's lady) are all revived now that he has sought them out here and courted their company.

In fact it becomes plain to everyone except Elizabeth and her father that Mr. Elliot is attracted to Anne, not her sister; and this provides a complication of its own when the Crofts and Musgroves come to the Spa city in their turn. For it transpires, as Anne learns in a letter from Mary Musgrove, that Captain Benwick and Louisa Musgrove have decided to marry; and Captain Wentworth comes to join the others in Bath at the same time. He is now a free man, therefore, and Anne begins to suspect that his interest in her is renewed; yet Mr. Elliot's gallantry at a concert party they attend waylays the *éclaircissement* between them which otherwise might have unfolded, and Wentworth retires, doubtful of her affection, jealous of her cousin, supposing Anne likely to be swayed (as in the past) by the prejudices of Lady Russell.

> 'Is not this song worth staying for?' said Anne, suddenly struck by an idea which made her yet more anxious to be encouraging.
>
> 'No!' he replied impressively, 'there is nothing worth my staying for;' and he was gone directly. (XX, 190)

Three days later, however, they are present in each other's company again at the Musgroves' hotel, the White Hart, where Captain Harville is also staying. His sister Fanny was James Benwick's original intended bride, the match was broken off the previous summer by her sudden untimely death; and he is hurt at his comrade's ability to 'forget her so soon'. The moving conversation between him and Anne on the subject of constancy in love is overheard by Captain Wentworth as he sits writing at a table further down the room, and he again proposes to Anne in the form of a letter penned under cover of the missive the others have supposed him engaged upon.

Anne's spirits are almost overpowered, the newly reassembled family company deem her stricken ill and only with a struggle does she manage to safeguard her right to walk home and with it the chance of meeting her lover and offering him some symptom of favour. This opportunity is realized, nevertheless, in Union-street, on her way back to Camden-place with her brother-in-law, who leaves her to Wentworth's care:

> . . . and soon words enough had passed between them to decide their direction towards the comparatively quiet and retired gravel-walk, where the power of conversation would make the present hour a blessing indeed; and prepare it for[1] all the immortality which the happiest recollections of their own future lives could bestow. There they exchanged again those feelings and those promises which had once before seemed to secure every thing, but which had been followed by so many, many years of division and estrangement. There they returned again into the past, more exquisitely happy, perhaps, in their reunion, than when it had been first projected; more tender, more tried, more fixed in a knowledge of each other's character, truth, and attachment; more equal to act, more justified in acting. . . .
> (XXIII, 240–41)

Previous to this resolution of all *her* woes, Anne has discovered Mr. Elliot's true character, his being a cold-hearted hypocrite, from a schoolfriend Mrs. Smith, who lives there now in poverty and sickness, and whose husband during time gone by Mr. Elliot helped to ruin. A similar light is thrown upon his gentility and professions of loyalty when he hears the news of Anne's forthcoming marriage to Another, quits Bath, and the Elliot family next learn of Mrs. Clay as his mistress established by him in London. So much for Sir Walter and Elizabeth's capacity for cultivating worthy friendships:

> They had their great cousins, to be sure, to resort to for comfort; but they must long feel that to flatter and follow others, without being flattered and followed in their turn, is but a state of half enjoyment. (XXIV, 251)

These cousins are 'the Dowager Viscountess Dalrymple, and her daughter, the Honourable Miss Carteret'; and her family's reaction to them has embarrassed Anne:

> Had Lady Dalrymple and her daughter even been very agreeable, she would still have been ashamed of the agitation they created, but they were nothing. There was no superiority of manner, accomplishment, or understanding. Lady Dalrymple had acquired the name of 'a charming woman,' because she had a smile and a civil answer for every body. Miss Carteret, with still less to say, was so plain and so awkward, that she would never have been tolerated in Camden-place but for her birth. (XVI, 149–50)

Such a world of no-meaning snobberies, depreciation of all real values, of insults and humiliations, Anne is very happy to leave behind with her marriage and the new friends it bestows on her; for she is 'tenderness itself, and she had the full worth of it in Captain Wentworth's affection.'

R. S. Crane makes a valid point concerning this relatively short work in the Austen canon (it is of about the same extent as *Northanger Abbey* and not much more than half the length of *Mansfield Park* or *Emma*) when he says, 'For a novel depicting such a simple series of events, there is a fairly large cast of characters.'[2] This, as with *Sense and Sensibility*, offers a representative cross-section of human types, and contrasts with the various temperaments so exhibited the kinds of awareness which characterize the hero and heroine. And of course Austen does it with a consummate incarnation of the art which conceals art. Not only are new social groups and individuals brought in without strain and with absolute thematic appositeness; as Miss Lascelles has remarked, '. . . the introductions of the several characters are so contrived that they contribute to this impression of an expanding world.'[3]

With the saving exception of the heroine, the Elliot family comes before us as a trio of character studies (sketches brief but accomplished, and quite sufficient) in extreme kinds of inattention to life at large, to other people; the simplest forms of egoistic preoccupation. Most people in this life are self-absorbed and indolent. The only other beings in whom they ever show interest are their parents and their children—namely, those who are extensions of themselves; and sometimes concern does not even extend so far. They are not always very malicious or ill-disposed toward their fellow-creatures, but the real spiritual work of taking imaginative account of the other person's condition they are willing to undertake only very rarely. This means that they do not have the experience of authentic friendship, or a good family life, a worthwhile marriage—or, really, anything at all. They move through existence as creatures drugged, inert upon the opiate of their intellectual sloth.

This is one of Austen's major themes, here and throughout her work; thematic in the sense of being (repeatedly and never more so than in *Persuasion*) an issue with which she attempts to come to terms, and something exhibited continually across the canvas of her social pictures. It is the dominant moral impression we bring from reading her; her works' continuous *exposés* of the world as a theatre of myopic egotists.

Sir Walter Elliot, his eldest and his youngest daughters are so idle that the kinds of self-endorsement to which they devote all their powers are particularly factitious. The exalted esteem in which all three hold their own rank and the two elder ones their good looks, 'merits' that in fact are not worthy the name and with the achievement whereof none of them has had anything to do, signifies the intellectual and emotional vacuity of *their* lives as very complete.

They are self-defeating even at a worldly level of assessment, and comic as well as unpleasant. Their relation to The Other,

167

the external conditions of their lives and of other identities, is
one long fantasy and therefore they keep coming a cropper. The
baronet and his Elizabeth are deceived at every turn: in their
belief that they figure as personages of consequence held in
esteem by their dependants (*vide* p. 137) and much talked of in
society (p. 168); in Mrs. Clay and Mr. Elliot; in the very terms
of existence itself:

> . . . and Sir Walter might be excused, therefore, in forgetting her
> age, or, at least, be deemed only half a fool, for thinking himself
> and Elizabeth as blooming as ever, amidst the wreck of the good
> looks of every body else; for he could plainly see how old all the
> rest of his family and acquaintance were growing. Anne haggard,
> Mary coarse, every face in the neighbourhood worsting; and the
> rapid increase of the crow's foot about Lady Russell's temples
> had long been a distress to him. (I, 6)

Their egocentricity being so extreme, dense and ineffectual,
they even achieve the pathos of it in our sight. As a woman,
Elizabeth *is* aware of getting older; as thoroughly and un-
intelligently egoistic, she lives by an unconscious double
standard which, when we last take leave of her, seems fair set
to offer her the future of a thwarted (and fairly impecunious)
old maid.

> She was fully satisfied of being still quite as handsome as ever; but
> she felt her approach to the years of danger, and would have
> rejoiced to be certain of being properly solicited by baronet-
> blood within the next twelvemonth or two. (I, 7)

It does not occur to her that if her object in matrimony is
status, then the kind of spouse she hopes for is not likely to be
soliciting her hand. Unwedded baronets with motives to match
the calibre of her own are liable to seek a wife with a fortune—
which she and her father, especially through their imprudence
and losses, cannot offer; they are not likely to be looking for a
lady endowed merely with her good looks.

Marilyn Butler has criticized the Elliots' role in the work
more drastically than many:

> That weakness, a failure to integrate the novel's two planes of
> reality, becomes more acute when in the second volume the scene
> moves to Bath. . . . enveloping this nineteenth-century novel of

the inner life is an eighteenth-century novel in search of a centre. The cold prudential world of Sir Walter and Elizabeth properly belongs within a two-dimensional tradition of social comedy, such as Fielding's. Within such terms they would convince: put in the same novel as Anne, they seem out of focus, and for various reasons. One is that the pain they give Anne, and the spiritual isolation they impose on her, are out of scale in comedy. Another is that beside Anne's consciousness their very being seems sketchy. In no other Austen novel since *Sense and Sensibility* is the social group surrounding the heroine so thin as the Elliots' circle in Bath.[4]

But Sir Walter and his eldest daughter are one piece in the mosaic, as Bath itself is here; these figures are not supposed to have the function of a whole arabesque in the pattern of the novel. Their restricted dimensionality of being, so that they are treated like 'humours' characters in Fielding, is the author's intention—since with them she is portraying egotism as it makes for blindness, insensitivity towards others, in the aspect which is self-delusion. The Elliots *père et fille* are so exclusively attentive to themselves and no-one else, they inhabit an unreal dream of their own relation to the world, the dupes and gulls of anyone who cares to deceive them. Their stasis as *dramatis personae*—their non-development as characters and their (apparently) minimal deployment in terms of the plot—does not make them alien figures in the book's imaginative dynamic; it embodies the thematic revelation their attitudes consist in (which I have treated of above) and their intrinsic fate, in one and the same function.

As we move out from their immediate vicinity into the 'expanding world' of the book's social picture, it is Mary Musgrove who supplements their value, the 'note' they constitute as an element in Austen's debate, with her wearisome fancied injuries and querulity. This other Elliot daughter makes apprehensible the difficulty and pain of living at close quarters with someone shallowly egoistic, and also fleshes out for us still further the nature of the self-defeat which such persons make of living.

We first encounter Mary Musgrove in Chapter 5 when her sister Anne Elliot goes to stay at Uppercross Cottage; and the sample of her conversation given there tells us all about *her*

169

inconsistency and trivial value. Indeed it does this so effectively, brings the character so livingly into being, that this seems an appropriate moment to consider the general fact of Austen's success in human portraiture through this 'scenic' method. Her reliance on such a method may well have contributed to the hero's belief in Kipling's story 'The Janeites' (1924) that she did not leave the English Novel without a successor in kind; that her artistic heir is Henry James. But if we compare a passage where James is similarly introducing two characters, making them talk and so reveal themselves to the reader, with this duologue of Austen, a cardinal difference comes into view:

'I should like to come in for the grand *finale*, but I rattled over . . . a little, I confess, in the hope of a glimpse of Lady Grace: if you can perhaps imagine *that*!'

'I can imagine it perfectly,' said Lady Sandgate, whom evidently no perceptions of that general order ever cost a strain. 'It quite sticks out of you, and every one moreover has for some time past been waiting to see. But you haven't then,' she added, 'come from town?'

'No, I'm for three days at Chanter with my mother; whom, as she kindly lent me her car, I should have rather liked to bring.'

Lady Sandgate left the unsaid, in this connection, languish no longer than was decent. 'But whom you doubtless have to leave, by her preference, just settling down to bridge.'

'Oh, to sit down would imply that my mother at some moment of the day gets up—!'

'Which the Duchess never does?'—Lady Sandgate only asked to be allowed to show how she saw it. 'She fights to the last, invincible; gathering in the spoils and only routing her friends?' She abounded genially in her privileged vision. 'Ah yes—we know something of that!'

Lord John, who was a young man of a rambling but not of an idle eye, fixed her an instant with a surprise that was yet not steeped in compassion. 'You too then?'

She wouldn't, however, too meanly narrow it down. 'Well, in this house generally; where I'm so often made welcome, you see, and where—'

'Where,' he broke in at once, 'your jolly good footing quite sticks out of *you*, perhaps you'll let me say!'

She clearly didn't mind his seeing her ask herself how she should deal with so much rather juvenile intelligence; and indeed she could only decide to deal quite simply. 'You can't say more than I feel—and am proud to feel—at being of comfort when they're worried.'

This but fed the light flame of his easy perception—which lighted for him, if she would, all the facts equally. 'And they're worried now, you imply, because my terrible mother is capable of heavy gains and of making a great noise if she isn't paid? I ought to mind speaking of that truth,' he went on as with a practised glance in the direction of delicacy; 'but I think I should like you to know that I myself am not a bit ignorant of why it has made such an impression here.'(*The Outcry*, Bk. I, Chapter 1)

Even in this novel, which was a play originally (1909), then converted into prose-fiction (1911), James the narrator is present as Austen is not. Even though he has retained from its original theatric avatar the presentation of Lady Sandgate and Lord John (and all the other characters in the tale for that matter) as it were from an external point of view—the work's convention being that we learn of them only what can be observed from without, we are not taken 'behind' by the author to be informed of thoughts, feelings and motivations which even the most intelligent scrutiny could not discover for itself—in fact much of their individuality, their aspects and attitudes is delivered by his own voice (his own voice of storyteller, that is to say):

. . . said Lady Sandgate, whom evidently no perceptions of that general order ever cost a strain.

Lady Sandgate left the unsaid, in this connection, languish no longer than was decent.

Lord John, who was a young man of a rambling but not of an idle eye, fixed her an instant with a surprise that was yet not steeped in compassion.

She clearly didn't mind his seeing her ask herself how she should deal with so much rather juvenile intelligence . . . [etc.]

By contrast once Mary Musgrove has had a paragraph of introduction, Austen's interventions in the eighty-five lines of dialogue between her and her sister following (pp. 37–9) are no more, in sum, than these: '. . . replied Anne', 'Anne said what was proper, and enquired after her husband', 'replied

171

Anne cheerfully', '. . .—and after a moment's pause'. And the introduction itself is made in a mode so impersonal, authoritative—rather like the tone of Samuel Johnson's essays—that this too does not insinuate a presence between character and reader, commenting and 'character-building'.

> Though better endowed than the elder sister, Mary had not Anne's understanding or temper. While well, and happy, and properly attended to, she had great good humour and excellent spirits; but any indisposition sunk her completely; she had no resources for solitude; and inheriting a considerable share of the Elliot self-importance, was very prone to add to every other distress that of fancying herself neglected and ill-used. In person, she was inferior to both sisters, and had, even in her bloom, only reached the dignity of being 'a fine girl'. She was now lying on the faded sofa of the pretty little drawing-room, the once elegant furniture of which had been gradually growing shabby, under the influence of four summers and two children; [and, on Anne's appearing, greeted her with,
> 'So, you are come at last!' (etc.)] (V, 37)

By not assuming, however fugitively, anything less than absolute omniscience while speaking directly about her personages—when telling, not showing—this author becomes the most perspicuous of mediums. The narrative devices of most of her successors in this same fictional form—and those of James *par excellence*—are more tentative, acknowledge a subjectivity of viewpoint; the writer is *primus inter pares* among his characters, he admits to being a fallible intelligence in a not securely knowable world, and his mediating consciousness constitutes the palpable means through which we make acquaintance with his personages, as perceptibly as the instrument, wire and voice-distortion in a telephone-call, or the frame around a picture. Austen disappears when she brings her characters forward, by pretending to entire psychological competence while the scene is setting, and then vanishing in the manner of a good playwright. Julia Kavanagh's remark of more than one hundred years ago is sweeping, but one can see how she came to make it: 'She does not paint or analyze her characters: they speak for themselves.'[5] Austen moves from one impersonality to another; that of a reliable oracle to that of a talented dramatist.

Talented is the word. Her skill in rendering identities

through their speech has been much remarked, and best of all by W. A. Craik and Norman Page:

> Just as Jane Austen has no need to describe physical features, she has equally little need to describe expression; her power of creating conversation—the actual cadences of the speaking voice—are such that incidental details of gesture or grimace are superfluous.[6]

> . . . this is dialogue which subjective experience shows to be constantly making an appeal to the mind's ear: it belongs to that category of speech which is 'written to be read as if heard'. . . . we learn to know these figures through their distinctive idiolects, which very skilfully combine individuality with plausibility.[7]

Mary Musgrove's speech, coming as it does in bursts of exclamation, reflects equally the impatience of her imaginary grievances and her incapacity for sustained attention to any topic in a rational way. The word 'I' is hugely overworked at this early stage (though later it thins out somewhat, as her ill humour is worked upon by Anne's 'patience and forced cheerfulness'). Generally the paratactic style of Mary's utterance expresses self-preoccupation and utter triviality of mind. She swings from one concern to another entirely unrelated except with respect to her personal comfort and endorsement, because this is at once the symptom and the self-inspissating habit of indiscipline intellectual and moral.

One of the profound irritations of her company is that there is no way for a polite intelligence to respond to her—I mean without verbal or physical violence—which can, of its own example, inspire her with the wish to 'buck up' and be less badly behaved. Anne Elliot well knows this of course—the conversation is also so contrived as to reveal how the heroine is already once more consciously having to undertake the management of Mary's temperament while under her roof—and she herself has to participate in this ethos of selfishness, albeit enacted at one remove, this bogus talk of conscious merit and martyrdom, in order to force Mary out of discourse which is whining and depressing.

> 'Oh! Anne, I am so very unwell! It was quite unkind of you not to come on Thursday. . . .'

173

'. . . I have really been so busy, have had so much to do, that I could not very conveniently have left Kellynch sooner.'

'Dear me! what can *you* possibly have to do?'

'A great many things, I assure you. More than I can recollect in a moment: but I can tell you some. I have been making a duplicate of the catalogue of my father's books and pictures. I have been several times in the garden with Mackenzie, . . . [etc.]' (p. 38)

More closely and habitually than any other author Austen represents the personal and social cost—in ethical and even psychosomatic terms—of being the recipient of remarks like (for instance) 'Oh! we did have a lovely time at the dinner party in your house last year. You must come round sometime and dine with us.' There is no way of receiving this blithe, contentedly impercipient kind of rudeness, no manner for coping with it, which does not mean diminution to the victim's own spirit. Yet of such interchanges social life is much composed. If you genuinely do not care about the affront, very well and good; but that is dangerously near being blasé about living altogether. If you are a saint and simply think of the offender 'Poor errant lambkin! that's a sad way of going on'— that too is precariously near to an aloofness, priggish, self-righteous, which is armour-plated with spiritual pride. My father deals with such occasions by taking out his pocket diary and a pen and saying 'Splendid. How nice! Exactly which day will suit you?' My mother may fix the other party with a very fierce glower: 'You have made this remark three times during the past six months. Why go on insulting me like this?' (Which means at least she is not humiliated by the same people in that fashion again.) I just give a sickly grin and limp away.

But each of those options, when you think about it, has its serious limitations, its snags not much less hurtful (in spiritual terms) on both sides than the teeth of a snare or gin set to catch hapless game. One of Austen's 'points' in this early scene between Anne Elliot and her sister is what her whole treatment of Fanny Price in *Mansfield Park* was designed to show at its most tragic. There is no way of associating with the selfish and unworthy at such close quarters as society enforces, without being contaminated or hobbled, even if oneself is perfection (and none of her heroines is that), by the impossi-

174

bility of responding to them other than on terms which are themselves humiliating and disabling.

The extraordinary livingness of her characters, then, derives from Austen's consummate artistry as a creator of individual speech, as a writer who realizes the personages of her fiction through their own utterance and this skill retroactively and prospectively in its turn confers authority upon her status as 'oracle', as impersonal narrator, when she is speaking of her individuals to us directly. It is for this reason that her human figures seem to have more independent life than, say, Henry James's; which is not to depreciate James's different kind of achievement, one of the principal pleasures of which is its very distinctive narrative voice, nor to have set up the last of his completed novels as an easy Aunt Sally in comparison with Austen working at her best. (In my opinion there is more to *The Outcry* than has hitherto been acknowledged, and its total neglect strikes me as sad.)

Anne Elliot's lot then, dealing with a Mary Musgrove weeks at a time, is a hard one; a very hard. The woman is a tedious wearying pest, contact with whom is inevitably a little withering. But a worse fate, as this first colloquy between them has given us to see, is Mary's herself. One does not have to be religious to believe in the existence of Hell and that one of its direst features is the impossibility of development, of personal change and growth. Like her elder sister Mary Musgrove achieves pathos as well as our great irritation, for what we thus come to realize we are looking at, in her case, is practically one of the damned.

Unintentionally she can also be very funny, of course; *vide* her letter which so roundly contradicts itself, sent from Uppercross to Anne in Bath (Chapter 18). In certain aspects the screams from the ranks of the destructively self-defeated *are* amusing, and this long epistle is one of the great comic set-pieces in the Austen canon. But the author's treatment of her theme is irresistible, whether it assails us in humorous mode or solemn: the question of consciousness, the preferability (putting the alternatives at their worst) of walking barefoot through an endless cruel thorny desert of a life, lonely, bloodied and bowed altogether, rather than possessing an outlook with the calibre of Mary Musgrove's. Unless, this is to say, being intrinsically unlovable, and quite incapable of any happiness worth the name, counts as an insignificant penalty for her sort of mental life, which is like the scratchings of an insect's legs together. We cannot but notice how Mary is one of those people nobody spontaneously talks to. In the course of the book we never see any other character deliberately originating conversation with her or participating in it more than they have to. Except on one occasion. Her finest moment comes when Captain Wentworth takes her seriously enough to make response to one of her fussings and laugh at her:

> Putting all these very extraordinary circumstances together . . . we must consider it to be the arrangement of Providence, that you should not be introduced to your cousin. (XII, 106)

Of course she does not see this as her nearest approach to significance. She is a nuisance, comic and, also, really very sad.

The general tendency of my argument will now be clear; and I shall not heavily labour it out with a blow by blow analysis of each other character's presentation and psychology in this novel. Suffice it to say that what is brought before us is an admixture of human types representing various kinds of moral/intellectual competence and inadequacy. It is done with a delicacy of delineation so inward and acute, any critical account has inevitably to be a serious crudification of the author's achievement. Nevertheless as one poet in more recent years remarked,

> : unsayable certainly feels, close to,
> unlike not-hitherto-said[8]

so here are anatomies much more skeletal than the ones Austen actually presents. The Musgroves senior, for instance, are worthy folk and likeable enough; but so lacking in discrimination there can be little meeting of minds when one talks to them. Their younger offspring are not sufficiently disciplined and *quiet* (something which is always a *bête noire* with this author—who was a deeply popular relative with *her* young ones, her nephews and nieces as they grew up); their family life almost bounds their horizons; and they are not in fact much good, therefore, at truly valuing it and holding at a proper estimate the real worth of their relationships with their children. Thus it is that when Anne Elliot plays dances for the company on the Uppercross pianoforte, though we are told 'she played a great deal better than either of the Miss Musgroves', 'Mr. and Mrs. Musgrove's fond partiality for their own daughters' performance, and total indifference to any other person's' is expressed in the form of their (well-meaning) compliments to her: 'Well done, Miss Anne! very well done indeed! Lord bless me! how those little fingers of yours fly about!' (VI, 47). This is also the point of the reference to their dead son 'poor Richard':

> The real circumstances of this pathetic piece of family history were, that the Musgroves had had the ill fortune of a very troublesome, hopeless son; and the good fortune to lose him before he reached his twentieth year; that he had been sent to sea, because he was stupid and unmanageable on shore; that he had been very little cared for at any time by his family, though quite as much as he deserved; seldom heard of, and scarcely at all regretted, when the intelligence of his death abroad had worked its way to Uppercross, two years before. (VI, 51)

The pained demurs to which this passage regularly gives rise among Austen critics are little to the purpose. 'If you cannot stand the heat, get out of the kitchen.' It is no good picking up the least sentimental, most authentically honest of occidental novelists and then complaining that she hurts; least of all, by the by, if you happen to be, like Austen, a Christian. Think of the beatific *gentilesse*, the delicacy of a light that never was on sea or land, the heart-broken, heart-breaking gratitude and the cool, calm, relaxed quite un-selfconscious ferocity which alternates through the Magnificat; or through the sayings and life of its speaker's Son; an alternation, a quality—albeit there in much higher moral form—which is characteristic indeed of the sort of universe where we find ourselves. Lovers walk together hand in hand along sunset escarpments, their feelings a symphony of wondrous delicate mutualities and appreciations; while off in deep space star-systems clash without a tear. The very greatest figures of Europe's religious *muthos* can be breathtakingly dry-eyed.

What we learn about Dick Musgrove is that he has been a

sort of psychic fly-switch of mere shuffled appetites; a being not even rising, unlike Sir Walter Elliot and his daughter Mary, to the dignity of error. Now confessedly, Don Armado's remark—'sweet chucks, beat not the bones of the buried: when he breathed, he was a man'⁹—*has* its relevance, but if we flinch at the fierceness of *this* mariner's treatment, is not that a part of Austen's best success here, a terror (in part) for ourselves? The same novel which shows in its heroine and hero what heights of sensitivity human beings can dwell at, what values they can *be*, also intimates how equally near we all are to making our existences deeply fatuous and properly forgettable.

> . . . from the Laconia he had, under the influence of his captain [Wentworth whom he mentions thus as 'a fine dashing felow, only two perticular about the school-master'], written the only two letters which his father and mother had ever received from him during the whole of his absence; that is to say, the only two disinterested letters; all the rest had been mere applications for money. (pp. 51, 52)

Mr. and Mrs. Musgrove would have been more truly hurt by his life than they have been by his death, had they minded his neglectfulness towards them, were they now still aware it had been an inadequate relationship, and generally been sad at the poverty of the familial bond in his case. But such a penalty, emotionally speaking, would have been a function of their having an attitude to relationships, to life altogether, which was meaningful; and this they lack. Their reactions to their dead child then and now reflect alarmingly on the quality of their consciousness of their living progeny.

Charles, the eldest of these and heir to Uppercross, is an improvement. Like so many married people, he is in the not happy position of seeing his spouse spoil *their* children, as much as she may, but he has at least the sense to know this and to act accordingly (*v.* para. 2; VI, 44). He is 'really a very affectionate brother' and hangs over his sister Louisa, after she stuns herself on the Cobb at Lyme, 'with sobs of grief' (XII, 110). He is more aware of identities other than his own, *their* needs and feelings, than several of the characters we behold in this novel's foreground:

> . . . and as Anne followed her up stairs, she was in time for the

178

whole conversation, which began with Mary's saying, in a tone of great exultation,

'I mean to go with you, Charles, for I am of no more use at home than you are. If I were to shut myself up for ever with the child, I should not be able to persuade him to do any thing he did not like. Anne will stay; Anne undertakes to stay at home and take care of him. It is Anne's own proposal, and so I shall go with you, which will be a great deal better, for I have not dined at the other house since Tuesday.'

'This is very kind of Anne,' was her husband's answer, 'and I should be very glad to have you go; but it seems rather hard that she should be left at home by herself, to nurse our sick child.' (VII, 57–8)

Nevertheless his limitations are serious. Despite his own disclaimer, he does view everyone from within fairly blinkered absorption as a hunting, shooting and fishing young squire; as can be seen here:

. . . I hope you do not think I am so illiberal as to want every man to have the same objects and pleasures as myself. I have a great value for Benwick; and when one can but get him to talk, he has plenty to say. His reading has done him no harm, for he has fought as well as read. He is a brave fellow. I got more acquainted with him last Monday than ever I did before. We had a famous set-to at rat-hunting all the morning, in my father's great barns; and he played his part so well, that I have liked him the better ever since. (XXII, 219–20)

In respect of this same Captain Benwick, Austen offers us insights the most complex of any afforded by the story's lesser figures. When we first make acquaintance with him, he is leading a secluded life lodging with the Harvilles in out-of-season Lyme, wrapped up in the devotions of a long and deep mourning for his dead fiancée Fanny, Captain Harville's sister. Evidently the visit of the Uppercross party brings the first eligible, attractive, likely young ladies into his ken whom he has met in a long while. Austen skilfully shows him becoming interested in Anne Elliot, then later we hear of his engagement to Louisa Musgrove; and Captain Harville is frankly hurt by the event:

And with a quivering lip he wound up the whole by adding, 'Poor Fanny! she would not have forgotten him so soon!' (XXIII, 232)

The implication would be what Anne herself remonstrates in answer to this on the subject of male constancy:

> No, I believe you capable of every thing great and good in your married lives. I believe you equal to every important exertion, and to every domestic forbearance, so long as—if I may be allowed the expression, so long as you have an object. I mean, while the woman you love lives, and lives for you. (Ibid., 235)

But what we are also given to observe is the somewhat shallow quality of Benwick's sentiments; not in the sense of their being insincere or unreal, but as not deeply rooted.

This is shown to us in the matter of his reading. It is of a piece with that part of Austen's talent which makes her *the* novelist of details, the one who most bothers to get them right, and her so profound artful intelligence that, with her characters she here refers to 'the richness of the present age' in poetic writing—which calls up that whole galaxy of names in the grand efflorescence of English verse c.1795–1815—and then picks upon Walter Scott and Lord Byron as the objects of Benwick's special interest and study. She has spotted how, though so recently published and famous, those are the two among the period's great authors who deal in factitious 'romantic' emotion, stoutly empathized but inauthentic feeling, when writing serious verses; Scott the novelist, Byron the author of *Don Juan* are not in question here. That is the point of her choice of texts, Anne and Benwick

> . . . trying to ascertain whether *Marmion* or *The Lady of the Lake* were to be preferred, and how ranked the *Giaour* and *The Bride of Abydos* . . . (XI, 100)

and her friendly wink, her unfooled but not ill-disposed giggle in Byron's direction, at the cult of the exotic-oriental and the inauthenticity which that of itself betokened: 'and moreover, how the *Giaour* was to be pronounced' (ibid.).

The way she penetrates, even by these apparently slight means, to the heart of the romanticism those poets offer is as astounding for a contemporary reaction as the lucidity, the critical aptness of Proust in respect of *his* age (so eerily intelligent that the *Recherche* never exalts a then new young name which history since has not done well to canonize for per-

180

manently substantial and valuable—except that of Aldous Huxley—and the whole novel itself, though conceived, part-accomplished and part-published by 1913, at the deepest level of creative inspiration anticipating the world war which was to be the major catalyst in its own later action).

We are not to infer that these two poets' notes of *Sturm und Drang*, of arcane exoticism, their images of the heroic solitary, bereaved and outcast, lack a value simply. But just as they regularly adopt a pose—and with great success, to great public applause—so this particular student of their lays is not so much in love as with the idea of being so. James Benwick's emotion is a partially self-attentive posture as are those of Scott and Byron in their bardic roles. That is why he reads in order to feed his pre-existing states of mind, and looks in poems for what he already takes to them: 'Lord Byron's "dark blue seas" could not fail of being brought forward by their present view', Austen kindly and archly, sympathetically and critically half-jokes (XII, 109). He is not resorting to imaginative literature so as to discipline and *transmute* his experience; as those most truly in love, the desperately bereaved—and indeed on all occasions the most truly intelligent reader—would hope to do.

That is the author's implication and if we will see her responding to her age's finest kind of poetic achievement, the same vicinity of Lyme furnishes forth an occasion. 'A very strange stranger it must be' who does not enjoy the description (Chapter 11) of its 'immediate environs' as the company first enter the place:

> The scenes in its neighbourhood, Charmouth, with its high grounds and extensive sweeps of country, and still more its sweet retired bay, backed by dark cliffs, where fragments of low rock among the sands make it the happiest spot for watching the flow of the tide, for sitting in unwearied contemplation;—the woody varieties of the cheerful village of Up Lyme, and, above all, Pinny, with its green chasms between romantic rocks, where the scattered forest trees and orchards of luxuriant growth declare that many a generation must have passed away since the first partial falling of the cliff prepared the ground for such a state, where a scene so wonderful and lovely is exhibited, as may more than equal any of the resembling scenes of the far-famed

181

Isle of Wight: these places must be visited and visited again, to make the worth of Lyme understood. (XI, 95–6)

There is a breath here from 'Kubla Khan' following an almost Wordsworthian notion—the unwearied contemplation of the flow of the tide: Nature affording processes of recreation with intrinsic laws quite different from those utilized by men and women 'mid the din/Of towns and cities'. The novelist could not offer a richer appreciation than her deployment of these other authors' experiences, thus integrated, to her own purposes; which are related. The extravagant forces of Nature and comparative dwarfing of man equally by its scale, its energies and before the long backdrop of Time, aeons and aeons of the 'dark backward'; and yet the power and value of the imagination, the fact that for those with a proper response, Nature is undefeating—these are no mere 'extras', a rare leaf inserted to garnish, or a pinch of exotic spice to flavour the dish. They partake and are redolent of the novel's thematic essence.

Jane Austen is not against second attachments on principle, either as *desiderata* of doubtful taste in themselves or as supposed proofs of infidelity to a previous commitment on each and every occasion; and in this instance her attention is by no means simply critical. Anne Elliot is 'persuaded that any tolerably pleasing young woman who had listened and seemed to feel for him, would have received the same compliment. He had an affectionate heart. He must love somebody' (XVIII, 167); which is not all un-appealing, though a hidden factor, the cost of Benwick's kind of attitude to love comes high:

> I confess that I do think there is a disparity, too great a disparity, and in a point no less essential than mind.—I regard Louisa Musgrove as a very amiable, sweet-tempered girl, and not deficient in understanding; but Benwick is something more. He is a clever man, a reading man—and I confess that I do consider his attaching himself to her, with some surprise. (XX, 182)

Thus Frederick Wentworth upon the match, and we feel this is an authoritative insight into the serious weakness in the alliance and their future together.

Just how severe the pain of a thwarted passion can be, Wentworth and Anne know better than anybody else in the novel; because they have hearts able to feel more deeply than the other characters'. This is the essence of *Persuasion*'s theme: that their kind of consciousness is the best worth having, whether it prospers in its hopes or fails; and, by comparison, the sort of awareness which characterizes, say, a Mary Musgrove's involvement in living, it really is not worth having come into a state of existence to possess. There is no need to get bogged down with the vexed question, whether the heroine should not have broken off her engagement to her lover eight years and more ago; the point is that matrimony did not then betide, yet both parties were of a calibre of outlook and feeling to recognize each other's worth and the depth and import of each other's mutual response. Accordingly he has not been able to marry another woman since, nor she another man. And this is not, on either side, due to some morbid fixation. Once the possibility of wedlock between them seems permanently to have lapsed, both are willing—keen—to be able to care for another potential spouse. But they are too aptly discriminative to find such a person with any ease, or to forget the quality of their own attitudes to one another. One of Austen's indications in showing us her so peopled canvas across the eight months and several differing scenes of the tale's action, is that identities of their quality are indeed rare.

That they are not a couple of Miss Havishams we are clearly notified. Anne is observed toying with the idea of another partner on more than one occasion, in this period when she too, to Lady Russell's relief, is being once again thrown into more and new company. On meeting Benwick she finds him

> most considerately attentive to her; and, united as they all seemed by the distress of the day, she felt an increasing degree of good-will towards him, and a pleasure even in thinking that it might, perhaps, be the occasion of continuing their acquaintance. (XII, 115)

When her brother-in-law speaks the Captain's devotion and the belief that this admirer will follow her from the sea-side back to Kellynch, 'she boldly acknowledges herself flattered, and continues her enquiries' (adapted; XIV, 131) and

> There can be no doubt that Lady Russell and Anne were both occasionally thinking of Captain Benwick, from this time. (Ibid., 133)

Likewise the Uppercross party's encounter with the distinguished-looking stranger near the beach at Lyme (who later proves to be her cousin William Walter Elliot); this too she enjoys. She can do with male admiration, and the fact that his tributary regard adds its own small useful effect on Wentworth's rekindling impression in her favour, is not the whole of its value or that of her acquiescence in it. For one thing she would like to be married, and the thought of being installed in her dead mother's place at Kellynch-hall, when this possibility is dangled before her, has no small allure. But

> The same image of Mr. Elliot speaking for himself, brought Anne to composure again. The charm of Kellynch and of 'Lady Elliot' all faded away. She never could accept him. And it was not only that her feelings were still adverse to any man save one; her judgment, on a serious consideration of the possibilities of such a case, was against Mr. Elliot. (XVII, 160)

In more elaborate fashion—and it constitutes half this phase of their story—Wentworth on his part attempts to fall in love again, or to make at least a satisfactory marriage; in the event all that his association with Louisa Musgrove can do is to set off and illustrate for him the far greater worth and charm of his lost flame. The fact that he comes into Anne Elliot's society to seek another wife equally provides the author with her action, her story's plot, and is artistically speaking a fine touch. Wooing a pair of younger ladies, or rather making himself particularly agreeable to them, before his former sweetheart's eyes, expresses the hurt resentment which he still feels towards Anne on account of their rupture in the past, but does not acknowledge to himself for the greater part of the tale; it signalizes a wish to prove himself unfettered by embarrassment, to show as his own free agent, and it brings into view that *cruelty* of which love (thwarted) is capable ('Love is too young to know what conscience is').

Yet he too cannot delude himself into settling for an alliance which is so much of a second-best kind.

> He found too late, in short, that he had entangled himself; and that precisely as he became fully satisfied of his not caring for Louisa at all, he must regard himself as bound to her, if her sentiments for him were what the Harvilles supposed.
> (XXIII, 243)

D. W. Harding opines that 'Captain Wentworth's release from Louisa . . . has the arbitrariness of lighter comedy'[10]—but with this view I cannot agree. All through, as in subtle ways we have been shown and as Wentworth himself specifies in the scene where he and Anne declare the history of their feelings to one another, he has not seriously wanted to marry the younger woman. Partly out of grievance, partly flattered by the warm attentions of the whole Musgrove clan and its two pretty girls especially, he has compromised himself—but against his own deepest inclination. And Louisa on her side is too good-natured, too sensitive to the filaments of reciprocity, the energies of mutual emotion, and too capable of transferring her affections, to settle for a union where her partner's heart is not in it. Had James Benwick's ministrations or the like not interposed, we may credit that the situation would have been more deeply embarrassing for both parties, but yet that Captain Wentworth and Louisa Musgrove would finally have agreed to go their separate ways.

The most significant single trait in this novel's hero and heroine is that they do *not* fall in love with somebody else, that they are not able (though Wentworth tries) to devalue each other's nature or the quality of their mutual regard; and this is expressed in the fact of their remaining single, by choice, during the years following the breaking-off of their engagement. Thus their experience has a pattern, a meaningfulness, missing from most of the other characters' lives. Events in Anne Elliot's life are portentous, not simply because—as it were arbitrarily—Austen has elected her into the role of heroine and the book's chief focus of interest but because, for all her apparent quiet insignificance in terms of the outer world's view of things, she is a heroine as other females in the story could never be; her interior history has a substantiality theirs lack. And this in its turn is how she and her real lover serve to answer the implicit leading question of the novel's debate: What resources after all *do* the goodly have—the intelligent, worthy, sensitive, responsible; what estimable advantage, when all is said and done, over their moral inferiors?

Their habit of discrimination is both the burden and reward of their lives. Like all the Austen heroines Anne Elliot looks forward and back, weighs the past with the present, has a critical sense which will not be lulled with easy anaesthetics, goes off on her own to evaluate the experiences by which she is begirt; and this in a measure to which only Frederick Wentworth's attitudes approximate, among the eligible men of her acquaintance:

> 'Yes, here I am, Sophia, quite ready to make a foolish match. Any body between fifteen and thirty may have me for asking. A little beauty, and a few smiles, and a few compliments to the navy, and I am a lost man. Should not this be enough for a sailor, who has had no society among women to make him nice?'
> He said it, she knew, to be contradicted. (VII, 62)

The relation of these lovers therefore is, at its worst, not the same as that of Edward Ferrars and Elinor Dashwood. Elinor is secretive about what she has heard from Lucy Steele—with her family because their hectic sympathy would itself be an additional burden; with Edward for the same reason that *he* does not broach the all-important matter with *her*, because she fears what open acknowledgement between them of his pre-engagement to Lucy will accomplish: a final rupture, the very death of their hopes. Her behaviour is much more legitimate than his, however; for Edward Ferrars has been wrong to entertain and develop their growing mutual interest in the early days at Norland when he knew he was previously committed; in that sense he plays fast and loose with Elinor's affections all along, as neither of the lovers do in *Persuasion* with each other. In fact Miss Dashwood's husband behaves almost as badly as her sister's first suitor; it is part of Austen's point in *Sense and Sensibility* that her heroines marry whom they best can, not men they deserve.

Thinking out conduct and its consequences, attempting honesty about motives (their own as well as other people's), these wakeful responsible minds are more able to be hurt by the self-absorption of others than most, *because* they are more discriminative and feeling. And that such a 'burden of consciousness' is heavy—is positively a Pilgrim's pack of a commitment to carry through the world—Austen needs not belabour as a theme. It is stitched into the nature of her every sentence and paragraph, throughout her *oeuvre*.

D. H. Lawrence, on reading *A Passage to India* when it first appeared, made a comment to which most students of Forster will from time to time be moved to give a feeble cheer:

> It's good, but makes one wish a bomb would fall and end everything. Life is more interesting in its undercurrents than in its obvious; and E. M. does see people, people and nothing but people: *ad nauseam*.[11]

The enormous attention to the individual's responsibility continuously to be morally evaluating, which is every step of that author's fictions, will occasionally weigh almost to weariness upon our spirits. But that is because life itself properly lived (on Forster's view and as he defines proper living) is like that. We can feel the same way about Austen's work but it has certain features which lighten the load still more, or with more complete success, than the compensating elements in the later novelist. One is the same constant moralistic perception as it makes for a comic release, the psychic re-energizing (to put this mercurial matter with inevitable pomposity) afforded by its own potentialities of humorous insight. Austen well knew the penalties of dwelling in a restricted dissatisfying circle—and for human beings as intelligent and caring as she, aren't they all?

> She said no more, other subjects took their turn; and the rest of the dinner passed away; the dessert succeeded, the children came in, and were talked to and admired amid the usual rate of conversation; a few clever things said, a few downright silly, but by much the larger proportion neither the one nor the other— nothing worse than every day remarks, dull repetitions, old news, and heavy jokes. (E, XXVI, 219)

Yet when we get this sort of commentary in her letters:

> . . . Charles Powlett gave a dance on Thursday, to the great disturbance of all his neighbours, of course, who, you know, take a most lively interest in the state of his finances, and live in hopes of his soon being ruined . . .' (No. 13, p. 36)

or, later in the same month and mode—

> . . . Charles Powlett has been very ill, but is getting well again;— his wife is discovered to be everything that the Neighbourhood could wish her, silly & cross as well as extravagant . . . (No. 14, p. 39)

187

though we shall agree with Yasmine Gooneratne that 'for her as well as for her heroines the experience of living involved a continual process of adaptation . . . to an unfriendly social environment',[12] we shall also feel that somehow the environment has not won.

Likewise with her less direct ironies upon the inanition, the (not really allowable or forgiveable) commonplaceness of most social intercourse. In that extract from *Emma* just quoted her response (for it is there considerably shared between author and heroine) is unusually desperate and flagrant, though by no means a 'false note'. Here and in most of her work, it is more complex:

> . . . How do you like this cold weather? I hope you have all been earnestly praying for it as a salutary relief from the dreadfully mild and unhealthy season preceding it, fancying yourself half putrified from the want of it, and that now you all draw into the fire, complain that you never felt such bitterness of cold before, that you are half starved, quite frozen, and wish the mild weather back again with all your hearts . . . (*Letters*, No. 33, pp. 116–17)

This is good-humoured and friendly as well as exasperate; with its charitable as well as contemptuous feeling it typifies the extraordinarily subtle fine-shading of her more characteristically frequent reactions.

And this is the role, the value of humour in the novels; both their broader comic effects and the play of mercurial discrimination in Austen's narratives. It is a counter-agent to the shown difficulty of living for the wakeful, the burden of ethically attentive consciousness. The comic in Jane Austen dramatizes the positive, energic resources of the discriminative mind and in that sense is all-prevailing, even in those works (*Sense and Sensibility*, *Mansfield Park* and *Persuasion*) which are deemed more solemn of tone than their companions.

This quizzing fullness of humorous critical reaction is at work in *Mansfield Park* when, near the conclusion (to give an instance at random) we have this:

> To talk over the dreadful business with Fanny, talk and lament, was all Lady Bertram's consolation. To be listened to and borne with, and hear the voice of kindness and sympathy in return, was

every thing that could be done for her. To be otherwise com-
forted was out of the question. The case admitted of no comfort.
Lady Bertram did not think deeply, but, guided by Sir Thomas,
she thought justly on all important points; and she saw, therefore, in all its enormity, what had happened, and neither
endeavoured herself, nor required Fanny to advise her, to think
little of guilt and infamy. (XLVII, 449)

Thus Lady Bertram on her child, Maria's publicized adultery.
The matter is serious enough, 'comprehending the loss of a
daughter and a disgrace never to be wiped off' (ibid.); yet we
cannot but be excited by the author's stunning management of
her own tone handling it. She is evidently quite conscious of
offering these phrases in a deadpan manner—that itself is a
note; and they *can very easily be read* as straightforward serious
reportage. The passage's vitality of wit, and this is thoroughly
characteristic, inheres in the achieved, the measured insecurity
of the reader's acquaintance with the narrative allegations.
'. . . But, guided by Sir Thomas, she thought justly on all
important points . . .': it is a little too portentous, too pious and
straightfaced; and a supportive clue for our so interpreting this
element is the hint that Sir Thomas has to do his wife's thinking,
even much of her feeling, for her. 'The case admitted of no
comfort': but how is this if you do not think deeply (and
therefore cannot suffer so greatly as many would do in the
circumstances) anyway?

The joy of such writing, it is no less, derives to us from our
conviction that Jane Austen has got the matter—so finely
filamented on a psychological crux as it is, so easy to crudify in
one way or another—exactly right. She is like an augur working
the oracle behind an altar of old, regularly dropping for our sole
privileged benefit an all but imperceptible wink. And thus it is,
as many have remarked, that the reader seems to be involved in
a more personal relation with this novelist than most. Katherine
Mansfield was correct: '. . . every true admirer of the novels
cherishes the happy thought that he alone—reading between
the lines—has become the secret friend of their author.'[13] With
their quiet manner, the narratives are designed to appeal to an
intelligence no less awake and refined than their author's own,
in acts not of mutual gratulating but alert amused recognition.
It is tonic.

189

The same unwearied honesty is on the *qui vive* throughout *Persuasion* and here again the heroine comes within its critical purview:

> Anne could not immediately fall into a quotation again. The sweet scenes of autumn were for a while put by—unless some tender sonnet, fraught with the apt analogy of the declining year, with declining happiness, and the images of youth and hope, and spring, all gone together, blessed her memory. . . . and after another half mile of gradual ascent through large enclosures, where the ploughs at work, and the fresh-made path spoke the farmer, counteracting the sweets of poetical despondence, and meaning to have spring again, they gained the summit of the most considerable hill. . . . (X, 85)

Anne Elliot is convicted of self-pity there, of willed pessimism (so as to simplify things and indulge herself with an attitude like Mrs. Gummidge's, in *David Copperfield*: 'I am a lone lorn creetur' and everythink goes contrairy with me'[14]), and the author there is moved to give her a little shake. But the cardinal difference between her and her lover on one side, and most of the other folk in her story on the other, is that Frederick Wentworth and his future bride take thought about, connect, the past and present as the others (mainly) do not.

Henrietta Musgrove, for instance: Austen makes a lovely kindly point, instinct with the beautiful fidelity of psychological observation which I have just been commenting upon, and mediated to us in the *mots justes* of her so economic utterance, when she brings her to Bath:

> Henrietta was exactly in that state of recently-improved views, of fresh-formed happiness, which made her full of regard and interest for every body she had ever liked before at all. . . . (XXII, 220)

But this is the same young lady whose converse with Anne at Lyme (Chapter 12) spoke the pretty fundamental self-absorption which marks most of the Austen characters—her themes there being Dr. Shirley the rector's health at Uppercross and the need for him to get a 'dispensation' to retire and install a curate (i.e. her fiancé) in his place there (*ergo* on a good salary wherewith she and Charles Hayter may marry). She has to have such exterior stimulants as these, her dearest hopes have to be successful *for* her to be 'made . . . full of regard and interest for every body she had ever liked before . . .'. Anne Elliot and Captain Wentworth by contrast, exert their spirits to be awake to other identities and careful of alien concerns when the springs of elation fail as well as when they are at flood. As R. S. Crane has observed, therefore:

> The happiness of Anne and Wentworth is 'rational' as well as 'rapturous'. . . . It is the happiness . . . not simply of lovers but of moral individuals—a happiness which can be achieved only by persons of superior minds and characters, and to which, consequently, when we are convinced that this is indeed the case, we tend to respond in a more complex way than to the merely 'sentimental' resolutions of ordinary love tales. What we feel is an effect compounded of sympathy and moral approbation. . . .[15]

This essentially is why Louisa Musgrove insisting on being jumped down the Cobb at Lyme was wrong, but Anne Elliot in originally breaking off her engagement was at worst mistaken. John Davie, in his introduction to the text, refers to the novel's title as a leading thematic clue:

> Mrs. Smith does, however, fit well into the pattern of *Persuasion* in one way. Like most of the other characters, she is persuaded—by herself—into at least one action which is not, by Jane Austen's fine moral standards, either right or the best she can do: she is prepared to conceal from Anne her knowledge of Mr. Elliot's true character. Captain Benwick and Charles Musgrove, though both amiable, are happy to persuade themselves into marrying someone other than their first choice; Mary Musgrove can persuade herself that she is right to go to the Great House when her son is sick; Elizabeth Elliot persuades herself that she need not invite the Musgroves to dinner in Bath. Sir Walter's vanity is of course one long self-delusion, but he also shows himself vulnerable to the artful persuasion of Mr. Shepherd and his daughter Mrs. Clay. Even Wentworth has persuaded himself wrongly over his feelings for Anne and comes to describe himself as a greater enemy to himself than Lady Russell has been.[16]

Unlike these others Anne Elliot's 'persuasion' was not a concomitant of self-regard.

Indeed if we have a problem with Anne it is, I suppose, her perfection. Quiet as she is, capable, conscientious, always right; one comes back to the author's own comment for the aptest brief response of all—'she is almost too good for me'[17]—

whether or not this was a considered *summum*. It is something of the same difficulty we have with Fanny Price and for a similar reason; we are trapped inside the character's rectitude, all we appear asked to do is assent to her acts and feelings; and given her role as the Cinderella, Patient Griseld etc. of the piece, combined with the mediation of its whole world to us through her point of view, we come near to tiring of the part of captive appreciative audience which on our side this imposes. This is something we do not suffer in *David Copperfield* for example. Especially in his juvenile days the hero there is a sane mind, the normative embodiment of wholesome healthy youth cut adrift in a loony world and his wide-eyed wonder, his (at first very credulous) innocence is the critical yardstick by which everybody and everything else are rightfully measured. But the David's-eye-view is perspicuous. Dickens looks through Copperfield and directs our attention more at this character's environment than upon the workings of his own breast— though these do have an important part in the whole and *it is his novel*. With Anne Elliot so much of the narrative deals directly or indirectly with her feelings that we seem locked into the *self*-concern of a heroine who after all is allegedly not egoistic. Her uprightness becomes too self-conscious for us, her virtue the theme too much of *her* vision.

It all results from an inescapable and insoluble technical problem. Austen needed to write her novel from a point-of-view—her heroine's; the issue which has to be dramatized and brought to life for us is the quality of individual perception in a world where knowledge is partial. But she equally needed not to cast her tale in the form of a first-person narrative; in which case the nature and calibre of her heroine's reactions to what is going on around her (and what has taken place in the past, not least) would be too indirectly and subtly adumbrated to be securely focused by the reader. But in effect this necessary fault seems to me to have its own virtue. Just as Fanny's unlikeableness in *Mansfield Park* was all grist to the mill, was thematically a positive value, so in its smaller way—for this *is* a smaller matter, we do like Anne with a pretty unreserved admiration—in *Persuasion* we come almost to sense the heroine's rectitude as a consequence of her exiled, devalued state. The matter is subliminal, inarticulate, but not less real for that; isn't it as if

Anne makes for herself an identity out of being Cinderella? that she is 'flawless' in order to have the good of that role as it were, as well as the bad? Such an achievement was probably un-deliberate on Austen's part, and her own possible disquiet about her creation has already been noted—though it is hard to press interpretatively on that cryptic comment of her letter of March 1817. But when we appreciate Anne's character over the story as a whole, and take in the process of its revelation, some such sense concerning one of its virtue's sources comes upon us I feel; which would illustrate once again how the artist who is greatly talented (in Jane Austen's case at full human por-traiture, conveying all the essential lineaments of a human identity) can do better than she is aware of or consciously contrives.

Anne Elliot's goodness is principally a *donnée*—that wants insistence. But what the book's very method also suggests is an element in her committed to righteousness for the sake of a compensating image of herself amidst the emotional dearth which is her life at home. And that is all to the point. *Persuasion* is about the varying ideas of selfhood which inhabit different lives. Sir Walter Elliot finds his—if we take him for a comparison—in the 'Baronetage' and his looks. An important implication of this shadowy other realm of the heroine's inner life and our con-sideration of it, is therefore that she will really most bloom when once fully, properly beloved; that the niggling undertow of a wrong kind of self-consciousness will then lapse beside a really congenial hearth.

Less welcome and artistically justifiable, on intrinsic grounds, though no less inescapable, may be the flaw of Lady Russell's characterization. Here again it is a case of a dilemma with horns. The novelist had to provide Anne Elliot with a friend/mother-figure confidant and for various reasons—principally so that there has been and is someone in her life she could respect sufficiently to have been creditably influenced in the past against her own will and the continuance of her engage-ment with Frederick Wentworth. Yet if this lady were to loom large in the work—were she even to feature much at all—the novel's centre of gravity would inexorably shift. If Austen regularly represented her as having long intimate amicable conversations with Anne—and something of the sort would be necessary actually to flesh out the alleged reality of their mutual regard—instead of being the story of the love between the heroine and the hero, *Persuasion* would really become a history of the relation between Anne Elliot and Lady Russell, with the lovers' attachment to one another early and late an illustrative episode therein.

In the event the author has elected to endure the lesser of these evils, namely that of keeping Lady Russell 'down'; and she mitigates her difficulty as much as possible by calling upon us to recognize the importance of the older to the younger woman in the manner of honouring an agreed social law. Quite a bit of ground does get covered this way. In the world of fixed emotional conventions and orthodox behaviour which her work takes for a basis of narrative strategy and ethical debate, we almost concur in the assumption that their dependence *would* be substantial from the very fact of its being stated. This writer's fiction is an idealized sphere ('idealized' in the sense that Molière's comedy exhibits an economized heightened picture of upper-class life in *his* society). Just as in this *oeuvre* no major personage is convicted of theft or murder, so we accept that a young woman here *would* rely upon the only likeable and respect-worthy female of elder date in her immediate circle. But this does not bring vitality to the portrait:

> A sufficient number of virtues and weaknesses are given, indeed, to equip this character with the outlines of a human personality: we learn of her intelligence, her honesty, and her sympathy, and find that these are counterweighted by a tendency to be swayed by social prejudice. What Lady Russell lacks is the illusion of life. . . .[18]

Not faulty are the characterizations of Mrs. Clay, her father John Shepherd the lawyer, William Walter Elliot—or Mrs. Smith. Once more it may indeed be at one level a case of authorial inadvertence that they have a peripheral and intermittent life, these personages, in the work as a whole; the Mr. Elliot–Mrs. Clay intrigue is sketchily worked out, implausible and at the end 'we realize that we have never, in effect, had anything but [Jane Austen's] word for the whole affair.'[19] Sir Walter's agent at his introduction (Chapter 2) is fully endowed with personality—an amusing interesting one—only to disappear for good early; and Mrs. Smith's conversations with Anne can be read as Austen's only exercise in the eighteenth-century novelists' regular resource, the tale within a tale, the added contiguous episode explanatory or space-filling. But these features seem more felicitous to me, whether or not they were so deliberated by the artist.

What the whole of the rest of the book shows is that in comparison with sentiences like Captain Wentworth or Anne Elliot, lives like her cousin's or Mrs. Clay's are the scrapings and scurryings of insects who lack intrinsic significance. Now of course the likes of Mr. Elliot, when empowered with great economic or political privilege, can do much harm in the world—*Persuasion* has something to say about the absolute exterior realities (such as Death) by which worthy individuals can be assailed—but the novelist's quite offhand despatch of him and his Penelope (nice joke in that name) is somehow apt, signalizing the empty uninterestingness of such beings. The other parts of the tale enforce in us the same sort of feeling about them that the goodly have to feel towards the power struggles of the political combinations in this country. Westminster parliamentarians and the lobby correspondents who also inhabit their same little world (for it is a little one) mostly suppose that the nation is hanging breathless from hour to hour upon the internecine broils, the executive squabbles, the leadership contests of the Conservative and Labour Parties; but upon such paltrinesses the intelligent and noble are not to waste their attention; nor are the public at large one tenth so absorbed as their M.P.s assume them to be. The privilege of a vote in elections to our sovereign legislature and the importance of every individual's active involvement in the political process are in my view paramount. But that is not the same thing as giving much thought to the ambitious clawings and strivings of worldly fools (albeit successful) for the top jobs. Hitler himself would never have got to power if the majority of German people had been virtuous.

Well may Mary Lascelles say of 'the secondary pattern of subterraneous progress and visible incident' in *Persuasion*, namely the doings of Mr. Elliot and Mrs. Clay, that it is 'so much less satisfactory' because Austen 'was not interested in the intrigue herself'.[20] Their alliance, like the no less incredible pacts and associations which are formed monthly within the political parties, is uninteresting because they are, in an ultimate sense. They may carry all before them, they may rule like the Pharaohs; but they have not had a life worth living nor worth attending to with any real respect.

The treatment of William Walter Elliot and Penelope Clay is appropriately scanted, because they are gibbering unreal figures in deep spiritual truth. And it is as well that Mr. Shepherd the 'civil, cautious lawyer' appears before us in a complete portrait only to lapse at a little distance later because otherwise this novel would approach nearer to the condition of being a tale where the other characters are somewhat trapped by their own author's ingenuity. When every personage in a story is allowed a full role there from first to last—sometimes this is valuable as an effect (as in Henry James) but it would make Anne Elliot's world ineptly claustrophobic. Even the Wallises after all, Mr. Elliot's friends living in Marlborough Buildings, Bath, are not just a gay, giddy society couple on the perimeter of the action but a conduit of significant information at the level of the plot.

Likewise with Mrs. Smith's featuring on the sidelines of the drama. In fact she performs several integral functions. It is all to the point that Anne Elliot should be warned off her cousin and in that sense be 'rescued' from belief in him, as the rest of her family is not, in consequence of her own method of respecting the past, *viz*. not forsaking old friends who have fallen on hard times. Her father and sister think of themselves as the arch-traditionalists, the impressive gentry with the keenest devotion to ageless ritual and unchanging affiliations. But since their conservatism is just another manifestation of their proud egotism, we see them blown about on the wind of time with no more coherent steadfastness to anything than a couple of withering leaves. Theirs has been the extravagance which necessitated the letting of Kellynch-hall to strangers, and once they get to Bath they are vastly preoccupied by the consequence of their lodgings, with an inconsistency apparent only to Anne:

> . . . and she must sigh, and smile, and wonder too, as Elizabeth
> threw open the folding-doors, and walked with exultation from

one drawing-room to the other, boasting of their space, at the possibility of that woman, who had been mistress of Kellynch Hall, finding extent to be proud of between two walls, perhaps thirty feet asunder. (XV, 138)

Anne in short is the only member of the family whose interest in the past is not merely another sort of exploitation incurred in the service of her vanity.

Yet the reward of this is not only the information she gains from the former Miss Hamilton her schoolfellow who is now a sick, bed-ridden widow in the Spa city; her renewal of the acquaintance is (of course) its own recompense, especially as Mrs. Smith, the extremest case of deprivation in the novel, exhibits the story's chief intuition at the very cutting-edge of human suffering; namely, the rich strengthening value and meed of possessing a consciousness of high calibre:

> She had been very fond of her husband,—she had buried him.
> She had been used to affluence,—it was gone. She had no child
> to connect her with life and happiness again, no relations to
> assist in the arrangement of perplexed affairs, no health to make
> all the rest supportable. Her accommodations were limited to a
> noisy parlour, and a dark bed-room behind, with no possibility
> of moving from one to the other without assistance, which there
> was only one servant in the house to afford. . . . Yet, in spite of
> all this, Anne had reason to believe that she had moments only
> of languor and depression, to hours of occupation and enjoy-
> ment. How could it be?—She watched—observed—reflected—
> and finally determined that this was not a case of fortitude or of
> resignation only.—A submissive spirit might be patient, a
> strong understanding would supply resolution, but here was
> something more; here was that elasticity of mind, that dis-
> position to be comforted, that power of turning readily from evil
> to good, and finding employment which carried her out of
> herself, which was from Nature alone. It was the choicest gift of
> Heaven. . . . (XVII, 154)

and at the very end we again have a reference to Mrs. Smith's 'cheerfulness and mental alacrity' as 'these *prime* supplies of good' (emphasis added) amongst all other possible kinds of benefaction.

W. A. Craik complains that 'Mrs. Smith, dealing so much as she does in hearsay and gossip, herself contradicts the good impression Jane Austen makes for her at first',[21] but it seems to me that Mrs. Smith's fondness for Nurse Rooke's gleanings of tittle-tattle, like her variations of policy, some of them quite self-interested, in respect of Anne's supposed forthcoming engagement to Mr. Elliot, makes her a credible human being and therefore adds to her value in the story. Jane Austen is not here offering us the image of a paragon, a saint in distress, but of a more ordinary human being coping with affliction. It is almost inevitable that Mrs. Smith in her situation, therefore, will make the most of her sources of gossip—they are one of the few kinds of entertainment offering—just as in her weak economic position she is bound to be glad to use Anne as a means of getting her financial affairs disentangled; not least because she thinks she is doing so innocently (it is certainly not for her to warn her friend against Mr. Elliot, when they appear very likely soon to become betrothed). Yet at the same time these traits usefully heighten, by contrast further fill out, our developed and thus still developing sense of the value of Anne's finer behaviour and scrupulosity on all occasions. His widow has to have been less intelligent than her visitor—and in this aspect of morally sensitive scrupulosity—to have married the Charles Smith she has to reveal to us, in the first place.

That is intelligence as Austen most applauds it and, correspondingly, she is not snooty about its intellectual manifestations in lesser degrees than her own. Hence the role of the Crofts in the story's scheme. They represent good will, albeit housed in more limited minds; and significantly theirs is the other good marriage within the book's purview. When the Admiral wishes Captain Wentworth would marry one of the Musgrove sisters, concluding amusingly 'And very nice young ladies they both are; I hardly know one from the other', Mrs. Croft replies

> 'Very good humoured, unaffected girls, indeed,' . . . in a tone of calmer praise, such as made Anne suspect that her keener powers might not consider either of them as quite worthy her brother . . . (X, 892)

and their passenger notes in this same scene her 'coolly giving the reins a better direction herself' when they are about to take a post in their carriage journey home and her 'once afterwards judiciously putting out her hand', as 'no bad representation of the general guidance of their affairs . . .' (ibid.).

Cruder as their sensibilities and affinities are than those of the naval couple on which the novel's focus is to conclude, like Mrs. Jennings in *Sense and Sensibility* the Crofts are outspoken and coherent in their loyalties, rational, unfussy and also altruistic; and have a host of friendships about their lives' outskirts, every least one of which is worth all the acquaintance cultivated by the besotted baronet of Camden-place and his eldest daughter. They embody the validity of what the work intuits as a whole, at the level of their less discriminative powers and insights; and they give us to know something of the hard work of happiness, the month-to-month reality of the married life Anne Elliot has in store (as in, for instance, the conversation between Mrs. Musgrove and Mrs. Croft: VIII, 70–1).

In one respect *Persuasion* is a political document representing a decisive commitment of allegiance, on the part of the author and her heroine alike, away from one class to another and from the settled mode of life to that of chance, uncertainty, adventure. Malcolm Bradbury has best expressed this:

> . . . the landowning virtues and responsibilities are not to be had among the class that should embody them, that is, among the Elliots themselves. They are not, however, to be had in a direct sense among the second main group of agents in the novel, in the seafarers, with their luck and pluck. . . .[22]

What is raised is 'the question of who shall inherit England':

> . . . in this book Jane Austen seems to want to persuade us that the moral life and the life of the classes are intimately connected. . . . It is not just that Wentworth has insufficient appreciation of the role of caution and prudence, and that Anne has not sufficient of Wentworth's confidence to take a risk in marrying. . . . Not only are [the seafarers] freer and easier, but they can actually keep up estates better; and Anne's severance from her family is conducted by means largely of this sort of insight and her realization that here, in this [the naval] group, there are much more supportable values, values basic to the moral level of persuasion in the book.[23]

Yes. Anne explicitly rejects the chance to become Lady Elliot of Kellynch-hall and turns her back on the established life of her forefathers.

> . . . by the end of the action therefore Anne has moved out of the world of stewardship we are familiar with in Jane Austen ('Anne had no Uppercross-Hall before her, no landed estate, no headship of a family . . .') and the reader is now persuaded that this is to the good.[24]

Indeed I would press this critic's points further than he does himself. As I see it, on one side the novel affirms the entrepreneurial life as represented in its sailors (the nation-defenders-*and*-prize-capturing-adventurers of Austen's day) here elevated for our admiration; and on the other the whole ideal of the life of safety, security, fixity in one place etc. is depreciated.

> Generally the sailors are presented to us as members of a profession shaped by their life of duty and yet making the most of their chances. 'These would have been all my friends', thinks Anne; finally they are. The play given to values associated with energy, steadfastness, and even luck (when it takes the form of 'honourable toils and just rewards') is here crucial. Because the action is about mistaken persuasion, we find a stress on the will (but not wilfulness). Because it is about status unearned, it is about the importance of luck that has been earned.[25]

Austen is not implying a radical change in the moral constitution of things. She is too perceptive, sees through everybody too thoroughly, to indulge that species of wishful thinking. No. Lloyd W. Brown has got it right:

> By limiting individual maturity to women who are demonstrably unusual in their circle Austen implies a somewhat sceptical view of the possibilities of change in society at large. On the surface at any rate it would appear that this scepticism has been softened or replaced in *Persuasion*, where Anne's marriage is not exceptional within the novel as such, but is actually complemented by the marriages of the Harvilles and the Crofts. But naval marriages like these bear a suggestively outside or alien image because their naval background somehow establishes a symbolically physical distance from prevailing social norms for marriage. And in a more literal sense, sailors and their women *are* outsiders: their occupation and environment represent a spatial openness which

seems to encourage a more liberated sense of self and others than one encounters in the fixed, narrower conventions of the rest of society.[26]

Anne Elliot decisively rejects her cousin and with him Kellynch-hall, its title etc., as a possible future for her, before she is at all sure of having regained the chance of marriage to Frederick Wentworth. She does this because her insights are founded in honesty, honesty with herself, a discrimination which connects the present with the past, a habit of evaluation which (humbly) takes account of all that comes into sight and eschews the partial self-flattering view of things in which most of the other characters to some degree wrap themselves. (Having set her face against Mr. Elliot's addresses, significantly Mrs. Smith's illuminating history of him follows. Anne finds, as always, that good judgement, severe truthfulness with oneself, brings with it greater escapes and still happier blessings than could have been anticipated.) This is the value she and Captain Wentworth represent, and theirs is correspondingly the most richly happy marriage in the tale.

Indeed the beauty of their relation is not marred even by their living in a world dominated by Time and change. The reference to contemporary poetry in Anne's conversation with Captain Benwick is not the author's only ironic note achieving a deliberate contemporaneity. The whole novel has a specific location in historical time, and the 'Peace' mentioned in Chapter 3 as 'turning all our rich Navy Officers ashore . . . wanting a home' was in fact temporary. The action of the book takes place between the Armistice of 1814, the apparent defeat of Napoleon by the confederated European allies and his escape from custody, with the consequent renewal of hostilities; his doom in fact being finally sealed at Waterloo in 1815. Writing after that event the author is implicitly reminding her readers of the fragility of human assurances. All the world had thought France defeated for a generation, yet military conflict flickered up again before the tyrant was indeed permanently caged on St. Helena. Anne and her husband-to-be do not know this is in store for their world in the February of 1815 where we leave them; but the novelist and her contemporaries could foresee it. Whether it is better, according to the old philosophical

201

poser, to be a contented pig or an unhappy human being Austen has not undertaken to argue; that is not a knowable matter, a possible enquiry—we do not have a pig's sensation of things. But what she has addressed herself to elicit—whether it is better or not to be a Frederick Wentworth or a Sir Walter Elliot, *or* a Mr. Elliot (base and successful); whether it is preferable to be Anne Elliot or even Henrietta Musgrove, let alone some of the other females of her social vista; this is abundantly shown. The two lovers upon whom the tale centres are capable of a condition of relationship and—when thwarted in this—a consciousness which is far superior to most others' and which is validated even when set over against the destructive possibilities of life. The important thing is the sense in which these two live and have lived as their companions have not; with a meaningfulness, a significant beauty, which the chances and changes of this transitory existence cannot debase.

Hence the lack of the supernatural in Austen's work. What she is concerned to argue are the interior logics of human behaviour, and the secularity of *Persuasion* matches its theme in this ultimate aspect—the value of a certain kind of living over the very fact of Death.

She is sane equally in not enlisting the Unseen, the possible after-life and preternatural into her characters' accounts; and in not extirpating such elements as with a deliberate conscious platform-stamping materialism. Indeed the degree of religious outlook, of Belief inherent in her personages and narrative rhetoric is ideal for the purposes of an artistically constituted philosophical debate in her chosen form. We have neither on our hands the thinness of the modern de-cultured novel (Atheism four-square or the 'There may be something in it' attitude which, boiled down, is pretty fatuous after all and which to my sense even *A Passage to India* suffers from); nor the question-begging of pious fiction: both these options being diminutions of reality and our complicated relation to its (variously inapprehensible) complexity.

One hope I do cherish for this study; that each of my arguments about Jane Austen's fictions may have set off in relief the case against biographical forms of artistic criticism.

Mr. B. C. Southam affirms with the majority of critics and scholars that

> there is a proper and natural critical activity in considering the relationship between the author—her character and personality; and the circumstances and events of her life—and certain elements within the novels.[27]

But this is mere assertion; I have never seen this argued satisfactorily in respect of any *oeuvre* and I am certain it cannot be so argued. The world of the artist's work and that of his actual life have too many crucial differences in their constitution, for information about one greatly to illuminate the achievement of the other. This is evident not least from the way in which the *makar* is often not 'conscious'—at least at the level of ready conversation—of the fullness, depth and whole value of his created work. Even Austen I suspect of this, supremely awake as she was in an intellective manner, and have so tended to argue in the preceding pages.

For the same reason the very letters of a creative mind, if they do survive (which ideally is not to be wished), need to be handled with extremest reservation. We can misinterpret them at the simplest level: that bothersome crux about *Mansfield Park*—'Now I will try to write of something else, & it shall be a complete change of subject—ordination'; does this identify what the author thought of as the essential theme of her new work or is it that by this date (29 January 1813), Jane Austen having already advanced beyond what was to be Volume Two, Chapter 7 of the published book (i.e. Chapter 25 in modern editions), she was talking only of Edmund's ordination, a local focus of interest within the developing text?[28] Yet more comprehensively there is the objection that we are liable to invest with authority throwaway remarks, musings themselves not carefully pondered, neither deliberated, really meant nor accurately reproduced, ideas imprecisely articulate.

The privacy of the artistic life should be absolute—it would be the millenium if all authorship were suddenly anonymous—not for the sake of the begetting originals but for their readers' (auditors' etc.), who otherwise festoon themselves with a whole tangle of obfuscating material which obscures rather than leading into the works' finest intuitions.

203

It is of no help to us if we archly shake our heads over the fourth chapter of *Persuasion* in (possibly quite fatuous) belief of its personal application: 'She had been forced into prudence in her youth, she learned romance as she grew older—the natural sequel of an unnatural beginning' (p. 30). Identifying Jane Austen herself with this novel's heroine will only take us further out, away from what it has to offer, which is all of general (i.e. highly particular) significance for human living; of how substantial an import is highlighted by the emphasis upon which the author chooses to close the work.

> Anne was tenderness itself, and she had the full worth of it in Captain Wentworth's affection. His profession was all that could ever make her friends wish that tenderness less; the dread of a future war all that could dim her sunshine. She gloried in being a sailor's wife, but she must pay the tax of quick alarm for belonging to that profession which is, if possible, more distinguished in its domestic virtues than in its national importance. (XXIV, 252)

This is very beautifully poised. Death is here nowise underrated. Rather it is that the quality of consciousness, the validity of being achieved by Anne and Frederick Wentworth, before as well as in their marriage, is such, the author knows she can afford to refer up against it the precariousness of human life and felicity, without her personages, her novel's leading intuitions incurring a drastic kind of defeat.

The mind was awake indeed, which could live at such a pitch.

NOTES

1. Chapman gives the reading 'prepare for it' in place of this of the original published text, with the not closely argued comment, 'This elegant correction [the attribution of which to A. C. Bradley he acknowledges] is perhaps not absolutely certain, but I have not been able to resist it.' My own view exactly agrees with D. W. Harding's, who in his edition reinstates the 1818 word-order and remarks of 'prepare for it',
    > . . . this is more like Bradley's elegance than Jane Austen's. It would imply that the lovers were preparing for the future recall of the moment; and this would be too much deliberated. Jane Austen's phrase means that they spontaneously made it so perfect as to be worthy of the long remembrance which she knows it was destined to have. (*Op. cit.*, p. 395)

That said, there are few such divagations in Chapman's texts, some of his changes seem necessary, others are arguably so; his notes take but little reading (those to *Persuasion* cover only 3⅓ pages of his volume's printed matter) and all alterations are properly featured. One can easily scan them, in short, and decide such matters for oneself. What one cannot do is justify the waste of resources spent upon supernumerary hardback editions of these texts. The funds are too much needed to launch many other titles suffering from scholarly neglect.

2. *NA Casebook*, p. 172.
3. *JA and her Art*, p. 181.
4. Marilyn Butler, *Jane Austen and the War of Ideas* (Oxford, 1957), p. 279.
5. *NA Casebook*, p. 137.
6. W. A. Craik, *Jane Austen: The Six Novels* (London, 1968), p. 27.
7. Norman Page, *The Language of Jane Austen* (Oxford, 1972), pp. 119, 147.
8. J. S. Cunningham, *The Powers That Be* (poems; Oxford, 1969), p. 54.
9. *Love's Labour's Lost*, Act V, sc. 2.
10. *NA Casebook*, p. 197.
11. Aldous Huxley (ed.), *The Letters of D. H. Lawrence* (London, 1932), pp. 605–6.
12. Gooneratne, *JA*, p. 18.
13. Katherine Mansfield, *Novels and Novelists* (London, 1930), p. 304.
14. *David Copperfield*, Chapter iii.
15. Some students of Austen's works are still deluded by an old mistake, the belief that the name *Persuasion* was invented by Henry Austen. Certainly the author did not see this book through the press herself and to that extent we lack an absolute creator's *imprimatur* for the title. But note *JA: Facts and Problems*, p. 81 and its reference to an ms. in the Pierpont Morgan Library (reproduced in facsimile in R. W. Chapman's edition of *Plan of a Novel*, Oxford, 1926): 'The chronology of the novels which were begun at Chawton is fixed by a memorandum made by the author and still extant:
    Mansfield Park. Begun somewhere about Feb[ry] 1811. Finished soon after June 1813.
    Persuasion. Begun Aug[t] 8th 1815. Finished Aug[t] 6th 1816.
    Emma. Begun Jan[y] 21 1814. Finished March 29 1815.'
16. John Davie (ed.), *NA and P* (Oxford 1971), pp. xviii–xix.
17. See note 30 to Chapter 3 above.
18. Gooneratne, *JA*, p. 189.
19. *JA and her Art*, p. 207.
20. Ibid., pp. 206, 207.
21. *JA: The Six Novels*, p. 182.
22. *NA Casebook*, p. 218.
23. Ibid., pp. 219–21.
24. Ibid., p. 223.
25. Ibid., p. 222.
26. *JA's Achievement*, p. 37.
27. *SS Casebook*, p. 12.
28. See Hugh Brogan, 'Mansfield Park' in *The Times Literary Supplement*, 19 December 1968, 1440.

Index